Dirt Press, LLC
New York | San Francisco

Dirt Press, LLC
New York | San Francisco
www.dirtpress.com

Special thanks to:
John Szot, Philip J. Ryan, Robert Szot, Shane Beagin, Jack and Jean Hendrickson,
and the many friends and family who have supported this endeavor

Library of Congress Control Number: 2005903097

Dirt: Volume One / edited by Su Hwang and Brian Lemond—1st Ed.
    Includes index.

ISSN 1553-2135
ISBN 0-9763368-0-4

design by: Brooklyn Digital Foundry; www.brooklynfoundry.com
published by: Dirt Press, LLC; www.dirtpress.com
printed by: Friesens, Altona, Manitoba, Canada

Dirt: Volume One

Su Hwang & Brian Lemond, Editors

Issue 1.0	February 2003
Issue 1.1	June 2003
Issue 1.2	November 2003
Issue 1.3	February 2004
Issue 1.4	June 2004
Issue 1.5	October 2004

Dirt Press, LLC
New York | San Francisco

MISSION

We all seek permanence—a firm ground to call our own, a means to embrace and preserve our individuality—but the passage of time, our emotional and physical growth, and the evolution of philosophies are ever marked by movement, variables, schizophrenic trajectories, and at times, conflict. *Dirt* is the articulation of these indelibly transient sensibilities—an attempt to record and relay the snapshots and voices of the malcontent, the optimistic, the lost, the actualized, the misunderstood, the forlorn, the exalted, the damned, the everyday.

Dirt is formally a journal, but the spirit of the endeavor has no such explicit boundaries. The depth and breadth of this collective is manifested in the mere expression of thoughts, the act of stream of consciousness or drafted writing, and the artistic composition of positive and negative space; its only limitation defined by the confines of bound paper (and web pages).

Dirt is perhaps the brainchild of individuals, but functions on the principle of mass consumption, marked by the constant, free-flowing dialogue with the public at large. All forms of expression—traditional genres to experimental—are welcome from emerging and established writers and artists, as well as those who simply have something to get off their chest. We want to be engaged, moved, taught, intrigued, dismayed, galvanized, repulsed, stimulated. In return, we will disseminate the dirt to those who recognize that each work is like a fingerprint—unique and essential—in the annals of our humanity.

SUBMISSION

For submission and contact information, please visit our official website at **www.dirtpress.com**. For complete details and guidelines regarding the Hendrickson Memorial Prizes in Short Fiction and Poetry, please visit the **contest** link at **www.dirtpress.com**.

For all other inquiries, please contact *Dirt* at **info@dirtpress.com**.

INTRODUCTION

Dirt: Volume One marks many things: the unveiling of a comprehensive anthology of work from talented contemporary authors and artists, closure for the inaugural series of online issues, and Dirt Press' first foray into the printed medium. Issues 1.0 - 1.6 featured the work of 105 contributors from around the world, and we will continue to add to our international roster of contributors and readers with the launch of the 2.0 series and beyond.

Dirt is proud to offer a dynamic forum for emerging artists and authors to gain exposure, for established contributors to share their latest work, for a global readership to be engaged, and for relationships to be founded. We'll always be grateful to the contributors who joined us in these formative years; they took a chance on what at the time was an unknown journal. Their offerings have ultimately defined *Dirt*; they have provided the flesh, the character, and the courage – the soul by which we hope *Dirt* will be judged. Their work has also directed our editorial and curatorial energies. *Volume One* showcases the work of 32 featured artists, 37 individual artists, 23 poets, and 23 writers of short fiction, including the winners of the first annual Hendrickson Memorial Prize in Short Fiction: Richard Austin, Jesse Donaldson, Deivis Garcia, E.S. Oldrin, and Anthony Tognazzini.

Several contributors are featured in multiple issues – we like to think they like us as much as we like them. Camille Napier's elegiac poems grace the pages of two issues, as do Marshall Sokoloff's photographic abstractions of texture and pattern. Oliver Dettler's collages of found material appear in two issues; J. Robert Beardsley repeatedly delves into the rhythmic meanderings of fear, passion, and youth; Joseph Maddaloni brings his unique translation of office culture in three comical installments; Derek Ableman transcends style and form in four issues; and last but not least, Dewayne Washington's urban histories invigorate a record five issues.

These pages brim with variations of theme, of method, of purpose. But for all their diversity, these stories and poems, these paintings, collages, and photographs tell a remarkably consistent tale. As a collection, these authors and artists offer a glimpse of who we were during the past two years – of where our interests lay, and of how we sought to capture and convey our feeling through form, shape, rhythm, and diction.

We hope this book is a testament to the creative impetus in all its diverse manifestations. Thank you for your interest and support.

— Su Hwang & Brian Lemond, Editors

FEBRUARY 2003

Alfredo Ferran Calle, *Dones*, glicee print, 2002, courtesy of Bailey Fine Arts, Toronto

POETRY

FICTION

FEATURED ARTISTS

INDIVIDUAL ARTWORKS

COVER ART

L'Oeil
Ai-Hz

Eye Hz, giclée print, 2002
Lumiére Dans la Ventre, giclée print, 2002

Metro Toner, giclée print, 2002

facing page:

Clockwise from top: *Porte au Neon*, giclée print, 2002
Mr. Marcadet, giclée print, 2002
Trichrome Centre, giclée print, 2002
Molécule Air, giclée print, 2002

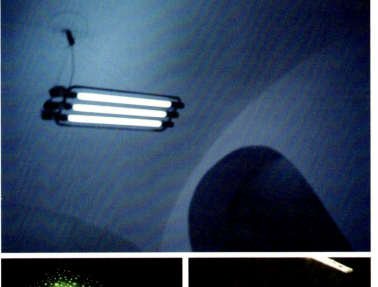

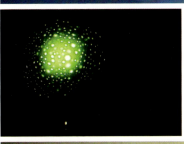

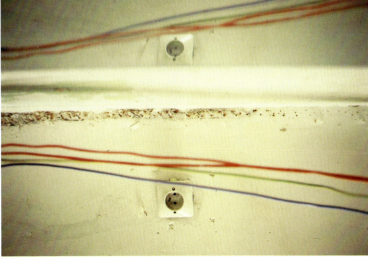

A View From The Side
Byron Barrett

The Templeton, Ilfochrome, 2002
Bodyshot, Ilfochrome, 2002

Untitled, Ilfochrome, 2002

facing page:

Culture, Ilfochrome, 2002
The Men's Room, Ilfochrome, 2002

Lotto
Maura Barthel

I'm just an average guy. You know, I like beer and I love basketball. I've got a pretty good job at this card store working the lotto machine. The strip's got an A&P, a liquor store, a pizza place, and the card store. The liquor store has a lotto machine too but most of the good customers, the high rollers, come in here. They think I'm lucky because we've had so many big winners over the last few years. I don't think it's luck, I don't believe in luck. I think it has to do with sales.

It pretty much goes without saying that I type in the numbers faster than anyone else in town. People line up and they never have to wait too long. I've got it down. I use my left hand and I've got the regulars' numbers memorized to speed things along. The way I see it, you sell more; you have more chances of selling a winner.

See, I only have three fingers on my right hand but that doesn't stop me. You only need one good hand to type in the numbers and then I use the other to rip off the tickets. Sure, this way everyone notices my three fingers. They can't help but notice cause that's the hand I give them the tickets with but they think it's lucky. I know what they say outside when they're chatting and smoking cigarettes.

"Going to play my numbers. Let's hope Three-Fingered Mike punches in a winner this time!"

Yeah, they call me that. It's not so bad, don't feel bad for me, I mean it's just the way it is. I only have three fingers on my right hand.

The customers come in, pick up some smokes and the paper, then fill out their tickets. I send them through the machine.

Then I'll say, "Hey, Willy, why don't you try playing numbers today? Play today's date."

"What the hell," Willy will say. People are always tempted by my suggestion. They think it's fate. "Give me a 007 $1 straight and $1 box. I love James Bond." And he'll walk out smiling.

Or if I see someone looking at the machine, thinking about it, I'll say, "All you need is a dollar and a dream." I use that one on Wednesdays when the Big One is real high. Everyone has a dollar and a dream. They always buy a ticket or two. I don't play much. I save my dollars and my dream is Nicole.

Nicole is this black girl. She's pretty. No, she's not pretty, she's beautiful. 'Take my breath away beautiful,' that's what I told my brother. She's about my age I guess. Not a big gambler. She plays her birthday once a week and that's it. She comes in on Thursdays and plays 824 50-50. That's 50 cents straight and 50 cents box. That means any way the numbers come in she wins but if they come in in that order 8-2-4 she wins big.

August 24th, last year. Last year I swore I'd ask her out. I was all

Miguel Lasala, *NYC Montage*, photomosaic, 1999

ready. I was going to ask her to the movies. I decided we'd go to a scary movie to scare her into my arms. That was my brother's idea. Anyway, when she came in, I punched in the numbers 824 and said, "Hey Nicole, how about…" and her cell-phone started ringing. She picked it up and I lost my nerve.

Well that's not going to happen today. Not this August 24th. I've got it all worked out. I know exactly what I'm going to say. I'm going to give her a free scratch off ticket. I think that's a nice touch. Something I thought of in May. Anyway, then I'm going to say "Happy Birthday!" type in her number and then I'm going to ask her out. I'm thinking romantic comedy. Something with Meg Ryan or Tom Hanks or maybe both if they're still doing those movies they do. Nothing's going to stop me.

My brother asked me what makes me think a beautiful girl is going to go out with a guy like me. Well, she's got this little kid. Don't get me wrong, he's a good kid. He never grabs at the candy and begs for things like the other kids. He asks nicely if he wants something and is silent if she says no. She usually lets him get a candy bar though. She lets him get a Snickers or something. I usually hand him the ticket and he says, "tank you," like little kids do and looks at me with his big little kid eyes. Anyway, I figure she's got this little kid working against her and I've got the whole three-fingered thing going on, so maybe it's even. I'll sit to the right of her at the movies, that way if she wants to hold my hand she can hold my good hand.

So, today is August 24th and I'm waiting. You gotta be in it to win it, right? Besides, I'm not so bad. I'm a friendly guy. I've got personality. I'm easy to talk to.

I use my personality to increase sales. I talk to the customers and they appreciate it. What do I talk about? Anything, the weather, how good or bad the Knicks are doing, something I heard on the news. It really doesn't matter. The boss likes me for that. He says, "Mike, you're doing a good job." He's thinking of getting two machines because of the lines, but I tell him don't bother. I can keep the line moving.

Another thing I do is give advice. That's where I run into trouble. I run into trouble cause I tell it like it is. I can't help it there. Like, this one lady, she comes in with a yellow hat with plastic birds on it. Me and Ginny, that's the girl who works the register, we call her The Bird Lady. Ginny tells me she buys greeting cards for Pavarotti. Once a week she picks up a card for him. She's always humming too, which gets on my nerves. Anyway, she plays The Big One. She doesn't pick her own numbers. She lets the machine pick them. Where's the fun in that?

She stands there humming and I notice she has between 15 and 20 thick black hairs coming out of her chin. So I say to her, "You know, there are things you can do about that hair on your face." I know this cause I have sisters. I tell her, "You can go get them waxed off and it doesn't hurt much, you can just pull them out with a tweezer yourself." I mean honestly, she can cut them with scissors if she thinks about it.

And then she says, "I don't think there's anything wrong with a woman having a little facial hair, do you?"

And then I say, "$1 please. And good luck." She needs it.

There's also Henry. He lives at the old folks home and the old people send him down to play their numbers for them. He's not that old. Not old enough to be at an old folks home anyway. I ask him how old he is and he says, "Sis, they tell me I'm 186."

I tell him, "Henry, please don't call me Sis." I really hate that.

Ginny tells me not to worry. Ever since she cut her hair real short he started calling her Tinkerbell. He calls the guy from the A&P Superman cause when he's on break he wears his red deli apron backwards. He picks us up coffee and runs errands for the boss. He's not a bad guy. Just a little off.

So I ask him, "Henry, why do you call me Sis?"

"I don't know." He laughs. "Cause you have three fingers."

Well, that just doesn't make any sense! He's a good customer though, comes in 6 or 7 times a day. Pretty much assures us all the business from the old folks place so I let it slide. I just hate when he does it in front of Nicole.

Oh, here she is. She has on these big black sunglasses. I love it when she wears them cause she looks like a movie star. I hate it cause I can't see her eyes. Her kid isn't with her today. That's good. That's a good sign, right?

"Hi Nicole." I punch in 824 and wait for it to print out.

"Hi, Mike, 824…"

"50 straight 50 box, I know. Happy birthday!" I rip off the Lucky 7 scratch off ticket to give her as a gift.

"Oh, It's not my birthday," she laughs, "it's my son Terry's. He's three today."

I'm stuck with the scratch off in my hand. "Well, happy birthday to him then." I can't give a three-year-old a scratch off ticket. That's against the law. You have to be 18 to play. I hand her her numbers and take her dollar. My stomach turns. I start sweating. Honestly, I don't know what do to.

"Well, when is your birthday?" I ask. God, I hope it's soon.

"July 31st, why?" she lifts her glasses and I can see her beautiful hazel eyes. "Mike, are you okay?"

"Me, yeah, yeah, sure I am. Good luck, Nicole. I have a feeling today is your lucky day." What a stupid thing to say.

"Really, why's that?"

I don't know. I don't believe in luck. Why did I just say that? Oh God, here comes Henry.

"Hey, Sis, can I get you a cup of coffee?"

"No, Henry, no. I don't want any coffee." I'm shaking. Damn it. July 31st is a long ways off.

"Okay, Mike," she says, "I'll see ya next week." And she leaves.

"Sure, Nicole," I say, "I'll see ya then."

And I watch her walk right out the door.

First Lady of Space
Maura Barthel

He calls me the FirstLadyOfSpace.
Half here.
Half there.
Full of tricks.
"Obsessed with the awful responsibility of time" he says.

because I can open my eyes wide
focus ahead
and still
watch
the heavens unfastened and open
right before me

because I can close my ears
and no human voices will wake me
from the wet slapping
reminding and slapping
reminding, reminding, reminding, me

because I can pull my knees up close to my chest
bury my feet in my sand
my head in my hands
and wait for it to creep
up
to pull me
in
to slip
away
to
drown.

But he comes right in after me!
Drags me to shore.
Shows me the moon.
Says "I feel like that sometimes too you know."
And puts his warm hand on my cheek.

our shore
like all shores
is temporary
as are his fingertips against my ear

but the sky
above
and my sky
(in my mind)
is infinite…
infinite,
Infinite.

Vacationing with Steve McQueen
Shane Beagin

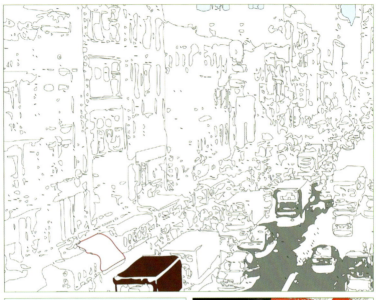

 *Chinatown 2*, silkscreen on paper, 2003
Chinatown 1, silkscreen on paper, 2003   *Celine*, silkscreen on paper, 2003

Pineapples, silkscreen on paper, 2003
Production, silkscreen on paper, 2003
Chinatown 3, silkscreen on paper, 2003

Under the Bed

Dave Bernstein

This is the story of nine-year-old Jed
Who didn't believe in the sounds neath his bed
Who slept with his closet doors open and wide
Who kept his shades drawn so no light got inside
For sounds in the darkness, were only just that
A mouse in the wall or a prowling black cat
He was never once scared of that faraway *bump*
Of that scraping, that scratching, that cold, heavy *thump*
He was not one to cower when closing his eyes
Or imagine those monsters, their horrible cries
He was bold and cerebral, too old for such things
For clowns who ate children, for goblins with wings

And so he declared, as he gave a great yawn
As he lay down to sleep, not so long before dawn
"I am not so afraid of you sounds neath my bed
All the moaning and scratching from things that are dead.
For I'm fearless Jed Black," he said, puffing his chest
"And I'm shutting my eyes for a full night of rest."

Well the clown in the closet did listen and fume
For young Jed in the bed, he'd made plans to consume
The clown mumbled softly, "I'll tear him apart.
I'll teach him a lesson, he thinks he's so smart."

But Jed did not stop, he continued to gloat
Then he let forth a cry from the back of his throat
"You are nothing!" he yelled to the very dark room
"You are figments and shadows, you can't bring me gloom."
With that he turned over, he shifted his hips
And the clown in the closet did lick at its lips
It waited an hour, till young Jed was still
Then crept from the closet, moved in for the kill
It stood right above him, the room became cold
Then little Jed woke and was no longer bold
He looked all around as his world fell apart
And was suddenly scared of that bump in the dark

And on that cold night in the heart of December
Young Jed in the bed was quite neatly dismembered
And eaten

Tagalong
William Clifford

At the only occupied booth an elderly couple sat whispering things about me. They did their whispering the way old people did most everything: conspicuously. So don't think I'm some kind of Sam Spade or something. I mean, from where I was sitting, they might as well have been using a bull horn. And the attention had started the second I walked into the place, wide grins and eyes that followed my every step to the bar, as if a second before my entrance an announcement had been made: *Ladies and Gentlemen, The President of the United States.* Then came the whispering. They droned this and thats while they sat on the same side of the booth gawking at me like old folks stare at the internet on a computer screen: with a thrill and disbelief such a thing actually exists. I squirmed on my bar stool. I wasn't even facing them—but I could feel them.

I had planned on starting my week stint at The Sunshine Inn by blowing a sizable portion of my summer savings at the ideally barren hotel bar "Happy Daze," but the not-so-sneaky chitter-chatter was getting under my skin. Well, I figured, I can just as easily drink Heinekens in room 313 as I can here—watch HBO instead of the ocean while wondering if I made a mistake by enrolling in grad school right after college—so, so what.

"Check, please."

"Oh, hi. Actually, I was just about to tell you, Mr. and Mrs. McCarthy just asked if they could buy you a drink."

The barmaid ("BUNNY", according to her stitched-on name tag) was about my age and had mentioned something about me looking a little bit like Edvard Munch pre-mustache, so I figured she had a good brain and gave her the are-you-serious eyebrows. (Not to mention she was dynamite looking in that impossibly pretty beach-girl way: strawberry blond hair, a few freckles down a ski-jump nose, green eyes as vibrant and inviting as a couple of senseimillia nickel bags. And she had a body that told you she *surfed*.) Anyway, she surpassed my expectations by giving me the subtle, but unmistakable, what-the-hell-a-drink's-a-drink eyebrows. Not bad, this Bunny.

Now, this is not the way stranger-bought-drinks typically transpire in lonely beach bars, but still, I played into the offer like a beach comber looking to score.

I look over my shoulder the way a driver looks over his shoulder at an accident on the turnpike: *am I really doing this? How bad is it?*

And there they were, boy. The McCarthy's: grinning like a couple of wax figures; sagging, tanned skin; white hair for her, none for him; American-built dentures. The Mister gave a come-on-over wave. Like an idiot, I looked back toward the bar in the hope that he was gesturing to someone else, but there was no one else.

Bunny put a Bud (what else, right?) in front of me. I picked it up, turned back to the table, and politely raised the bottle. The Mister gave another wave, a bit more emphatically this time. They wanted me over there. I took a deep breath, a last look at Bunny, and acquiesced.

"Thank you very much. Ma'am. Sir."

"Not at all, young man," the woman said.

And the man: "No, that's right. Not at all, son...*hell*."

I sat across from them and drank up appreciatively in hopes of placating their need to keep flashing their horror-movie gums at me(the McCarthy's Polident needed a workout). It didn't work. They sure were happy.

"Well good goddamn it!"

The old man said (yelled) this, and then we sat there sucking on our beers looking like some Norman Rockwell in Hell painting. Done drinking, they stared at me. I stared at my almost empty Bud and concentrated on the smell of the place: beer, fishy sea-air, Oil of Olay.

"Goddamn it, indeed. 71 years of age and would you look here at this. It's like them sheep, wouldn't you say, Peg?"

"Yes, Gil."

"Baaaaa," he said, imitating a sheep.

"Okay, Gil," said his wife.

Gil shook his head and started laughing and slapping his own knee like some possessed caller of square dances. The woman, *Peg*, started tittering and rubbing Gil's big forearm; so I finished the Bud and just started laughing too. When in Rome. Bunny suddenly appeared with three fresh Buds.

So, there we were, Bunny back behind the bar now, Gil, Peg, and myself, all laughing our heads off, rocking back and forth, looking from face to face to make sure we were in, whatever it was we were in, together.

Great, I figured, old folks, just a little batty with age (not to mention the Buds—Peg, the trouper, was half way through her newly arrived brew). They were probably happy to buy a youngster some drinks, probably going to tell me stories about falling in love back when things were simple or something. Well, I was down here to clear my head anyway, what better way than to listen to a twighlight-of-their-life couple spin some yarns—snap me out of my self-pitying, worrywart crap. Maybe the Mister and Misses here would lend me a little perspective: laugh, laugh, laugh because, hey, *you're alive!*

"So," I giggled, "where are you two kids from?"

Whereupon Peg burst into wild theatrical sobs. Her face met her palms. As she wept her fingers rubbed against her forhead in small scratching motions.

Gil turned pale and Peg garbled something completely unintelligible into her hands, to which Gil said, "I know, I know."

Bunny came running over (with three more beers, the angel) and helped Peg out of the booth. Peg stood with great effort, weak with weeping. With her arm around Peg, Bunny walked her slowly into the ladies room.

"Sorry about that, son, you see, Christ—we didn't even get your name."

"Uh, Stuart, sir. Is Mrs. McCarthy going to—"

"Stu, lemme explain. Peg's an emotional person. You see, so her crying jag is no prob-lay-mo. Just pictures in her head. Bunny'll clear things up. Women understand such matters."

"But—"

"Right-o, Stu. You see, we got a boy 'bout your age … whaddaya, 27, 28?"

"Actually, 23. I just graduated and—"

"Right, so our boy and you, well..." He inhaled for what seemed like an hour. Gil was a stout man. "Well you're the spittin' goddamn image. I still can't get over it."

"Oh," I said, only a little relieved, still a bit foggy. "That's really...great, I guess. So, where is your son? What did you say his name is?"

"I didn't, Stu. And that's because the little tagalong fairy is dead to us."

He lifted and drank his entire Bud in one long, methodical swallow. When he finished, he slowly put the bottle on the table, his hand still gripping it (withered, giant hands; white hairs by his red knuckles; thin, blue veins—exactly: red, white, and blue). He stared at the bottle unblinkingly and gave a short, derisive snort.

"Dead as dirt," he reiterated.

Peg materialized, sort of singing, "Right as rain!" Gil stood to let her in. She looked like she had just come from a health spa. Her make-up melted face restored to perfectly painted old lady. I think it was at that exact moment—seeing Peg so cheerful and rejuvenated—that I suspected I might be falling in love with Bunny.

"So, did Gil fill you in on ... Timmy? Little Tim?"

"Uhhh....sort of."

"I gave him the skinny low-down. Boy's name is Stu, hon'. Stu, I'm going to ask you a question and I want you to give it to me straight. Straight, get it, Peg?"

In lieu of answering, Peg drank her Bud.

"We got a deal, Stu? Hey, Stu, you need another? We run a tab down here. Been coming down here for thirty years, if you can believe that."

"Gil, maybe the boy doesn't want another one."

"Peg, he's young, that's all they *do* is drink! *Hell*. Right, son!?"

With surprising quickness Gil smacked me on the shoulder. He hit me so hard I dropped the empty Bud I was holding. It clanked and spun across the table, settling on a point and turning round and round. I thought of the game Truth or Dare I used to play when I was young. I wondered what was coming, a truth or a dare.

"See, looky there, empty." Gil said, indicating the bottle. "Honey!"

Bunny came over with three Buds. Gil was whispering in Peg's ear. Maybe that's just how they talked.

"You seem to be having fun," Bunny said to me, and went back to the bar. I watched her go.

When I turned back, Gil was mugging at me with an inane, dirty-old-man leer. A regular Benny Hill. I immediately regretted looking at Bunny's behind. Actually, I always hated when I saw other men playing that ugly game.

Like the last time I had dinner with my parents. It was two years ago, my sophomore year, at a Thai place near my university. My dad decided to start checking out our waitress—*in front of my mom*. Fuck it, in front of *me!* Mom pretended not to notice, which only made me twice as embarrassed, twice as furious. I went to the restroom for ten whole minutes (I know because I sat behind the locked stall door, belt buckled, looking at my watch, trying to determine how many minutes it would take to indicate a sort of punishment—I came up with ten). After I emerged, I didn't give my dad a word or a look all night. Later on, when they dropped me off near my dorm, my dad said, "So, why's our book-thumper suddenly so tongue-tied, sport?" In the murky lights of the parking lot, I just looked at him, a sickly yellow halo of sodium-vapor light around his face. My silence, my look, let him know I was old enough now to notice his sneaky glances, and to understand that those glances yearned to touch, as he had no doubt touched before. My mother sat in the car, looking straight ahead. I think we all felt ashamed. They drove away and got a divorce seven months later. When I started my senior year, I stopped talking to them both.

But with Bunny, well, there were the beers, and, I don't know, she had a particularly sensational ass. Besides, the only wife around here? Well, she sure wasn't mine. So there you go, my actions: rationalized, justified.

"Fun, fun, fun!" chanted Peg. "I want to have nothing but fun. No more crying!"

She drank her Bud.

"Hubba, hubba. Huh, Stu?" Gil motioned towards Bunny.

"Uh, yeah, she's really pretty. So," I said, wanting to switch gears before Gil said something like "trim" or "tail," "are you two just down here on vacation?"

"Hell no," Gil boomed. "Vacation, that's richer than a movie star's cheesecake."

"We own, honey," said (slurred) Peg.

"Plus a farm up in Fresno. Son, my question is simple: you like a nice piece of tail, right?"

Whaddaya know.

"I'm...I'm not sure I know what you mean."

"Son, I'm no red-neck, I made a lot of money on Wall Street, met a lot of different men. If I talk like a good old boy, well, that's what a smart, college educated person like yourself would call *an affectation*. I, in fact, respect diversity."

Here Gil sighed and (this is when I started planning my nice-to-meet-you, so-long-now, wow-are-you-two-fucking-insane lines) put his hand on my wrist. "With my death so imminent, I mourn for your entire generation. Today, it's a bandwagon full of fags. And it's OKAY, it's PC, hell, it's all but legal now; ram anybody you want, right up the Hershey Highway, that's violence and violence is a sickness. Thank God for Bush. A sickness.

Biological or environmental? Well, Stu, you're educated, scientists are cloning sheep, doing embryonic stem-cell research, spending millions of decent people's tax dollars curing AIDS, for God's sake—and you don't find the notion of them just not being able to identify that one tell-tale gene just a tad dubious? Well, I'll tell ya: there is no gene. Not from my stock and barrel. It's total environment, psychological. It's a fucking pep-talk. Every other TV show with a swishy homo in the lead role—that's Hollywood propaganda at its finest. *Gay pride? Queer nation?* Kiddo, you do the math, it's Hitler all over again. Charisma can blind men to what they really believe, who they really are. And now they wanna tie the knot, have what me and Peg have? Please. It's a joke. A sick one. I'm not saying hey-ho for violence, I don't think stringing a fairy to a fence and puttin' his lights out works. But maybe it's a start. Hey, I propose ... nothing. This is a *theoretical* discussion. For a little peace of mind before the grave. Stu, we lost a son to a used-car salesman; that's a metaphor, you understand. And our boy got a jalopy, a lemon of a life. Sounds heavy, but it be the truth. A lemon of a life. Sin. Depravity. Waste. Whatever happened to two roads, huh, Stu? And that's why God sent you, so we can see Tim as a real man, right in front of us for a few Buds, before we go. A healthy, virile man. Timmy, right in front of us."

Right. Fantastic. Nicely said.

"Mr. and Mrs. McCarthy ... thanks for the drinks. I actually have to...use the men's room, and then I should be going."

I had meant that "men's room" thing to sound really sarcastic, a real snarky fuck-you from the college kid, but Gil just smashed his huge hand against my shoulder again and winked.

"You've caught on, son."

I had no idea what Gil was talking about.

I stood up and felt my head spin.

"Honey," slurred Peg. "You do like girls, right?"

I put my hands on the table to steady myself—oh so cool.

"Sure I do, Mrs. McCarthy."

Knocking a couple of bottles over, Peg stood clumsily and grabbed my face. Her hands felt like paper macheé. She puckered up and (swear to God) leaned in to kiss me—breath like a skunk—but I backed away (actually, I jerked into a Nosferatu-recoil, Peg's Revlon-Reds my crucifix). With her hands suddenly empty, she fumbled and lost her balance, crashing back into the corner with a cross between a scream and a sigh.

Gil was working on his beer, looking out the window at the inky waves, smiling.

In the bathroom I tried to clear my head. I read the graffiti on the wall: NO MATTER HOW HOT SHE IS, SOMEONE, SOMEWHERE, IS SICK OF HER BULLSHIT. I didn't think the scrawl was funny, but found myself laughing and hoping Gil might hear in case he'd read it too—why? I pushed open the miniature window which only opened half way because of warping from the salt air. The Pacific blew in: warm, heady breeze. I closed my eyes while I pissed. Soon, the sound of the tide spilling in and sucking out was mingled with my relief, and I felt myself drifting out, out toward Japan with Bunny. We'll swim naked on the other side of the

Pacific, skip shells off the sea's surface, hold hands and shriek on Space Mountain in Tokyo-Disneyland. Right, so much for clearing my head. I flushed twice. I went to the sink and splashed water on my face. Right. Quick exit. Last goodbyes to the the Homophobic American Gothic, a casual, *maybe I'll see ya later tonight* to Bunny. (Come to think of it, what the hell time was it, anyway? 11-ish? What day?)

I opened the door and the bar was gone. Pupils all haywire. I wondered for a second if I accidentally walked into a broom closet. But then I saw a silhouette moving in the shadows, a red neon HAPPY DAZE burning in reverse at the far end of the bar, and heard a voice, low and sweet against the waves: "Hey, thought you got lost. Mom and Dad are gone, off to dreamland, I'm afraid. The doors are locked. Can I get you a real drink?"

Bunny moved into a knife of moonlight, smiling, inviting. I wavered over.

"Do you know what the difference is between a tributary and an estuary?"

Before I could answer she purred a "shhhh" and produced a tall black bottle.

"Tributary," she said, pouring two big shots.

Flicking open a Zippo, she bent the hardware to our drinks where they caught fire: blue flame licked the rims of our glasses. Pier lights bounced off the water. The exit sign glowed beside us, violet light spilling across the beige carpeting.

"Estuary," she said. Her jaw went slack as if a dentist had just asked her to say "ahhh." I saw silver fillings in the back of her mouth. She took the ember-orange tip in her mouth and swallowed.

So, we were flirting.

"Hey," I asked, "what the hell was going on with those two?"

We were on our second (or third?) shot of whatever Bunny was pouring. Sitting close together on two Adirondak chairs on the closed-off patio, the bottle on a table between us, we were talking.

"They're here all the time. Same old story. I told her that if she still loved her son, it didn't matter."

"...What didn't matter?"

Bunny looked at me and smiled. Her cheeks ballooned out red and sweet like bazooka bubbles.

"Do you want me to kiss you?"

I looked up at her (*up?* wait a second, how did *that* happen?), and smiled.

"I'd love..." I tried to think of something clever to say about estuaries and tributaries and kissing and sharing spit and the roar of the Pacific behind us, but there she was with her flowery breath breathing down my throat, burning my tongue, getting me instantly erect so that I almost flipped over backward like some sideshow Rubber Boy. Slow, still kisses. My head was reaching up, and I could feel my pulse pounding against my chest and neck.

And then (just like that but probably hours later) we were in water.

Even now, months after, the end of this story seems present tense. I can't make it history. Every day, it happens again.

Seaweed snarls around my toes. Bunny pulls at my hamstrings. The tide sucks out each time I push, so our bodies sink deeper into the ground with each thrust. Like digging a hole in the sand, a little more falls in each time you dig. Her hair looks black now; it mingles with the water and California sky. Fat moon, big winds. I like women. I like Bunny. A five-footer breaks and foams in my drums; I dig; she scratches my back and I feel sand and dirt beneath her fingernails (eggshell blue); someone is yelling; a few hundred yards south, down around Santa Monica, I notice either fireflies playing tag, or, more likely, the floating cigarette embers of flanneled locals and slickered foreigners who are casting off into moonlight so their families won't starve, and more likely than *that*, it's just buzzed swirlies behind my squeezed shut lids; still, I think about the Santa Monica fishermen and imagine being a family man—a real stand-up guy with eyes for no one but my Bunny; I imagine this while Bunny and I fuck on the beach; I dig; Bunny loves me; I know it; we'll marry and "divorce" will be a never-heard-of word, a dirty word. I want to come right here in the waves so it rips out to nowhere and is swallowed by a thousand fish, impregnate the globe, the planet, the fishies in the sea (you betcha I like women—grampa, old hag); I see Peg's horrible mouth coming toward me, I bite down hard. I see Gil's perverted Benny Hill face, and I strike something; no bandwagon full of fags here, just Superman, baby; I see time creeping by, a slow red second hand, as I sit in a toilet stall trying to punish my parents; a slow red second hand, like a bottle, like Truth or Dare. I dig deep; Bunny; I dig deeper; Bunny...

She is suddenly grabbing my cock, which is about to explode. She is squeezing, twisting. She is screaming under midnight.

"STOP! DO YOU FUCKING SPEAK ENGLISH? YOU WERE

Eddie Alfaro, *Putrid Mucho*, marker on paper, 2002

HURTING ME! FOR THE MILLIONTH FUCKING TIME—STOP!"

I swallow a mouthful of black salt water. I cough, gag sick, sweet booze, reach for Bunny's hips, and get an ankle kick in the mouth; something crunches, my thick tongue searches, hoping to find Bunny's ocean soaked vagina, but instead—slick gum. My tooth is gone. Kicked it right out. Blood. Blood down my chin, across my chest.

Now she's on top of me. Blood spills from her mouth, too. I'm naked. Feels warm.

"Do you like that, motherfucker?" When she speaks blood spits from her mouth, striking my face. She snatches my scrotum and forces her middle finger perilously close to my anus. "Oh yeah, ohhhhh yeaaah," she mocks. I groan. She is writhing painfully atop my stomach, and I suddenly realize I'm extremely, woozily drunk. She removes her finger from where it is hurting me and clamps a bony hand around my neck. "Jesus Christ. So much for sweet college kids. What are you, some fucking psycho? I told Gil you were cute and we'd chit-chat, maybe make out, maybe even more, but I wasn't really in the mood to get fucking raped."

"They, they planned this...?"

"Like you didn't know. Shape up, pal. They see us, wanna play matchmaker. You're cute, I'm cute, who cares? No one gets hurt. Grow up. They get a false sense of pride and we swap spit, maybe get lucky and maybe even get along."

"You're telling me you..?" I said.

"Please." She laughs. "Don't try pulling out a bag of morals, 'cause you sold those for a few gay-bashing Buds. Right? What? Did Gil give you the tagalong speech? So what? You smile so you don't throw up and still feel kinda sorry for the fucker 'cause you know it's evil, you know it wrecked a family, and you know it's bullshit. But you fuck it up because you know what? Despite your crafty smart-boy smirk at their table, you inherently believed in Gil's pathetic schpiel. And you know why? And here my big speech will end...."

She stands up, naked. Her small breasts are wet and stained with goosebumped blood. I want to wash the blood from them, kiss it away, swallow it and beg forgiveness for something I can't believe I did. But did do.

She crouches down near my ear and hisses, "...because you're susceptible."

She stands up again, towering above me, and kicks a spray of sand into my face.

The water laps at my toes. Vertiginously, I watch Bunny stride back to the bar, pull on her bikini, fumble with something...disappear. The neon yields to empty tubes.

"Happy Daze" is gone.

An airplane speeds across the sky, perhaps from LAX to Tokyo, and vanishes through the constellations. Then I hear a rush, a soar, and hold my breath as a wave crashes over me.

Under the humming surf, I try to believe I am good.

Faithless
Joe Fielder

My girlfriend is on her knees, hunched over with her head buried in the toilet. I'm holding a ball of her long, flat black hair behind her neck with both my hands so it doesn't fall down into the mess below her face.

"I'm puking blood!! I'm puking blood!" she says. There's a near hysterical pitch to her voice, which echoes slightly in the bowl.

"Tina," I tell her, "you're not puking blood. Your blood's not pink. You drank too much Boone's Farm strawberry wine."

She's giggling when it starts again.

Cut back a few hours. We're attending a holiday party for my work at San Francisco's City Hall. The theme is "white trash." Hundreds of people are dressed in flannel shirts, sweat pants, wife beater undershirts, and the rest. An ocean of K-Mart and Goodwill's finest.

This is it, I think: The new racism. The last group that whites could look down on to feel superior: other whites. It was morally wrong to joke about poor people from other backgrounds, but poor whites were still fair game. The whole thing is a little less funny when you grew up in a trailer yourself, I guess.

Tina and I walk out into the crowd and she soon realizes that we're the only people there not dressed in costume. "Why didn't you *tell* me it was a costume party?" Tina asks me, sticking a finger under my ribs. A look of slightly veiled indignation plays across her face.

Tina has a thin, dark purple dress on. It's so loose that even Kate Moss would spill out of it occasionally, and men are openly staring at her already. I'm wearing a tuxedo for the first time in my life.

I get us drinks from one of the dozen different themed-bars that dot the hall (in this case, "Jerry Springer Cove") and come back to find Tina talking to a thin man in overalls. He slinks off with a smile and an abbreviated wave when he sees me. I think he works in Accounts Payable. Half of his teeth have been blacked out and he's wearing a straw hat, so it's hard to tell.

"Who was that?" Tina asks.

No one, I tell her. I look at her in the eyes, which is easy to do since in heels she's almost as tall as me.

"He's nice," she says, but I'm not convinced.

Tina's the type of woman that requires constant attention, particularly the kind from men. It's less that she's insecure than that she's constantly defining herself through those around her. You think that she's listening to you when you talk, but she's really just consulting the magic mirror in your eyes.

We walk around the party for a bit before I beg off to go to the

Shane Beagin, *Redondo Beach*,
silkscreen and gouache on arches, 2002

bathroom. As I head in the doorway, I'm stopped by my best friend David, who asks me if he can steal Tina for a dance.

"You just can't leave a girl like that alone, Danny."

He's not really my best friend. He's my best friend "at work." A prison yard alliance created to guard ourselves against others who might try to fuck us up the ass there.

I come back in a few minutes, feeling much lighter, and David is nibbling on Tina's ear. I sneak away to visit the three other bathrooms in the building. After each successive trip, I feel as if a great weight has been taken from me, particularly the small of my back. I head back to the party once it's all gone.

A hand drops onto my shoulder and I jump, but it's only my boss glad-handing me and asking how I'm enjoying the party. His ear-to-ear smile makes him look like The Joker with an expensive tan and he's wearing mechanic's overalls with the name "Joe" in cursive patched onto the front. The back reads "Alabama Motors."

I'm from Alabama, I say.

"Did you live in a trailer, Danny boy?" he asks, grinning behind his drink.

Over his shoulder I see Tina talking to a security guard with a machine gun. He's one of many hired for tonight because of the threats made by all the people we've laid off over the last year.

"Yes, I did," I tell him.

"Wuzzz yoar daddy a mechannnic?" he asks me, drawling profusely.

My girlfriend is running her finger around the security guard's badge.

"Yes, he was," I say. He used to wash the grease out from underneath his fingernails in the kitchen sink and say, "I'm a grease monkey, son. I'm a grease monkey."

Tina's touching the security guard's gun now. He's got a hat on, but I can tell that he has sandy blond hair. Tina loves blondes.

"Are you going home to 'Alabammy' for Christmas to see him?" My boss makes 'quote' symbols in the air with his index and middle fingers as he says "Alabammy." His drink makes this awkward.

The guard is demonstrating the proper way to hold a gun to Tina. His right arm is a crooked line from his shoulder, slightly bent to absorb the shock. His left arm and hand provide the gun with additional support.

"No," I say. My father worked to pay for my school so that I could come out here and get a job working for someone like you. "He paid my way through school and then he died," I tell him. So, no. I won't be going home for the holidays.

I look up and see Tina being led off somewhere private by the security guard. He has his arm around her lower back, loosely. Like an afterthought. His fingers are touching lightly on her rib cage just below her small, right breast.

Tina takes a few steps at his side and, as if on cue, makes an indelicate choking sound that I can hear even from where I'm standing. She covers her mouth with the tips of her fingers, and a string of vomit spurts out of her left nostril. She proceeds to puke on the guard's shoe.

I see his right hand reach involuntarily for the gun.

"I have to go," I tell my boss, already walking away from him. "I think my girlfriend's taken ill."

"Happy holidays," he says, grinning like the Buddha now. "Glad you could make it!"

Once Tina's finally done throwing up, she collapses like a manic toy now set to "off." It's all that I can do to not let her put her face on the toilet bowl and go to sleep right there. I slink an arm around her middle and hoist her out of the bathroom into her bedroom. The room is bright with hastily turned on lights.

Once we're clear of the doorway, Tina wakes up with a start. She hoists herself upright using my shoulder and kisses me full on the mouth.

"You're the greatest," she says. But I know that I'm only the greatest one there.

The part of her that is still awake directs her fingers to stroke the back of my neck, while the rest of her body goes limp in my arms again.

I take off Tina's dress, pull a pair of pajamas onto her, and cover her in sheets. Like I do every night.

She mutters one end of a conversation to me and, though I can't make out the name she's calling me, it's obvious that she thinks I'm somebody else now.

Standing back near the doorway to her bedroom, I touch the face of the detonator in my jacket pocket thoughtfully. It's bulky like a half crate of eggs, and has a collapsible antennae on one end. A few flicks and a press will send a radio signal across town that will ignite the three putty-like blocks of Semtex I placed at the party earlier this evening.

It's not too late, I think.

I make Tina take two aspirin and drink a tall glass of water before turning off the lights and walking out her front door. There's a plaque there left by a former roommate that reads, "The House of Moral Ambiguity." I try not to think about it.

The detonator slaps lightly against my side as I walk. I try to imagine that it's all in my mind for a moment. And maybe it is. It would be both easier and harder to believe.

I hike down the apartment's stairway and pull out my cell phone to call the girl who served us drinks during the party. She'd taken my phone out of my pocket, set her number into the memory, and given it back to me. Apparently, her name is "ANNAH."

Maybe Annah can help me decide whether or not to hit the button. Better to put it in the hands of someone I just met than Tina's or mine. She's in no state to provide accurate counsel and I'm no longer any sort of judge of character.

David Gulley, *Empire State*, Ilfochrome, 2000

A Night Before
Arren Frank

On that long walk through the city,
Through the dawn of a September morning
Nonsense-rhyming, roaming on down sleeping streets
Impelled by giddy lust for life (and lack of sleep)

Tugging on the veil:
Translucent imposition of the mind's familiar order
On surreal scenes of slumber
In the city 'fore the dawn

Conversation strays unheeded,
The sound of words becomes their meaning;
Laugh as they're misconstrued
For knowing their nature

After all, the sunrise sobers,
Levity lulled into portentous silence;
Feeling it must be broken,
A voice like a dagger swift and extemporized:

"I'll miss the days of walking when they've gone"

The Light of the Body is the Eye
Gabby Hyman

The last time Carol saw him, Steven Ennex was waiting for his lover to die. Carol and Steven were standing at the pig sculpture in the Pike Place Market and Steven said, soon as Chess went, he was going to start drinking again. Tourists flooded past them with their silly grins, which made Steven's pledge seem worse.

"You won't do that," Carol snapped. "You're just looking for sympathy."

It had stopped raining—a temporary condition at best—and she had pulled the hood down from her green slicker and shook out her hair. "You know I love you. There's no need to beg or threaten me for it."

"You're sweet," Steven said. "But I am. I am going to do it. I want to get obliterated. I'd drink now, it's just that Chess..."

Shoppers swarmed out into the wet avenues, their paper sacks gorged with produce. A Chinese fish monger tossed a silver salmon into the air, mugging for the tourists with their minicams. It was difficult for Carol, among the sprawling rows of cashews and pineapples, among chanterelles and persimmons, to imagine Chess now, ashen in his bed at the hospice, his arms worming with IVs. Just as tough, too, to think of Steven before his swaggering, sober cynicism as she once had known him, years back when he was silent, morose, diminished by Valium and gin fizzes. At least his current acidity gave him sparkle. It was heartening in a perverse way, his vain attempt to summon her pity.

"Of course, I promised Chess I'd stay sober," Steven said, steering her along the racks of international magazines and out into First Avenue.

"Some bargain," she said. "A short-term character farce before you drink again and cash in your life."

They ran out of words, waiting for their bus to Capital Hill, pressed together by circumstance under the Plexiglas transit shelter. Once she would have taken his hand. Now she looked off into the steaming distance of Pike Street. "Stinking buses."

"What's to live for?" he whined.

"Not much, I suppose, by your thinking," Carol said. "Maybe the opportunity to someday drop the melodrama."

He looked at balled-up newspaper in the street. "Poor old Chess."

"Okay, you might as well start drinking now," she said, lowering her voice among the crowd of gray and yellow slickers.

"What do you know about love?" Steven said.

Not much, Carol thought. Certainly not by evidence.

"Enough to stand by you," she said. "In the face of the most pathetic, moronic behavior."

"Every faggot needs a lady pal," Steven said. "It's like having a safety on the trigger."

The bus came and they squished up the steps and found seats beyond the exit door. Seattle was a tolerant little city where everyone walked the rainy streets, shoulder to shoulder, safe in hermetic bubbles of caffeinated stupefaction; then the bus threw you all together like a family of foul souls.

Carol sighed, put her head against Steven's shoulder and closed her eyes. In 1988, he had gone through rehab just to make Chess happy. Carol could see it coming in stages—his relapse. She could see stages almost as sharply as she could see the crystalline moments when lives take their irretrievable turn. Like she had intuitively known the moment Chess' AIDS had gone active on that July evening at Steven's mother's apartment in Magnolia, all of them happily arranged around the living room piano.

Carol and Steven and Chess had wandered over there in the euphoric opera-house afterglow of Die Meistersinger (or as Chess said, Der Singer Meister) and were sipping Chablis—Steven nursing dourly on his Cascade water. On the mantle over the fireplace, there was a black and white photograph of teen-aged Steven blowing bubbles through a wand. Mrs. Ennex raced around the room, targeting lamps on the artwork and turning the books in the shelves so that all the titles read straight up.

Her husband, Steven's father, had been a stress engineer for Boeing. He'd died running on a treadmill in the gym, and after that, Sandra Ennex had moved from Puyallup to fashionable Magnolia. Carol loved Mrs. Ennex, cautiously. She was honest and direct, yet you had to approach her. She had silver hair that began in dark roots and culminated with flaring violet tips; the corners of her eyes were fretted, and her smile ended not in an upraised apogee, but curved down as if by consequence.

That June night after the opera, the lovers were seated at Mrs. Ennex's aquamarine piano—the oddest thing you'd ever see—trying to echo some of the Wagner. Steven played the upper register while Chess bent into the bass lines and tapped the pedals. Mrs. Ennex was aiming one of the art-lights, and the beam struck against Chess' right cheek— that was when Carol saw the beginning spackle of the unaccountable, runaway rash, and she knew he was going to die. Watching him go, the way a hot day loses its lustre to the dark line of evening, was hard enough. And now, Steven had begun to issue his bizarre caveats.

The bus groaned up toward Capital Hill. Carol lifted her head from Steven's shoulder, tugged on the end of his tartan muffler.

"Seriously," she said, "you need to get active again in AA, or find yourself some HIV support group."

Steven glowered over his shoulder at the middle-aged woman behind them in the blue-stocking Seahawks cap. "Maybe we don't need to talk about it here. And maybe not anywhere else, Carol. Back off, will ya?"

Issue 1.0

So odd, this righteous tone in her. Carol hated to think of herself as the broadly promotional girl for self growth. She didn't have the drinking problem. She had the disappearing-act boyfriend, mind-killing clerical job problem.

"I don't need to back off," she said anyway. "Don't be an asshole. One death is enough."

"Then my friend just vanished into thin air," said the lady in the stocking cap, to no one in particular. "It happens."

"Thanks," Steven said, turning around. "As the lights go out over the world, your words will bear me through."

"Steven. You could be nicer," Carol whispered.

"So could you," he said.

They got off at the light and trudged up Broadway to the Gravity Bar for some healthy drinks: wheat grass and carrot juice cocktails. The waitress behind the counter wore a white cotton shirt with kiddy Band-Aids crisscrossed over her pockets. A gold ring was threaded through her left nostril, which looked infected. She was chopping cloves of garlic, took one look at Steven and said, "How about a Liver Flush?"

"Is it delivered rectally?" he asked.

The waitress shook her head, grinned feebly. "Garlic, olive oil, and lemon juice with a mineral water chaser. Revitalizes the daylights out of your immune system."

"What immune system?" Steven asked.

"Sorry for you," she said.

The waitress ignored them a good ten minutes, passing back and forth, before she came and took their orders, then went off to construct their spinach salads.

"You go drinking and pill popping after Chess dies and your love is all a lie," Carol told him, starting up again. "Don't think he won't know."

Two sorority lesbians wandered in, set their Nordstrom bags on the counter, and fell into a roller-coaster dialog punctuated with "likes" and "wows." One of them plucked chocolate chips from a huge cookie and fed them into her lover's mouth.

"Don't start your Angels-Up-on-High sonata," Steven said. "You don't go up high when it's all done, you go out sideways. A diaspora of atoms."

"It's almost too hard to deal," Carol said, "when you're as pissy as this. I can't find much to give you."

He put his hand—cold, brittle, damp with rain—set it on her own folded hands and looked at her. Carol felt a dim shudder move through her.

"Give me your silent regard," he said. "Maybe I won't do a thing after all, you can't tell. Maybe, afterwards, something will change." He spoke without conviction and Carol felt her back stiffen.

"Don't snow me," she said. "Just don't bother."

The waitress finally brought over their salads. She held the check in the air, looked sidelong at them, fishing around until, at last, Steven said,

"Don't ruffle your tail feathers, hon. It ain't catching. It's only a criminal lifestyle."

Carol laughed. He had always startled her into laughter. Go way back to Puyallup High days, when Carol and Steven had been sweethearts. The first time they were startled, fearful, and both of them ended up crying in each other's arms. But afterwards, they laughed even as they made love, delirious with the illicit and delightful end of their virginity. He could make her laugh at the idiotic rigidity of their Catholic families. But there was no glimmer of the brittle edge to his humor then, nor a spoor of the grave bouts of drink. They'd gone steady for a year and a half, until he said something was off kilter about it, and he didn't know what. She was a good kid, he said, but something was horribly off. Now, somehow after all the fractures and disappearing acts, they still were friends. He had given her something that in his retreat grew in consequence.

After inexplicable abstinence, almost ten years later, when his newfound sexuality had finally surfaced, Steven was beaming. He met Chess in the Seattle Men's Choir: Chess the erstwhile poet, the high school band director and math teacher. To Steven, who worked the night classical music shift at KUOW and tuned pianos, Chess was simply exquisite, and their match serendipitous. Most of their friends were alarmingly dead or becoming dead. One night after rehearsal, Steven and Chess went out dancing; Chess broke his big toe, and they hurried to the emergency room, then home together afterwards. Chess had recited Matthew Arnold: *Ah, love, let us be true to one another.* That was that, and in some way Steven's sobriety was linked to fidelity.

When Carol looked at Steven now in the Gravity Bar, she could only see a blank palisade behind his anger. That was the worst of it. She tried to be cheery, to mend something across her face.

The waitress had marched off to other campaigns. Steven saw Carol's look and grinned. "Come on. Every faggot needs a fuzzy friend," he said.

"I'm your hairline trigger," she said, her laugh coming out more like a hiccup. "Try and not take the afterlife so seriously. Chess wants you to live happily ever after."

"It's not the pain that I can't take," said Steven.

He folded his knife and fork across his half-eaten salad. It looked like a logo for something.

He rose and dropped his napkin on the counter.

"You can be one bitch of a nag," Steven said, simmering up to a grand exit. One thing about Steven, his glamour was always enlarged by flight.

Carol started after him into the street, but he'd flagged a cab so deftly she felt deflated, ashamed standing there in the wind.

She went back into the cafe and paid Miss Nose Ring.

"I guess I was a little stupid," the waitress said.

"Don't worry," said Carol. "With us it's hard to know the difference."

She trudged out to find a bus to Greenlake. The clouds brimmed up over the Sound and it had started to rain again. So thoroughly typical. And it was the last time she would ever see Steven Ennex.

Actually, it was Angie Cooper, another Puyallup High survivor who now worked at Jenny Craig, that told her about Steven's overdose the day after it happened.

They rarely phoned each other anymore, so when Angie called at Klass Title, Carol hushed her voice so her cubicle-mate would know it was important. It was her fraud to get a rise out of Payton. He was already leaning across his desk, pretending to look for something in all his papers, angling an ear at her. He'd treat her to lunch, or she could play it mum and reel him in all week long on a line of curiosity. At bottom Carol knew, guiltily, that she was still pissed at Bill Austry for running off without fanfare. Ten months shot to pieces. Carol knew she was working Payton like a Sousa Medley. Hell, what could you do—Klass Title was a shitty satellite office for a gloomy company located in San Diego.

The receiver crackled; Angie Cooper was giddily toxic with gossip. It apparently happened following Steven's visit to Chess at the hospice. He had gone down the hall to the critical care unit and when the nurses stepped out, Steven had disconnected a sleeping patient's I-V drip and fed the trickle of morphine into his own arm. The first dosage, while scant, made his task easier and somehow sensible. So the next logical step was to take down the entire assembly and climb into the patient's commode so the full bottle, now reassembled for quicker deployment could drain into him. All the while, six rooms down the hall, Chess was watching TV, clicking with drastic boredom from talk show to talk show on the remote control.

Steven Ennex: Into the silent sideways diaspora of atoms.

Angie, idiotic as ever, apparently had no clue that Carol and Steven had remained so close. She rambled on stupidly a moment—Steven had paid the price of his wicked lifestyle, she said—then hung up. Carol continued to talk into the receiver: Fine, she said. Nice of you to call.

She dropped the telephone into its cradle and stared at Payton. His smile lifted up his brushy mustache. She smiled back. It was a nice afternoon, he said. Almost time for lunch. She plucked a paper clip from its plastic caddie, unfurled it with her fingers and jabbed its first quarter-inch length into her biceps.

It certainly looked odd, jutting out like an antenna from her arm, and she began to laugh at the small purpling bubble that drew out of the puncture.

"Good god," Payton shrieked.

Carol let him come around her side of the desk and lift her from her seat. Then he walked her by her good arm down the hallway where the tacky beer calendars fluttered in their wake, down the arcade of sputtering fluorescent lights to the men's room where he sat her on the commode and trussed a wet paper towel on her forehead. He dropped the paper clip in the trash and pressed his thumb over the punctured welter. She let him dance about, administering to her arm with superfluity, running the tap and asking if she'd had a tetanus booster.

"I might have a Band-Aid," he said, flustered, rummaging in his wallet when a red-foiled condom flap-jacked to the floor.

"Just forget it," Carol said, absently looking at the graffiti in the stall. Someone (she hoped not Payton—but who else sat here?) had drawn a rather distorted representation of female anatomy. She reclaimed her arm, let him re-assemble his wallet.

"I'm really okay," she said.

When they had gone back into the office proper, Carol sent Payton out, ostensibly for decaf lattes and gyro sandwiches, and she telephoned the hospice.

"Sorry. I don't know who to call first," she said when Chess picked up the extension. "I don't know whether to come over."

"I didn't call anyone," he said gently. "Don't take it personally. Sandra was terrified of publicity and it still got in the PI and Times. Nothing to do or say, we've already had him cremated."

"Can we do a memorial service or something?" she said. "I kinda feel left out."

Chess was quiet a moment. She could hear the plink of Christmas jingles over his intercom in the background.

"Chess?"

"I feel left out myself," he said. "You know, it ends up that Steven was the most self-centered little zit on earth."

"I'm coming over."

"Not yet," Chess said. "But you ought to call Sandra. You can do something for her."

"Like what?"

"Hell, I don't know. You'll have to go and see," he said. "She's too nice a sport for all this crap."

Carol said good-bye and clocked out, and then she walked into the low December sunlight. At the corner of Eighth Avenue, Payton stood in front of the latte cart, hitting on a woman in a gray pant suit. Carol crossed over, walking briskly against the wind. She sat in the back of the Magnolia bus, rubbing her arm, wondering how Chess would hold up, laughing suddenly at the insanity of that notion, wondering how in god's name you even looked at the world the same way.

Up the hill, at the apartment in Magnolia, Sandra was apparently not at home, and Carol bitterly tore at herself for not phoning ahead. As she turned and descended the stairs to the street, Carol heard the faint rich supplication of a piano. She went back and rang the bell, but no one answered. Well, perhaps the music had come from an adjacent apartment. The wind bit away at her cheek. The cold air tickled her throat and by the time she stepped off the bus at Phinney Ridge, she had developed a cough.

Carol ate a supper of mushy days-old salad and cold vermicelli from the icebox. She took a broad swig of cherry Ny-Quil—a leftover from the last flu—and slipped into bed before the winter sun went down. Her arm ached, and the wind pestered the window panes.

Later, around midnight, the phone roused her from blank, narcotic sleep. She rolled over in bed, fumbling to put her mind together. It was Payton, most assuredly smashed.

For a moment, undeniably, she thought of having him come to her bed, if for no other reason than to get the ugly thing over with and move on ahead into dark resentments and a search for a new job. She missed Bill Austry. She missed him on the wall-side of her bed, though she missed not so much his feckless intimacy, but the inebriating promise of it.

"You have to leave me alone," she told Payton. "You can't make it better."

"If it's about working at Klass, I'll quit," he said. "Please go out with me." She could hear the sound of talk, glasses clinking in the background.

"There aren't enough jobs out there," Carol sighed. "Otherwise, I would have left Klass a year ago. Besides, Payton, I just can't see you. Not socially."

"Then see me anti-socially. You don't want to, it's not can't."

"Okay. I don't want to."

"Then fuck you very much, Miss Office Tease. You know what sexual harassment is? I do. You can't feed me to the lions."

While he continued his sloppy tirade, Carol wondered about lions she had seen on Wild Kingdom and how the meat dangled and shook from their mouths as they fed. Then she thought of the drawing in the men's room and hung up on Payton. Her cough started anew. She unplugged the phone and went in search of the Ny-Quil bottle.

The urn that held Steven's scant ashes stood on top of the hospice armoire, a Japanese brush painting of vermilion carp behind it. Sandy Ennex stood in the sun-blazed window frame, tilting a water can over a Wandering Jew. Her face was smooth and peaceful, as if it had been rectified. Nearly a week had passed since Carol had first spoken with Chess, and in the interim he'd freighted himself with Steven's death. A pale green oxygen tube had been fastened into his nostrils, and he was propped up with pillows. His voice had a thin, nasal timbre.

"Old musicians don't die," Chess was saying, "they simply decompose."

"Good one," Carol said from her chair next to his bed. She had brought him a Sunday copy of *The New York Times* and a *Seattle Weekly*, both folded in her lap. "You have any others?"

"Sure," Chess said. "I was thinking he didn't go back to the bottle, he went into one."

"Yes. Brilliant."

"At least *I* was sober when *he* died."

"Come on, Chess." Carol popped him on the shoulder with the paper. "That's enough."

"Oh, indulge him," Mrs. Ennex said, turning from the window. "He'll be done in a minute." She looked over at Chess. "Won't you, dear?"

"She loves me like the daughter she never had," Chess said.

Carol grinned, "I'd gladly take that job."

Sandy Ennex put up the watering can and smiled at her. "Carol, you were the one who was supposed to marry Steven," she said, then winked at Chess.

Carol hid her face behind the newspaper, mugging. "I guess he just forgot me at the altar," she said. "One of us forgot."

Chess folded his hands behind his head. "If that had happened we'd have been in a helluva state," he said. "Tails wagging dogs. Anyway, Carol has good old Billy."

Mrs. Ennex looked over, sharply rapt, but said nothing. From the window behind her, the sun kindled the tips of her hair and gave her a faint, purple corona.

"We can't stay as long today," she said. "I'm taking Carol over to Westlake Center to look at the decorations. We might even buy you a present."

Chess nodded at the urn. "Maybe you could take him along. He needs a walk every so often."

"Good lord," Carol said.

Chess shut his eyes. He reached up with his hand and ripped the oxygen tubes from his nose.

"I hate these goddamn things. I have boogers the size of rocks, and my chest feels like a building fell on it. I mean it. Sorry, Mrs. Ennex, but would you please take what's left of your son the hell out of here?"

At Westlake Center the traffic was ugly. Carol had held the urn in her lap until they had found a space in the parking garage, then she nested it carefully between a cashmere sweater and a yellow towel in the rear seat of Sandy Ennex' Honda. The sky was swept clear by the wind, and the air sizzled with Westlake neon. People jostled each other on the sidewalks. Mean little world of indifferent traffic, Carol thought, running circles inside this surreal big one with former lovers in urns. Customers were lined up five-deep at the coffee kiosk just outside the center, and Carol and Mrs. Ennex drank their caffeine fix at a white table beneath the red umbrellas. Bike messengers huffed by on the cobblestones.

"Seattle is a city for the zealous," Mrs Ennex said. She looked at Carol blankly. She stood up from their table and Carol hopped to her feet, and they pressed ahead through the throng.

Inside the mall the air was thick with cinnamon and tallow. On the mezzanine, there must have been two dozen Santas mulling about. It was something. Carol stood on the up-escalator and took Sandy Ennex's arm.

Carol said, "Chess didn't really mean it, you know."

"Oh, yes he did!"

Mrs. Ennex opened the top-most buttons on her Burnaby parka. In the sudden heat, her eyes had begun to moisten. "There's nothing I don't know about Chess. I haven't been spared information about anyone."

"He just meant he couldn't stand it."

Mrs. Ennex pulled her arm free. "Let's stop this. We know how to get along fine, don't we?" They had topped the mezzanine, and Mrs. Ennex went into the bright spectacle. "Oh Carol, isn't that the most fabulous potpourri?"

"Sure," Carol said, lagging behind.

It was fine, this mindless shopping, except for the whole thing, and it went on for hours. Mrs. Ennex stopped in the chic-as-hell shop to buy cedar bars for her dresser drawers, stopped for another quick double mocha at Starbucks, looked rather hopefully at a Venetian glass tureen in an upscale studio, and finally settled on a pair of peach-colored sandals at Leeds.

While she tried them on, Carol wandered off to Brentano's and found herself dragging her hand over the titles on the self-help rack. The volumes ran over four shelves and she had to kneel to read the bottom row. *Women Who Hate*. She gave that one a thought, until she felt Bill Austry's shadow course through her with its icy amperage, then she stood up and looked around. The aisle was empty and gave out a hallowed hush.

Carol set off for the fine art books, but ended up in the metaphysical section and was reading something in Emmet Fox about "the light of the body is the eye." The phrase held her in a strange vortex. She was still lost, her eyes blurred when Mrs. Ennex swooped in beside her and took her hand.

"Find something?" Mrs. Ennex asked.

"Delight of the body is denial," Carol heard herself say.

"Don't be so rough on yourself, dear," Mrs. Ennex said. "Incidentally, I've had too, too much coffee. Now, you'll have to suffer me over to Nordstroms. Can you? It's only four and I'm not nearly ready to quit."

It was the break of evening when the dusk is glazed with secrets. Carol accompanied Mrs. Ennex into the chill air, and they fell into step beneath the blinking cadence of lights. Vapor rose from their lips as they chatted about pianos and how much Steven had liked to play. Now that they had finally gotten around to talking, Carol was vacillating. She told a harmless story about the afternoon that Steven had come home tipsy with spring fever from the University of Washington and played through half of the Ring on Chess' dining-room upright. They'd sat there all night long, trading places, Chess and Steven working the keys while Carol turned pages and brewed coffee and twisted fresh candles into the soft-wax base of the spent tapers, the three of them blissed out as the sun finally peeped through the shadow of the Cascades.

Carol and Mrs. Ennex were standing now before a great mirror at the perfume counter in Nordstrom, and Mrs. Ennex lifted an atomizer of Opium and squirted its potion into the air. Carol watched in the mirror as the mist dissipated into the background of lights and moving bodies.

"Such a nice story," Mrs. Ennex said, "and nice of you to tell it." She put down the atomizer and met Carol's eyes in the mirror. "You're not seeing Billy any more, are you dear?"

"I broke up."

"Naturally," said Mrs. Ennex. "Inevitable."

For a good moment they watched each other in the glass, then Carol took Mrs. Ennex by the arm and led her deep into Nordstrom so they could buy something for Chess. They looked for a long while before giving up.

It was pouring out and the howling wind made the lights flicker across the city. At Klass Title, Payton showed up drunk. He stayed long enough to call Carol a "no-time slut"—whatever that meant in his personal lexicon. Then he removed his sports coat, turned it inside-out and began dumping the contents of his desk into it. He went off like that into the rain, the coat-bag slung over his shoulder. A newly unemployed Santa of Malice.

Carol telephoned the home office in San Diego and informed Mr. Elliot that they'd need a new clerk. Mr. Elliot said he'd fly up after New Years. "Pronto enough?" he asked.

"Sure," she said, "I'm great at holding things down."

After she hung up, she went into the hall cabinet and took out a roll of paper towels and cleanser, and she burst into the men's room and scrubbed at the misshapen image of the vulva. By the time it was gone, her arm ached. The rain pelted the skylight, and the whole thing made her rather sad. From the outer office, the phones had begun to ring and she let them dash themselves out.

She was thinking of Chess as she passed back through the hallway with the half-spent roll of towels in her upraised hand. It came upon her like an intruder, her own shadow cast so large upon the wall that her heart blazed.

She sat at her desk, waiting grimly for the image to resolve itself: this sudden demonic figure with upraised weapons of sanitary fortitude. A regular Brunhilde of the bathroom, the latest in a series of false gods. Carol burst into laughter. Chess' gloom called for action of heroic proportions.

She telephoned Marty Abrahms at the Gay Chorus. Yes, he said, it would be a bitch getting everyone together on short notice for a Wagnerian wake. But Chess' life was ever contracting. Sure, one pithy segment followed by a huge party. His enthusiasm grew as they spoke. They could certainly gather a few costumes from the Seattle Opera, and he was suddenly confident Carol could learn the part by rote with his coaching.

As the last rain of the year whipped against the windows, Carol locked up the office and took the bus to Pike Place. She walked past the newsstand under the cover of the market, beneath the bare bulbs dripping with steam, past the herbalists and the fish mongers and the dangling roasted chickens. She took the ramp down, underground to the magic shop. They sold flash paper there, the kind that sparks up between your fingers like a burst of subatomic energy.

"Naturally, the costume calls for braids," Mrs. Ennex said.

Carol sat before a long mirror in the living room, the costume armor plate fastened over her breasts. A Valhallan hat with its curved horns sat beside them on the aquamarine piano.

Outside the apartment in Magnolia the rain had given way to a furious blow. The alder scratched away at the windowpanes, and beneath the mantle that held the black and white photo of Steven Ennex the flue moaned with an insuck of wind.

Earlier that morning Carol had conditioned her hair and it combed out easily, sparking with short embers of static as Sandy parted the middle with a blue brush. Carol could feel the heat of Mrs. Ennex's wide bosom against her neck.

Sandy divided the hair into thick bands, and she twisted up the shocks into twin, maiden braids. She smiled at Carol in the mirror.

"So where'd you place the urn?" Carol asked matter of factly. "I thought it'd be on the mantle."

"I had to take it back to Chess," said Sandy. She looked sternly at Carol in the mirror. "You know? I have to confess something."

Carol closed her eyes, then nodded.

"One afternoon I was standing right here," Sandy went on, "right before this mirror with that silly urn in my hand. I was looking for a place for it. Then the next moment I had the lid off and I was stirring the ashes with my finger. Well, sort of stirring. I just took a dab of him, see, and put him to my lips. Then tasted him on my tongue."

Carol reached for the hand that held her braid, and Mrs. Ennex stiffened.

"Oh," Carol said, "it's nothing to be upset about."

"I wasn't upset, dear. I'm upset that I never did as much for him before, even knowing where he was descending."

From the streets outside, the wind kicked itself up and the light began to flutter, and Carol felt the air begin to move inside her in strange euphony. Against her back, Sandy Ennex's body had begun to sway. Then, Sandy ran a hand through Carol's hair.

"You really are beautiful," Sandy said, "from within and without."

In the mirror Carol's eyes were brimming. Sandy reached up and let loose the knotted braid and began smoothing the long wisps of hair with her fingers, running her hands delicately down and across Carol's shoulders.

Carol tightened her eyes, then gave up with a distended sigh that ran through her body.

"I was worse. I knew he was going to do it," Carol said, weeping honestly now.

There was no end to the things everyone had failed to do. The news of her great iniquities rang from Carol's heart as the alder smacked against the window. All along, Sandy Ennex just kept smoothing her hair and smoothing her hair, and after a while the wind began to take the world away in pieces.

Witness Borne
Ross Johnson

Iceman, silver gelatin print, 2000
Caress, silver gelatin print, 2000

Snakeye, silver gelatin print, 2000

Ross Johnson, *Groundzero*, Ilfochrome, 2002

untitled 03-13-02
Josh Magnuson

some days i'm too thick with words
i'm all for love and warmth and skin
i can write about that too
but mostly
i hold it in
hoping it won't leak out

Hwy. 68 Overpass
Camille Napier

I was cursed with a standout name
in a small town
So that no boy would
spray-paint his love
or his luv
or his 💚 for me
in a banner across the highway.
I wanted to be Stacey or Kim,
a girl loved by John or Jim
in public anonymity.
I wanted a brazen boy
with great balance and some flagrant disregard for the law
to scale a silo
or lean over a bridge
and declare to the world we'd be
2-together
4-ever.
But I was Camille,
the only one in town
—or even in three counties—
and the boy would have been caught
though his name was plain.
And his love might not have lasted through 100 hours
of community service.

Absence
Catherine Eve Patterson

When Kitty met Mike she was still an eighteen-year-old punk working as a café waitress at an upscale eatery on Lower Broadway, close to her school and dorm. This was good for two reasons. First, it allowed her roommate to stay up snorting coke until two or three in the morning without annoying Kitty. Second, it paid for her clothing.

Mike, already and always older than Kitty, was a painter who'd been living in the East Village ever since his father died, and his mother decided to hide the will. What Mike remembered most about his father, apart from the fact that at some point back in the seventies his family had been singled out as the perfect American family and splashed on the cover of a lifestyle mag—all this before there were lifestyles—was that he spent the last two months of his life eating pints of chocolate chip ice cream in his hospital room, waiting for his soul to drain out of his shell and telling Mike not to get suckered like he'd been.

Mike moved to a tiny apartment next door to a Catholic soup kitchen and took a job as a delivery boy so that he could eat. Despite this, Mike was always hungry, iron-thin, and wired. Mike and Kitty spent an afternoon in a bar near Christopher Street that boasted bad bohemian art on its walls and an old 45 jukebox with the best jazz in town. It had started to rain as they walked there, and by the time they left it was pouring. It did not take more than this afternoon for the two to fall in love.

On 13th street Mike and Kitty kissed for the first time. It was raining and the billboard plaster they leaned against got into their clothes, their backs and hair. Mike took Kitty to his apartment on East First Street and both of them showered. The best thing about his apartment was this shower. Mike had built and installed it himself. When Kitty got out of the shower she jumped on his back and they spun around the room laughing until they crashed into a desk. When she fell asleep that night she dreamt she had fallen into one of his canvasses—blue poppies, flowers blooming endlessly around her.

Mike had come from a childhood of chores and American pastimes. He'd been a football player, newspaper boy, and builder in a small, wealthy town. His father would vanish and return like clockwork, the house style nuclear, then modern, then swinging and with shag, until finally his father developed cancer and died leaving a rich wife, two angry children, and Mike who came out of the deal all golden. This was something his siblings never forgave him for—his looks, charm, and running with the popular crowd.

Kitty's favorite story about Mike's childhood involved the time where he, serving as an altar boy, had stepped too close to someone's candle, his blond curls going up in flames as his parents aped to him silently from the pews that he should put out the fire on his head. Mike never combed his hair, neither did Kitty, and both of them loved reading and clean oceans.

Kitty's life, though very different from Mike's, included the same anchors of diligent dad, problematic mom, and being the one that got away. Away from what, Kitty did not know. She developed and continued an early habit of going away for many years until she finally figured that out. She was someone else's cuckoo clock until she pulverized the motor with a mallet.

Mike's favorite story about Kitty was the one in which she fell in love with an American boy, her first. She'd been raised elsewhere and drove her Tuffy bike in circles in the Delhi dirt yard until he came to find her. His name was Ricky. This boy she never kissed, but she knew she loved him and she loved his American lunch box. Kitty spent an orphaned childhood thinking about American things like Josie and the Pussycats, Velveeta, and Lucky Charms. All of these were as exotic to her as a basket full of genies, and Kitty always believed that if she got her mitts on any one of them, her whole life would change.

That summer, when the school year ended, Kitty moved to Paris to study French. Mike did not come. There are fourteen shoeboxes of letters and napkin art that testify to that period. Kitty for her part learned French but stopped speaking all together. She did not like or trust language or herself anymore. Everything had betrayed her.

The only friends Kitty made during her stay in Paris were a quartet of thieves who'd been working on her roof, and had taken a shine to her. She gave them melon that they hoisted up on a bucket through her skylight; they left her presents in her shoes. Language was not a required part of any of these transactions. Her favorite shoes were a bottle green pair of brothel creepers with purple embroidered flowers on their tops.

When Kitty returned to New York she went to the first pay phone she could find and called Mike. He met her at Café Dante at eight the next day. Each of them had cappuccinos with toasted ham and cheese. When Mike left, he went home and broke up with the woman he had been living with at the time. This was something that endeared Mike to Kitty before, during, and after they had been married. He was a stand-up guy. He did not mess around.

Mike brought Kitty to Nantucket where his family had a four-bedroom house on the water. He cooked them dinner, and lit the fire, they made love and G&Ts, and then fell asleep on the floor. Kitty dreamt that Mike's father was stepping over his corpse in the dark and that he'd come to pay her a visit. She knew that he wanted to know her intentions towards his son, and since she did not know her intentions she let him take her face in his hand and gaze down into her soul. After this, the corpse man walked away.

Mike for his part had a dream in which Kitty, getting out of an industrial elevator to his studio, had opened his robe to look at him. He let her look as long as she liked, even though there was sawdust everywhere and he was getting cold. Again, language was not part of

Miguel Lasala, *Corner*, photomosaic, 1999

either of these transactions.

Their first apartment was on 13th street in the West Village and here Mike and Kitty bought their first things. Rattan chair, fifties dining table—red Formica and chrome—and a bed on a platform that Mike built. The room was probably as big as your pantry but in it Mike and Kitty got along. They were all right. When Mike got his first show, Kitty bought him flowers and single malt, and when Kitty produced plays Mike built a giant hand for the stage that was an essential prop. His sister came to visit, a brown-haired savage girl, with tattoos of flies on both her hands.

Mike's sister hated Kitty. Kitty hated only her tattoos. She was a beautiful woman who'd grown up angry about everything. Life had been a cheater to this girl. Now that she was grown up she continued to keep her anger alive by putting herself into preposterous situations, a scientist working backwards to prove theories of vapor and rage. This kept her intact and allowed her to become a junkie, tattoo artist, and bitter disappointment to her mom. Which maybe was what she had been after all along. Kitty did not know. Kitty's family loved Mike. They were helpful and optimistic about her choice, and the only nagging doubt her mother entertained was that Mike had majored in literature at Kenyon and did not know his poets. Kitty's father enjoyed sharing a Scotch with Mike and a good laugh or cry about U.S. policies, domestic and foreign.

When Kitty and Mike were engaged, their wedding notice was written up in the *New York Times*, the paper of record and both families gathered for a celebratory cocktail at his mother Helen's apartment on 5th Avenue. She was entranced by Kitty's father, and jealous that Kitty's mother had a man.

Kitty and Mike were married on Nantucket in an Episcopal Church by a woman minister. The night before the wedding Mike and Kitty's brother got stoned, and Kitty went for a moonlight bike ride with her other mother, Cora. This was one of the happiest memories of Kitty's life, riding in the moonlight with sweet Cora. Cora did not like men, weddings, funerals, or babies—in no particular order—but had been a good sport about it all. She was happy that Kitty seemed pleased, and pleased that Kitty had chosen a suit that could be re-purposed if things didn't work out. The innkeeper and Cora hit it off, and later Cora went to visit him during the off-season.

Mike and Kitty received presents from people they did not know, of things they would never use. Cut fruit bowls, candy trays, and salvers. Kitty did not know or use the word salver, she used the word slaver, silver, and sliver. The presents were kept in boxes that were more useful than the gifts themselves, and soon they moved into a larger apartment on East 12th street.

Mike painted an outline of Kitty in the kitchen so that she would always be around, and Kitty produced a play about a woman who had lost her mother and found herself. The play was a success, which surprised them both, so well did they know its characters and contents, but they did not complain. They took the money and went to Mexico where they lived on the beach for two years.

Mike produced a series of paintings called Mexico City that he showed at a gallery in Los Angeles to great acclaim. Kitty got pregnant and they named their daughter Emma. When she walked on the beach Kitty would tell Emma about the things that she'd already seen, and that were waiting for her when she arrived.

When Emma was born Mike cried the first good cry he had in years. His face got all scrunched like the baby's and they looked so alike that everyone had to laugh. Emma was a blonde-haired, space-eyed munchkin with petal lips and fists that opened and closed like hearts. Mike and Kitty took Emma home and slept with her in the middle of a white bed with cotton sheets and a Mexican pink comforter. The baby was placid, and Mike thought that his life had made a complete circle as he lay in this bed, the tangled hair and breasts of his wife at his side.

Emma drowned in shallow waters the afternoon that Mike and Kitty took her on an outing. Even though they had kept lookout. Even though it was nobody's fault. When Emma vanished in the surf, the sun still shredding the horizon, Kitty threw herself face first in the sandy water and tried to lose her own soul. Mike picked up Kitty, a mummy of salt and sand, and took her into his arms.

Mike and Kitty packed up the cabin at the seaside and went home. When they left, Kitty burned all of her work. In New York she wrote another play about a mother who loses a daughter and finds herself. This she burned in the apartment sink. When Mike got home she had taken the ash and painted outlines of herself on all the walls, with and without Emma. Mike decided to drink.

Mike drank for five years with a scientific expertise he'd not known he possessed. The studio, with its usual smell of sawdust, paint, and thinners was permeated with the stink of whiskey. Sometimes Mike talked to his dead father in his studio, certain that he was around.

Kitty took a job writing fluff pieces for society mags and traveled around the country interviewing people she knew she would despise. She was never wrong. When people told her she had a glamorous life, being married to an acclaimed painter and meeting the famous, Kitty decided to stop talking to humans. They were not worth her spit. Mike and Kitty drifted apart, she to departure lounges, he to his drink and soon they reached a point where they spoke to one another like well-mannered strangers in the same elevator. Going up, going down, and standing. There was not enough oxygen for talk.

Kitty wondered why no one had taught a course on early onset cancer of the soul for high school and college students. This course, she felt, would be the only one worth taking—the one that talked about how a person carried their own destruction right inside them. Their own maze, their Minotaur, and their thread.

Kitty flew one hundred and fifty thousand miles in six months. It did not matter where. Every plane was well known, every airport alike and her destinations—taxi, hotel, lounge—were the same in every town. In Nevada Kitty was propositioned by an oilman from Colorado. She spilled her drink on his Stetson. In Chicago a man with fists like red Christmas hams grabbed her coat. Mike sent Kitty a card that said HAHAHA on it for New Year's. In January Kitty went home.

Mike was sleeping like a kitten in the shower. Kitty picked Mike up off the tiled floor and dragged him down the hallway to the living room where she managed to get him onto the Bauhaus chair. She did not care if he banged his head along the way. Kitty washed the dishes, and bought coffee and the paper while Mike slept next to the bamboo. It had grown into a wild, glorious jungle during her absence. Kitty waited doing the crossword puzzle while Mike slept and gurgled on the sofa. She was thinking about her intentions, and the ghost of Mike's dad on the beach.

Kitty knew that her intentions had never included having Mike cock-eyed on the Bauhaus in filthy clothes or in love with a ghost of their past. She knew that she still loved and would always love him, with or without the ghosts and bamboo. He had a direct line to her inside that would never go away. Kitty thought about how Mike got migraines and would lie on the floor trying not to vomit while she doused the lights, and about how he would still burst to tears in old toy stores.

Kitty knew life was full of cancers of every type and that the body was no more than a shell for something much deeper and pure. She did not want Mike to die, now or ever, so she took off her red coat, put it on his sleeping shoulders, and waited. Don't let them sucker you, said Mike's dad, eating his pint of double chocolate from the ICU. He waved his spoon at her and smiled.

I'm Pretty Blessed
Dave Prager

Standing in front of my refrigerator, a bowl of Corn Flakes on the table, I've just discovered I'm out of milk. "Dear God in Heaven," I intone, "O Lord, my refuge and my fortress, King of the universe, blessed art Thou who shines His countenance upon me and gives me milk."

And lo, did milk verily fill the empty carton. Hallelujah, praise God, amen.

My life has grown generally easier since I realized that God answers my prayers. I don't have to go out for groceries any more, for one thing. And the other day I tore my favorite sweatshirt, and God answered my prayer for the knowledge to fix it, as well as a subsequent prayer for the needle and thread.

It's only been a few weeks since I came to understand my relationship with God. At first, suspicious it might be some kind of test, I tried not to pray too much—I still paid my rent, I still went to the bathroom, and if I couldn't finish the crossword, I still gave up.

But as time passed, my confidence in Him grew, and I came to understand that unconditional love is just that—He heeds my prayers, and because He's God, there's no such thing as taking advantage of Him. Long story short: riches, fame, happiness, love, health, and most recently, a quart of skim milk.

So now, having everything a person could possibly want, I'm pretty content. Some people in my position might start seeking spiritual fulfillment, like praying for the meaning of life, or for knowledge of the true nature of God, or whatever. I'm not sure if I'll get to that—the other day I prayed for digital cable, so for now I've got like seven HBOs fulfilling me.

You should know, however, that I am planning to make a few altruistic prayers soon. I'm aware there is suffering in the world, and sometimes I feel like maybe I can do something about it. And I will, in July. Right now the Nuggets are 64-0, and I don't want to break His concentration—some miracles may be harder than others.

In fact, I had just started thinking about getting ready to determine how I should go about deciding what to pray for when the doorman buzzed up that God was here. I was surprised—in spite of all the attention He pays me, I never expected Him to visit. I met Him at the door, and with all appropriate genuflection and aversion of gaze, ushered Him in, asking Him to wait briefly in the foyer while I ran into the living room and prayed for a nicer couch.

As God settled into my new Herman Miller crushed red leather sofa, I marveled that after thousands of years of keeping humanity waiting, God had chosen to manifest Himself in my very presence. Realizing my awesome duty to mankind, I got all psyched up to ask Him to reveal the secrets of the universe, but then I realized that once everyone found out, they'd want to turn this place into a shrine or something, and I'd just moved in. So I offered Him a drink instead.

God asked for a Harvey Wallbanger. I went into the kitchen and prayed for the knowledge of how to make a Harvey Wallbanger and, once that was granted, prayed again for some vodka, orange juice, a splash of Galliano, ice shaped like little crosses and stars and crescent moons, a really, really nice Collins glass, and a coaster.

I returned to the living room. God sipped His drink, protesting that there was no need for me to go to all that trouble. I prayed His forgiveness, and He forgave me.

God studied His drink for a moment, shifted in His seat, and then smiled awkwardly. "Dave, as you know, My love is unconditional, and My power infinite," He began. Suddenly, I knew what was coming. I had gotten too greedy. I had prayed for too much. He was going to cut me off, or worse—what if He really was a vengeful god?

Frantic, I started preparing justifications and counter-arguments. But then I remembered that He's omniscient—He'd probably already thought of them. There was nothing I could do. As He cleared His throat, I desperately prayed He wouldn't bring up the subject.

"So how about those Nuggets?" He asked. "Tell me Jordan's not playing the best ball of his career! And I'm so stoked that Bird and Magic both 'chose'"—He made little quote marks with His fingers—"to come out of retirement." I agreed the team had a solid squad, and thanked Him for His influence in the matter. We talked some more sports, then a bit about the weather, and after I gave Him a tour of the apartment, we shook hands and He left.

I prayed His empty glass into the dishwasher and sat stunned. It's one thing when God answers your every prayer, but it's another to change the will of God… or is it? Needing some guidance, I called my sister's roommate's father, a rabbi. However, he asked more questions than he answered—"What did He look like?" "What was He wearing?" "Did He say anything about me?"—so he wasn't much help.

Deciding I should just get my mind off the subject, I picked up the crossword. After all, it's always easier to take things at face value—my prayers get answered, no one gets hurt, why rock the boat? A few seconds later I finished the crossword and turned on the TV, praying for something good to be on.

Since then, everything has been great. I haven't heard anything else from God (which I take as a good sign), and I even did something good for my fellow man by praying for it to not get so cold in the winter anymore. In fact, the only problem I've had was one attack of theological doubt last Saturday, when I awoke in the middle of the night, terrified, in spite of all logic, that I wouldn't get into Heaven. What if I died tomorrow? How would I be judged?

I realized shortly that God was the answer, and began to pray. "Dear God in Heaven," I intoned, getting down on my knees to show I was serious, "O Lord, my refuge and my fortress, King of the universe, blessed art Thou who shines His countenance upon me and grants me entrance to Thy kingdom of…" Then I thought better of it, prayed not to ever die, and with my soul at peace, went back to sleep. Hallelujah, praise God, amen.

Regis St. Louis
From Temp to Porn

As an aspiring writer, I've had difficulty finding a job that allows me time to write while still earning enough to get by. After a few unsuccessful attempts at waiting tables, I decided to try temping. I asked around, and a friend referred me to Supertemps, a placement agency that specialized in editorial jobs.

Although Supertemps assured me they often received jobs in publishing, initially the only work they offered me involved a great deal of discomfort and humiliation. Once, I was contracted by a law firm to solicit teenagers on the street and ask them questions about bowling. Another time, I dressed up as a giant avocado and handed out guacamole at a Super Bowl party. A few weeks later, I donned a bunny suit and served punch beside a giant egg-man at an Easter party.

After that episode I phoned Jack, my recruiter at Supertemps, and asked him about the publishing jobs he mentioned when I signed up. "I'm really not all that picky," I told him. "I'll even take a corporate job. If I have to wear a suit to work, I'd rather it be made of cotton/wool blends rather than green carpeting."

Jack stopped calling me after that, and I figured my employment with Supertemps had come to an end. Running out of options, I was on the verge of accepting a job selling hot dogs near Times Square when Jack phoned.

"I've got the perfect job for you," he said enthusiastically. "It's a copyediting position in a publishing house downtown. It's an open-ended assignment, so there's a good chance it could go permanent."

Visions of poring over manuscripts at a small literary pub danced in my head as I graciously accepted the job. I knew things would turn around, I thought as I hung out my coat and tie for the next morning. I wondered if I'd rub elbows with any other writers—maybe get the inside scoop on literary agents looking for new voices.

The office was located in Chinatown on an unlit street next to a row of massage parlors. I took the elevator to the second floor and walked up and down the hall, baffled by all the signs written in Chinese. Finally, I spotted the dimly lit corridor leading to a door bearing the placard, "Publishing." I knocked lightly, and then went inside.

An elderly woman with white hair and turquoise eyeglasses sat behind the tiny reception desk reading a paperback novel. She had a coat draped over her shoulders and when she looked up at me her eyes looked enormous behind her glasses.

"Hi, I'm from Supertemps," I said.

"The temp?" she said, eyeing my tie. "First desk on the left."

The whole place felt less like a publishing house and more like an accounting firm fallen on hard times. The walls were bare, the windows covered in grime, and the carpeting—once a cheerful beige—had been worn to a rusty gray. Behind the secretary three mismatched desks stood in a row, all facing forward like well-disciplined schoolchildren. The only other features decorating the office were a few adding machines and other aging office equipment, which slumbered like animals in a barren barnyard.

As I was putting my stuff down, the man who arranged the assignment came into the office. A giant of a man, he had droopy features and sloped shoulders, a few wisps of hair plastered to his otherwise bald pate.

"Hi, I'm Gary," he said, offering his hand. "Thanks for coming on such short notice. We're weeks behind on our production schedule and we could really use some help. Let me give you an idea of the type of thing you'll be working on."

I followed him over to his desk, where I watched him open up the bottom drawer and stick his meaty paw inside, rifling around for something. "I don't know if you're familiar with our product, but it really doesn't matter," he said. "The bottom line is this."

He shoved a small journal about the size of *Readers' Digest* into my hand. Only instead of an understated design with text adorning the cover, it bore a lurid photo of a young woman with blonde hair, her skirt hiked up to reveal her naked ass. The header read: *Dirty anal whores want you to plow their hungry holes!*

That's when I realized that this publishing operation wasn't exactly going to help me make the move to Oxford University Press. Supertemps had done it to me again.

"I doubt if you have much training working with this kind of material," Gary continued. "My job is to get you up to speed, so you can get editing as quickly as possible. Now this is what we call a digest; it's easily held in one hand, get it?" He made a jerk off motion with his other hand, staring at me blankly.

"Our subscribers buy this for one thing only—to get off. Your job is to make that as enjoyable as possible. This is no Hemingway, and we certainly don't present it as such. It's all about the fucking," he said. "As soon as a character starts having interior thoughts we cut it. And if the story gets too literary, chop it."

"Literary?" I asked.

"It's all about the fucking," he repeated. "Here's the format. Two-paragraph opening, where the characters and scenario are introduced, one paragraph closing, and three pages of graphic fucking—but don't let it get repetitive," he warned.

He ran down a list of guidelines, referring to them as the bible of porn etiquette, and he made a number of other allusions to drive his point home. "We're just grease monkeys here," he said. "We take this material—which is outdated, poorly written, flowery, and we fix it. We take a broken-down Dodge and get it running again. It's not going to be a Maserati when we finish with it, but at least it'll run."

I nodded.

"Porn writers used to get paid by the word, so there's a lot of useless, repetitive shit that we have to get rid of. You'll see for yourself," he said, handing me a stack of clean copy. "The only way to learn this stuff is by doing it."

I started reading the first story, titled "Hot Box Lunch." Written from the perspective of a janitor named Jim, it detailed his exploits working in an all-girls' college dormitory. Every day he ate out a different co-ed, and he kept a journal of each experience—the flavor, texture, size, color, and wetness factor (or viscosity—as the writer dubbed it). In fact, he considered himself a connoisseur of fine pussy, much like other men are scotch or cigar enthusiasts.

I struggled to follow the storyline as the narrator jumped from first person to third and back again. At one point the custodian even referred to himself as a woman. The transitions were also a little rough. In the opening scene, Jim creeps into a young virgin's room and pulls off her panties as she slumbers. He parts her labes with his mouth, tenderly licking her clit, and just as he's about to thrust his tongue deeper, suddenly he's buck-naked and "balls-deep in her asshole, pumping her like an animal."

The next story was written from a woman's perspective, the protagonist a happily married librarian with a house in the suburbs, two kids, and an insatiable appetite to fuck anonymous young black men. Although she kept no written record of her conquests, she happily described every detail of her encounters from the time she unhooks her bra to the moment she puts her panties back on.

I edited the best I could, clarifying the ideas, tightening the narrative, making the dialogue a little less clichéd and repetitive. After I finished the first batch, Gary examined my work, his eyes scanning the pages as he knitted his brow.

"Why'd you take out 'shitpipe?'" he asked. "There's nothing wrong with saying 'he rammed his cock up her shitpipe.'"

"I thought it seemed a little 'flowery,'" I said, trying out one of the words he'd used earlier.

"Listen," he said, "it's not a good idea to keep repeating the same words. We have to be inventive. Take the penis, for instance. We've got cock, dick and prick—those are the main ones, but don't be afraid to use pecker, hard-on, boner, shaft, crank, rod, prod, staff, spear, tool, joint, or fuckstick. And as for women, pussy, cunt, and twat are your power words. But there's also cooze, box, slit, slot, snatch, fuckhole, or on occasion, ditch or chasm."

"Chasm?"

"Some readers really eat that stuff up," he said. "Now for sperm, we've got jizz, jism, cum, spooge, spunk, sputz, goop, gunk, and crud. But be creative. Don't be afraid to use man-sauce, man-chowder or love lotion. The more graphic the better. And for the female stuff you really have to be inventive since pussy juice tends to get overused a lot."

"Right," I said, trying not to appear to be too much of an amateur.

"Pussy juice is fine, but try using cunt cream, snatch sauce, or just plain nectar or honey. Now, whatever you do, don't use penis or vagina. Too clinical. It's not exciting."

Gary went back to his desk and returned with another batch of unedited copy. "These are family stories," he said.

"Porn for the whole family?" I asked, imagining Mickey Mouse stuffing his prick up Goofy's rear.

"Incest," he said, groping the shelf for more digests. "They're some of our hottest sellers. *Family Touch*, *Family Secrets*—are you familiar with either of those titles?"

"I haven't read too many—"

"That's all right. You'll catch on. It's the usual fare—co-eds sucking off their dads, sons humping their moms, anal aunts, the occasional family foursome, that sort of thing."

I nodded, soberly taking the crisp white pages from Gary and laying them out in front of me. By that time, I was already beginning to imagine that those smutty paragraphs just ached to feel my red pen smearing all over them.

I felt a little dizzy as I read the first title: "My Grandma Is One Hell of a Toothless Cocksucker." Determined to maintain a professional distance from the work, I uncapped my pen and started editing. As per Gary's instructions, I dutifully left in words like shitpipe and fuckhole, and I came up with as many synonyms for jism and genitalia as I could. By the end of the day I was bleary-eyed, and in need of a stiff drink. I'd thought of nothing but hard-core fucking for the last eight hours.

"Not bad, not bad," Gary told me on my way out. "If things work out, we might have a place for you full-time. See you same time tomorrow?"

Aaron Pou, *Jealousy*, Ilfochrome, 2001

Where Something Blends Into Another
Amy Van Orden

By the fifth class of the semester, the college art professor would identify which of his female students he would take home. She had to be beautiful of course, with the fluidity of a nude in a Parrish painting, but she also needed talent: a true artistic intelligence and maturity, a knowledge of the maestros that had come before and paved the way for the masters of today. He would walk slowly by her canvas and watch her movement—the soft way she held the slim wood branch of her brush, the wide spread of her dark bristles, her gentle stroke in working the thick paint. In the way her hands flowed, he could see all he needed to see.

On this fifth class he would always wear his black turtleneck and small wire glasses and use the scent of sandalwood along the large curve of his jaw. He would call her to his easel at the end of class and push out the strong muscles of his chest through the dark ribs of his shirt and tell her he could show her his private collection, if she were interested.

When they would arrive at his home, the Gruyère would already be set out on the glass table, the Concord grapes propped up in full purple bunches. He would pour her a glass of single-vineyard '93 merlot and lead her to the walls of his salon and stand near the warmth of the small focused spotlights and talk to her about each painting while she balanced the bowl of the round glass perfectly in her palm, the stem straight between the thin of her fingers, a soft pink of lipstick on the crystal's fine edge. The last canvas he would show her would be "Turning Road" by Derain, a Fauve work of incredible color: the blue and red trees curving, the gentle bend in the yellow street. And these are the words he would always deliver in a softer voice as he moved from the light and into the place where her ear was hidden by the chestnut shadow of her scented hair:

So many people think that life is impressionistic, that when you get up close to it, it is nothing but tiny dots, nothing but blobs of color that sit and dry on the canvas waiting to become form, the rounded edges overlapping, and when you step back you see the full picture, and then you are either very glad you stepped back or very sorry, because sometimes the full picture—the whole scene—is exactly what you expected, and sometimes it is nothing like what you thought it should be at all. But no, life is not like that. Life is like a Fauve painting where the colors are powerful and bright, and the lines are clearly there, but the color has no reason to stay within them, or no desire to follow the rules set out by someone once, long ago, who said yes, you must stay within the lines. You must. But I have to ask, Why? In Fauve one paints emotions vividly, puts passion directly into being, heightens everything. Les Fauves, the wild beasts. There are stripes of fields that blend into sky, and flowers that wash over onto the table, and yes, isn't life like that, where something blends into another thing so graciously that one cannot help but think that nothing has an end or a beginning but does have a definite implication of form or shape, like you, like now, when you are leaning into me, when the wine sloshes to the wide brim of the glass like a crimson crest and the front of your ice blue blouse is dripping past its lines.

JUNE 2003

1182 Treat Street
Maura Barthel

Did you ever wake up and find a 4 foot by 4 foot orange painting of two owls perched on a branch hanging on the wall across from your bed? Of course you didn't. I'm sure there's only one of these paintings. But I want to tell you about this morning. So, I woke up and there's this painting, two owls with a big yellow sun behind them surrounded by a crazy orange sky. The owls are standing really close to each other, almost like Siamese twins, trying desperately to look into each others eyes. Love birds. And then I think, wait, maybe it's a moon. Maybe it's a big full moon and they're surrounded by this evil swirling yellow-orange wind and it's a crazy orange night sky. And they're huddled together cause they're scared, eyes searching for safety. Then I think, well, either way they are not alone.

Then I notice my bed's been moved. My dresser is in a different corner, painted terracotta red. In fact, every piece of furniture is in a different place and quite a few things are painted terracotta red. I've also placed all of my miscellaneous belongings into fancy baskets. I say fancy as in expensive because there is a receipt on the floor for $174.92 from Bed Bath and Beyond. There is also a new pair of Nike's, a cute pair of mules, and a Nordstrom's bag with a silk, polka dot, halter dress in it.

On the mantel above the fireplace is a half empty bottle of Pinot Grigio. (Half full?) No glass. On the wall above the mantel is a collage; Yoshimoto Nara's pissed off little kids (one writing "nobody's fool" on a piece of paper), a drawing of a joystick and a camera my friend Anthony made for me, Polaroids from college, a poem by Susan Minot, and a doll with a frown, freckles, and really messed up hair. I decide to take a picture. "Still Life, 8:12 a.m." That's what I decide to call it.

When I reach for my camera I see 8 rolls of exposed film which I later develop. The 8 rolls, 288 pictures, are all of the sky. Why the sky? I don't know. One day at work I email everyone I know and ask them to send me their favorite quotes about the sky in an attempt to figure it out. A lot of people respond with "excuse me while I kiss the sky" or google searches and those do me no good. Some of them are perfect though. One goes like this:

"here is the deepest secret nobody knows
(here is the root of the root and the bud of the bud
and the sky of the sky of a tree called life; which grows
higher than soul can hope or mind can hide)"

So, anyway "Still Life 8:12 a.m." Great title. I take the picture. Then it hits me. It's 8:12 a.m. and I have to go to work. It's Monday.

On my way out the door Clive-the-Evil-Landlord asks me what I

Philip Ryan, *Untitled*, digital C-print, 2003

was doing all weekend. Was I going to work today? How have I been feeling? Where do I go so late at night? I tell him, "Clive, why don't you try less talking and more fixing." The bathroom hasn't worked in over two months.

So I get to my office (I file, professionally) and I find out that it's been invaded by teddy bears. Everywhere. Next to every in-box, on top of every computer, even the receptionist has one with lei around it. There are purple ones, green ones, blue ones, purple ones, red ones, lots of purple ones. There are even a few brown ones with American flag sweaters on. I go to the bathroom, into the big handicap stall. In my 4 months at the firm, I've spent a lot of time in this stall. I tell myself it's all right. It's no big deal. They're just teddy bears. I breathe in and out. I put my head against the cold marble wall. Then I go to my desk.

I ask Jillian-My-Favorite-Co-Worker, "Where'd they come from?" My desk has piles of stuff all over it, coffee stains, pen marks everywhere and a bulletin board that keeps falling down.

"What are you talking about?" Her desk is spotless. Everything has a place, the paperclips, the hole puncher. Her binders are stacked neatly and labeled. She smirks at me because she knows what I'm talking about.

"The teddy bears Jillian. The bears."

"IKON. They're gifts. You want one?" Of course, IKON the copy company, they give out cookies so why not teddy bears.

"You are so funny Jillian. Really. You are. No, I don't want one. I hate them. They're all over the fucking place. This is insane." I turn my computer on.

Jillian is organized, calm, and confident. She blends right in with the mauve of the firm. She goes through the day nodding and doing everything in a timely manner. It's almost like she belongs there. Almost. The people at the firm think she is one of them. She's not. She's one of me. The thing is she says everything with this smirk that not everyone notices. I notice it. How she's always slightly amused. That's the trick to Jillian.

"Hey, Maggie was at your desk before. She thinks you're having problems with anxiety. It's all the rage. *Time Magazine* did an article on it. It was on the cover. Anyway, she'll probably say something to you. Just so you know."

I tell her thanks and Maggie walks over. Maggie is so nice. She really is. She's not even 5 feet tall. She bakes. She's really the sweetest lady. She's my boss. She comes to my desk with a piece of paper. This one is not to file. It's for me.

"Hi Therese. How was your weekend? Are you feeling okay?" She takes her voice down almost to a whisper, "My niece has some of the same problems as you and I saw this number on a billboard so I wrote it down for you…."

1-800-ANXIETY. I want to tell her thank you, Maggie. Thank you for being so god damn nice. Thank you for writing this number down for me. I can just picture it. I'm feeling anxious, what should I do? Oh yes! That number Maggie gave me. What was it? I can't remember. Oh, she wrote it down, it's here in my purse. Thank God! 1-800-ANXIETY.

"…and make sure that your doctor checks your thyroid cause that can cause all sorts of problems, and try yoga…"

Try yoga? Yoga is my enemy. It's on my list of things I hate, right below the pigeons that hang out on 24th Street by the McDonald's that try to attack me when I get off the BART. I want to tell her that people in San Francisco do so much yoga that the rest of the country doesn't even have to stretch. I want to tell her lavender is not a nice smell, nor will I put cucumbers on my eyes. In fact, what I'd like to do is pick up one of these fucking teddy bears and, and, and then I realize she's still standing there.

"I'm sorry I was out Friday. I'll catch up today."

"Oh, it's no problem, don't worry. Don't worry at all." She is so so so nice. " How was your weekend?"

"My weekend was good. Yeah, it was good. Very good. I, um," I move some folders around on my desk. "I got a lot done."

The Day Johnny Unitas Died
D. Douglas Goodman

After the news, my morning regimen continues with a cup of Starbucks premier brew-at-home espresso and a small bowl of cornflakes with a dash of cocaine sprinkled atop for flavor. When breakfast settles, I hop into a shower (a water-so-hot-it-burns-the-skin kind of shower). My skin emanates a scarlet luminosity when I'm finished, and my hair smells of Vanilla bean.

My mother used to tell me that I would burn myself in the shower.

"David, you're going to burn yourself in the shower."

Nowadays, the burning is what let's me know I am still here.

An apology: I sometimes become filled with self-pity right before I brush my teeth.

My gums are weak and diseased (a beautiful gift passed on to me by my father), turning the sink-water red. Mesmerized by the thick drops of crimson moving unharmed through the sulfur-and-chlorine-infested water, it occurs to me that I showered with my socks on. The weighted sogginess accompanying each step feels, at first, uncomfortable, but I have to say I am getting acclimated to it—they almost feel nice, protective.

When the phone rings and I trip over the elongated heels of my socks, I know it is Walrus. I grab the phone and jump back into bed, sending the socks sailing across the room and smacking moistly against the peach-colored wall. Pulling the comforter over my now frigid toes, I press *Talk* and feel the warmth of the bed invading my exposed feet.

"Good morning, David Egman. It's nine-forty-five. This is your wake up call." Walrus' voice is high and quivering when he tries too hard to be serious.

"The Walrus crows too late this morning, although the thought is greatly appreciated."

"Watch the news this morning?" I hear immediacy in his voice that worries me.

"I was. Why, did something happen?"

"Johnny Unitas died."

"The old football guy?" I fear the wound this non-thought-out question will cause: my knowledge of football is limited, and Walrus prides himself on the endless supply of sports facts amassed in the recesses of his brain.

"No, Johnny Unitas, the greatest quarterback to ever play the game of football." Walrus' voice is now hard and sincere, and he pauses to let me sigh deeply as an apology. "Yeah, well, he had a heart attack. I'm going to Fiddler's later for a drink. Want to come?" Walrus eats cereal, probably his usual Golden Grahams, and the intense crunching moves the phone away from my ear. "Hello?"

"Yeah, yeah, I'm still here. You mouth is causing some static."

He swallows hard like a cartoon *gulp*, and the bowl clanging against his glass coffee table echoes through to my end.

It is at this moment I remember my meeting with Boomer. That realization mixes roughly with the morning cocaine. I sneeze droplets of red from my nose. Second bleed today already. The unsettling thought of lunch with Boomer churns the acids in my stomach and I vomit onto the Oriental rug my mother gave me last Christmas. Dropping Walrus, I walk into the bathroom and grab a towel to wipe the pieces of regurgitated cornflakes from around my lips. I pick up the phone to nothing, and yell "Walrus" three times before a "one second" ricochets back.

His toilet flushes and he says, "Hello."

"Nice."

"You left, and I had to pee."

"You didn't wash your hands."

"Only the phone suffers."

"And all future phone users." I am the only visitor to his apartment, ever. Note: do not, under any circumstances, use Walrus' phone.

"So, you coming to Fiddler's with me or not?" he asks.

"I have a meeting with Boomer today. Sorry."

"Little weasel?"

"Enormous fucking asshole."

"Ah."

There is a heavy silence. I can nearly feel Walrus' breathing, fast and weighted like an asthmatic. He clears his throat, and I am sure small pieces of mucus and breakfast fly onto his phone (see earlier Note).

"What?" I ask, not because I condone his blatant manipulation, but because he's breathing nervously, which he rarely does.

"Have you thought about it?"

His foot tapping breaks the silence.

"Probably not."

"The meetings, Eg. I really think you should come with me."

I wonder, now, how long I can avoid this subject again. "I don't know."

Walrus is talking about his weekly Narcotics Anonymous meetings. He was quite the user in his day, before the dark times, before the Empire (thank you, George Lucas). In fact, and I'm sure the reason for his mother-like attentiveness to my (fallacious) attempt at going clean, Walrus was my first introduction to the world of coke. It was Memorial Day, 1997, our first year out of college: Walrus had a table full, and his life partner, Nabokov, had passed out. At that point, I didn't even know they were such heavy users, but Walrus did a line, fell over and said, "Eg, do one, it's cool." So, I did one.

Nabokov died the next year: Walrus found him with his face crushed through the glass coffee table. Walrus pulled his lover's head back to see a sprinkle of white swimming in the pool of blood on the freshly polyurethaned hardwood floor, the shards of glass in his face, and the one rogue piece that entered Nabokov's right eye and probably tickled his brain.

Walrus called me and cried and I did a line while he cried. Then, Walrus quit and I did a line when he called and told me he was going clean for good. I did a line before and after Nabokov's funeral, and I cried when Walrus did a line and told me he wanted to die.

"Not yet, Wal. Soon, though. I promise." I don't really promise, and I cross my fingers behind my back so no one can see.

"Bullshit. You're going to fucking kill yourself. I can't take that. Not both of you. Christ, think of your mother."

"I can wipe my own ass, thank you."

"You obviously can't, moron. You just threw up all over yourself. You're sick."

The silence hits again, interrupted by the most beautiful of sounds at this point in such a conversation—the Call Waiting beep. Yahtzee.

"I have another call. We'll continue this later."

"You're sick, Eg."

The click of his hang up hits hard into my ear and I flinch a moment before switching calls.

"Davey boy."

The flinch stalemates right in that spot between my stomach and hell. "Hey, Boomer."

Boomer is in denial about what a severe asshole he is. And, despite his increasingly evident faux-knowledge of the real estate business, I cannot deny him a meeting. The man has more money than God and Bill Gates' love child.

Strictly as a side note: Boomer also employs a man named David Smith (although not his real name, it is the name I am to call him—actually, it could be his real name; I don't really know), a bond consultant from whom I buy about five-thousand dollars worth of white lightning a week.

"How are you this morning?" I can tell that he's smiling that big, Jokeresque smile that scares the shit out of me.

"I'm fine. Very well."

"We still meeting today?"

"I was hoping so." I bet he has a horribly small penis, like circus-midget small.

"You sure? Because you don't sound too enthused."

"Yes, Boom. I want to see you. I already made the reservations."

"Not in some shithole, I hope?" He chuckles, and I imagine he swallows his own tongue.

"At Park Plaza. Is that satisfactory?" I don't care.

"Fine, fine. Couldn't have picked it better myself. Beautiful scenery. Sweet ass." He chuckles again, and I realize he still has his tongue.

"Yeah, I know you love the scenery." The "scenery" he speaks of is Amanda, a waitress, and he claims to have fucked her on more than one occasion. He lies. I bite hard on my tongue and feel a little blood trickling from the edge and careening down my throat. "Twelve-thirty. I'll see you

Liz Wolfe, *Untitled*, light-jet print, 2002

then." My index finger hovers above the *Off* button like it were a thermal detonator.

"How about twelve?"

Boom. "It's non-negotiable. The reservations are made. See you then." Hanging up at precisely this moment is vital because I cannot bear to hear another word.

"I—"

The clock ticks past ten forty-five, and although my hair is still a bit wet, I have the sudden urge to get back into the shower.

The water is hot and piercing and cleanses me of the conversation. I used to shower like this, sometimes five or six times a day, after my father died. It was the only time I didn't feel like slitting my wrists, which I did when I was seventeen. My mother found me in the living room and she screamed at me for staining the new, Italian sofa, then dragged me by my right ear into the bathroom and told me to clean up before we went to the hospital. I nearly passed out showering off the blood, water burning at the exposed nerves and tissue in my wrists. I still don't hear well out of that ear.

For Christmas this year, I think I'll buy my mother an Italian sofa: red, perhaps.

I am naked in the living room and the phone rings. Walrus' voice on the other end makes me smile.

"When, then?" He is cold, rigid.

"When-then what?" I am at a loss.

"You said *not yet*. When, then?"

In my silence, I swear I hear crickets chirping in the phone. "What do you want from me? I cannot make myself ready to stop if I'm not." It sounds coherent in my head.

"I wish you could hear how stupid you sound."

"Who the fuck made you holy?"

He's quiet and crying, holding his breath so I can't hear.

"I'm sorry, Wal." I'm still naked, and I wish I had a towel because I see my neighbor staring at me through the living room window. "When I stop, I stop. That's all I can give you. You used for a long time. I will be ready, just stop counting the days."

"It has to end, Eg. I won't watch you kill yourself."

The phone clicks dead, and I walk into the bedroom to get dressed. He's wrong. It's not an addiction for me; it's an inevitable part of life, like showering or brushing your teeth. Slipping a silver tie over my head, I have the sudden urge to choke myself to death.

I call the restaurant on the drive there to ensure a table outside, where Boomer's voice won't meander inside and frighten other patrons. The steps of this lunch are simple: park, sit, order, pretend to listen, feign interest, eat, leave quickly. No coffee, because it takes too long.

He's already here, at a table outside. Amanda smiles and waves to me, and I cannot help but sympathize with her.

"Davey, Davey, Davey."

"Afternoon, Boomer. How are you?" I extend my hand, and he shakes it like a Texas-oil tycoon.

"Damn skippy. Sit, sit. Sweet Ass will get you a drink." Amanda walks into the conversation and I ask for a Bailey's on the rocks.

"Tell me, Davey. You ever fuck a Leprechaun?"

"I'm sorry?"

"A Leprechaun, you know. Little Irish guy, loves his rainbows and gold. Only one kind-of guy likes rainbows and gold. Fags. You like fags, Davey?"

"I have no aversion to them. One of my close friends is gay, and he's a wonderful human being."

"Really? Fuck it all. I can't stand them. These two fags were playing tongue tennis outside of Pottery Barn earlier, and I nearly threw up on them. Disgusting if you ask me."

"People are free to do what they want. That's the beauty of life."

"Beauty my ass. I'm all for freedom, but not when that gives a guy the right to stick his dick up another guy's asshole. God made pussies for a reason."

The vein above my eyebrow pulsates in rhythm with my heartbeat and I contemplate sliding a warm butterknife through Boomer's forehead.

"So, why the meeting today, Boom?"

Amanda delivers the drinks and we order, I the Pork Tenderloin and Boomer the Blackened Cheeseburger. Boomer slaps her ass as she walks away and she ignores it, making me immediately proud of her.

"The property just off New York and Park, the big white job. I want it."

"It's not a sale property."

"I don't care. You get it for me."

"If the property is not for sale, I can't just *get* it for you."

"Everyone has their price, their button. Find the right one and push."

"I have to strongly advise against this. I don't feel comfortable approaching the owner of a three-million-dollar property and telling him he has to sell."

The food arrives and Boomer immediately takes a bite of burger twice the size of his mouth, if that's imaginable. Pieces of bun fly about carelessly as he opens his mouth to speak.

"Davey, let's cut the bullshit. I want this property. Get it and shut up. I couldn't care less what you're comfortable with."

I take a bite of the tenderloin, succulent and tender, but a piece of rosemary penetrates the bliss.

"So, you ever fuck this fag friend of yours?"

Sipping water then Bailey's, I excuse myself to the washroom. Boomer retreats into his burger.

The washroom is small and pleasantly fragrant. Someone has left the sink slightly turned on, and the slow, steady dripping sound ricochets off the walls. I sit on the toilet and pull out my razorblade and mirror, carefully arranging and cutting two perfect lines. One, in all honesty, could never be enough right now. The first goes down smooth, warming my sinus vacancy and then my chest. I breathe in deeply before the second, and immediately after, cut and partake in a third and fourth line. The fifth, unexpected yet reassuring, knocks me off the toilet and I rest for a moment against the porcelain before standing. My head swells like a muscle tear and I walk back towards the table. Pressure pushes against my face from the inside like a backdraft, and a warmth drips from my nose onto my lip. The last line hits my stomach as I get to the table, and a mix of coke, bile, cornflakes, and one bite of pork tenderloin breaks stomach then mouth barriers and rains down over Boomer and the table. A weight presses heavy on the space between my skull and brain and everything, except for the screams of Boomer reverberating in my recesses, goes away.

Walrus is unhappy. I tell him to smile, but he doesn't listen. He cries. When Walrus is sad, he eats Reese's Peanut Butter Cups. I say this because, as I wake up from what feels like the longest nap in history, I smell peanut butter and chocolate.

"Did you hear?" I ask, which comes out as a whisper due to the aridity of my throat.

"Hear what?" Walrus sits beside my bed, running his right hand through my hair and eating with his left.

"Johnny Unitas died."

Walrus smiles and licks the remaining chocolate from his fingers. "Yeah, I heard."

My eyes close again, and the sound of machines beeping and

breathing rocks me back to sleep. It is sometime later the voices wake me up.

"Can you tell me what happened?" Male Voice asks.

"Are you a relative?" replies Female Voice.

"He's my brother."

I don't have a brother.

"Mr. Egman suffered a severe hemorrhage in his sinus cavity." Female Voice is professional and stern.

"How did this happen?" Male Voice sounds tired, scared.

"We ran a toxicological screen, which came back positive for cocaine. More than enough for an overdose."

The voices mumble and I no longer hear anything distinct. The door opens then closes.

"Eg? Eg, can you hear me?"

I open my eyes to Walrus.

"Howdy."

"How you feeling?"

"Like a truck went through my face."

"It could be worse."

"It could always be worse, Wal."

"You were close this time, real close."

"How did I get here?"

"Amanda brought you in. Boom says thanks for lunch."

"Nice." It almost makes it worth it just to know he bathed in my intestinal fluids.

"You should call your mother. I don't want her to worry."

"She won't, believe me."

"What does it take for you to wake up? You're going to die if you do this again."

"Bullshit."

"The doctor told me, Eg. This is it. Dead."

"That's what they said last time and the time before that. Look at me, a strapping young lad."

"Stop or you die, that's it."

"*You* say. I'm fine."

"You will stop." Walrus walks from the room, slamming shut the door, and the IV shakes in my vein.

My eyes again fall heavy and I sleep. The doctor jostles me awake about two hours later, according to the alarm clock beside me. I notice my flaccid penis is exposed and so does the doctor, who looks unimpressed.

"Welcome back, Mr. Egman." She smiles and throws another blanket over my gown.

"Thanks. I should get the next visit free, I think."

"You just might."

"When can I leave?"

"You're free to go whenever you'd like. But, I have a drug counselor coming down to talk to you before you leave."

"Who? Bob or Anne?"

"Robert Carnes, I believe."

"Bob's a schmuck."

"Mr. Egman, you need to stop doing cocaine. Luck was all you had this time."

"Vegas always was my place." I finish putting on my clothes and leave shortly after the doctor, before Bob the Schmuck could make it down.

Rush hour. The car goes nowhere. You've got to love Orlando. If it's not rush hour, it's the tourists. I honk, they honk. Nothing. I could die in this car and no one would know for hours.

My cell phone rings, A Ha's *Take on Me*.

"Hello."

"Come over, please." The voice is firm and frozen.

"Wal?"

"Come over."

"What's wrong?"

"I have something to show you."

He hangs up and the dial tone chisels at my eardrum. Walrus is melodramatic when he wants to prove a point. It usually works, though. At the very least I feel totally embarrassed for him.

The music of Kris Nichols accompanies my ride to Walrus'. I pull into the parking garage adjacent to his building, The Waverly, which overlooks Lake Eola. When I approach his door, I hear his television, loud and obtrusive.

A trail of white greets me when I walk into Walrus' apartment. I've never seen so much coke. I yell for him, but the call drowns in the television. Little crimson drops are interspersed between the snow, and I follow them down the hallway into the living room. Walrus kneels in the middle of the floor, almost like he's praying. His nose pours blood, which covers his shirt, and his eyes have nearly rolled back white. I try to say something, an attempt to figure out what has happened, but Walrus covers his ears and screams. He pulls a gun from his back pocket and puts it to his temple, trembling. I step forward, but Walrus shakes his head *no*. He stares at me, his pupils fading, and doesn't even blink when he pulls the trigger and his blood and brains fly through the room and paint the walls a brilliant red. My hands shake violently, and my tongue discovers Walrus' blood dripping from my face and lips. The smell of gunpowder fills the room, and I look down at Walrus, noticing he no longer has eyeballs or a left ear, and I am suddenly very, very afraid of dying.

Don't You Forget About Me
Precious Jones

Don't you forget about me when I'm in Brazil whining through the streets of Bahia celebrating Carnival. I will whine through the streets of Bahia surrounded by the most delectable, sun-baked women celebrating their blackness, I will be whining through the streets of Bahia, so don't you forget about me.

I remember when you fell down the steps at Penn Station. I laughed and now I'm sorry. Don't you forget about me while I hold on to some Brazilian girl's ample waist and another holds mine and we'll whine through the streets of Bahia, a black woman's Freedom Train.

Remember me as I was when last I saw you on the corner of Fulton and Nostrand, not as I'll be, laid up in a hut, dressed like a slut whining on some fine brown Brazilian woman, remember my happy birthday email, not me as I'll be waking up to a cock...a-doodle-doo after partying all night with two Brazilian girls who each had their way with me and I with them and them with each other...

It was fun, but know you've been warned: don't you forget about me when I'm gone.

Philip Ryan, *1965*, digital C-print, 2003

Public and Private
Simon Höegsberg

Summer 2, Ilfochrome, 2001
Autumn 3A, Ilfochrome, 2001
Winter 5A, Ilfochrome, 2001

Summer 5A, Ilfochrome, 2001
Autumn 1, Ilfochrome, 2001
Winter 3A, Ilfochrome, 2001

Spring 7, Ilfochrome, 2001
Spring 1A, Ilfochrome, 2001

Brian Lemond

Revelation comes greyly
In the resolute pursuit
Of direct expression
Of primary experience
Of poetry, of sensation unfiltered

It is the narrative
The metaphor and symbol—the artifice
The enemy
But the tool of history and mastery alike
And it illuminates my folly

Perfection freed is imperfection bound
And chooses death over tether
What a dilemma!
To arrive at the opened heart
To touch as touched

Yet know it is yours alone
For to accommodate with words
To make this legible
To make this bearable
Through context

Is to soften each sharpness
To demean inspiration
To betray contact
With gods glimpsed and known
For dreams of human gain

Maddaloetry
Joseph Maddaloni

Window cleaners

to those of
you who
are seated near the windows,

please
remove drawings,
etc.
from tables
near windows
tonight,

as
window cleaners
will
be here
tomorrow
at 8:
45 AM

Bernard, let me know if you need a dumpster

Window cleaners (reprise)

window cleaning

Incomplete,

there was some windows
that could not be cleaned,
due to,
Drawings, files etc.
which was
not removed
or covered,

If in the future,
you need help in this matter,
please bring this
to my
attention

windows

Richard,
just to bring to your attention,
the upper window
near you
is cracked,

I will get a new window
put in
A.S.A.P.

Two new windows
were replaced
Tuesday,
near Thomas Juul-Hansen
& Sara LeBalch

I checked all other windows,
& they are
O.K.

However
if you notice any cracked windows
in the future
please
bring it to
my attention
this could be hazardous,

Years ago

on a windy day

one window

blew

in

Motel Confessions

Harlan Overlike

Untitled, giclée print, 2003
Untitled, giclée print, 2003

Untitled, giclée print, 2003

facing page:

Untitled, giclée print, 2003
Untitled, giclée print, 2003
Untitled, giclée print, 2003
Untitled, giclée print, 2003

Tim Carpenter, *Untitled*, light-jet print, 2002

Garbage Stacks Name Tacks
Sarah Paulson

Pieces of garbage have accumulated identities in transit. Pieces of garbage were valuables with direct destinations and relocations. We have carried and dropped, traded and chopped (our very own names). It is loss on a regular basis (plus or minus).

There are numberless numbers of piles.

The letters form identity; disposal sets all afloat. We become hair wisps and eye floaters. To dig is to uncover the bones of our ancestors, our equals, and our selves.

In some way and from something, the sorting process takes place on some level (maybe not physical—maybe just in the same way that the small child sings "Jesus Loves Me"). Names are stacked into their own piles. All Matthews are not grouped together. Instead, there is a pile for Matthew and a pile for Matthew and a pile for Matthew and a pile for Matthew . . .

It could be made up of paper or napkins or plastic or glue skins. The highest stack wins. There is an account of this, and in the existence of this account, where are we placed, and what are we named?

I have 1.25 miles less names than X. X has 3 feet less names than Y. Y has 7 feet more names than Y. The being is named and measured by the material, the written, and the physical.

Anecdotal
Graham Roumieu

I Love To Hate You, pen, ink, watercolor, 2002
Bad Day for Big Head, pen, ink, watercolor, 2003

All You Can Eat, pen, ink, watercolor, 2003

facing page:

Wheelbarrow, pen, ink, watercolor, 2001
Super Ass v. Bad Chair, pen, ink, watercolor, 2003

Puppet Show, pen, ink, watercolor, 2002

Ready, Fire, Aim
Ira Shull

2:00—you arrive on time, even though traffic was heavy and the directions on the website were wrong. It's a corporate campus, secluded from the highway along a parallel two-lane road. Inside the security gate, it's another world—low, whitewashed buildings with gables and reflecting glass, a movie theater, fitness club, a duck pond. You could be in college again, except for the logo—two vertical black lines with a white slash through the middle—that covers everything like kudzu.

Your appointment is with Marie, the HR director. The receptionist makes you fill out an application. She's young and pretty in a vague, professional sort of way, like a salesgirl at a Macy's makeup counter. She looks bored. Marie has your resume—that's why you're here. You ask about the purpose of the application. "She won't see you unless you fill it out," the receptionist says flatly. She hands you a pen.

You jot down the basic information from your resume. Your handwriting is bad because you're used to typing on a computer. It looks like a fourth grader's handwriting—scaly and uncertain. It's ten minutes past your appointment time. The receptionist's desk is next to a closed office door that must be Marie's. You wonder if she's actually in there.

A woman walks into the reception area. She's silver-haired, wearing a tailored peach suit and a strand of pearls, and sipping from a bottle of mineral water. She holds up an index finger, as if to say she'll be with you in a minute. Then she goes into Marie's office.

Another ten minutes passes. It's 2:20 and you haven't eaten lunch because of nervousness. Your stomach growls. Marie buzzes the receptionist, who says indifferently that she'll see you now.

Marie smiles and tells you to sit down. You hand her your application, which she drops into a basket on her desk next to your resume. You talk for a half hour about the job, about your background and skills, about your career. Marie seems impressed, though it's hard to tell what she's thinking. There's a brittleness to her face, to the lines around the corners of her mouth. It's like talking to someone wearing a putty nose or a bald skullcap. You wonder how many people she sees a day, how many she judges as unsuitable or inferior. She makes a few notes in what appears to be your file. She says she'd like you to meet with the Vice President of the specific department. That sounds fine, you say.

Marie says, "Let me run upstairs and get him." She asks if you would like anything to drink. You say, "Water would be great." Marie leaves her office and closes the door.

Marie's office is spacious and cluttered. Framed pictures of teenagers line her chestnut desk, and there's a copier and fax machine in the corner. Her window faces the duck pond, and you notice some male employees walking past it. They wear chinos and blue sport shirts with the company logo, and they look exceedingly content, like they've just finished a round of golf and are on their way to the clubhouse. It's mid-afternoon on a spring day, the sky is bright arc of blue, and the grounds are immaculate. It's hard to believe work actually gets done here.

Marie has been gone a while—almost twenty minutes. You think, how far away is "upstairs?" The place is huge; maybe she had to go to another building. Then again, why didn't she just call the Vice President to come down?

The office door opens. Marie comes in, alone and without your water. She seems a bit flustered; a few silver hairs hang in front of her face. "Well, I guess this is my fault," she begins. She stops; her face suddenly clouds over, the lines at the corners of her mouth crinkling like cellophane. "No, it's not," she declares, more to herself than you. She goes on to explain that the Vice President, Lance, is in a meeting and can't get out for at least a half hour. "If you want to go out and walk around, that's fine," Marie says. "As long as you don't leave our little oasis."

You thank her, though you're not sure why, and exit the office. You search for a water fountain, but can't find one. Outside the sun is brilliant, piercing. You head for the car, figuring you can wait there and read the newspaper. Benches are scattered along gravel paths, but you wonder how it would look, sitting outside in a suit. Yours is the only suit you've seen. It's certainly an awkward situation, but you're willing to give Marie and Lance the benefit of the doubt. Jobs like this one are hard to find, and the company's reputation is unparalleled. They're doing something right, you think, or they wouldn't have a set up like this.

A half hour goes by—it's 3:45. You get out of the car and walk to the main entrance, just like at 2:00. The receptionist greets you and phones Marie. "He's baaaaack," she says playfully into the phone.

You sit. The receptionist tells jokes to another woman sorting mail that you recognize from an old "Saturday Night Live" routine. Marie comes out of her office after ten minutes. "I'm going up to get Lance now," she says, smiling. Your skin itches and your throat clamps up from dryness. You ask the receptionist where the nearest water fountain is and she looks surprised. She tells you the building doesn't have any water fountains. "There's a fully stocked fridge with mineral water in the kitchen on level 2," she says. You ask where that is. She rolls her eyes. "You'll have to wait until Marie comes back."

Another five minutes edges by. It's 4:00. The receptionist answers a call and peeks in your direction. She says into the phone, "I think Marie's on her way up to see you." Five more minutes, and then another five…this could go on forever. You've now read every copy of *People* for the current year. The phone rings again.

The receptionist says, "She still hasn't gotten up there? OK. I'll page her."

Marie's name is announced over an intercom. You suddenly feel like you're in a hospital, waiting for a doctor to deliver bad news.

Marie calls in almost immediately. "Lance is looking for you," the receptionist tells her. Marie's response is unclear. But shortly afterward, she appears in the waiting area with Lance.

Lance is burly and slack-jawed, with a blue tie and a narrow layer of hair that looks like bear fur. Marie says, "Lance is just going to read you resume, and then he'll come out to get you." They disappear into Marie's office. Fifteen more minutes slowly tick away. You wonder how fast Lance reads.

Finally, Lance brings you in. He mumbles apologies while Marie excuses herself.

He could be 25, but he looks younger. You sit and chat, and he asks the same questions about your background that Marie did. Then, with all the panache of someone doing a telephone survey, he says, "How would you rate your interest in the position on a scale of 1-10?"

The tactic is straight out of a job interview textbook. The correct answer is 10, or possibly 11. The goal of the interview is get the job offer, even if you don't want the job, and then decide what to do. You make eye contact with Lance. It's 4:45. You suddenly imagine him groping women at a fraternity party, or passed out on a sofa with his pants around his ankles and a chip clip attached to his nose.

"Seven," you say.

"That's good," Lance says. "It gives me a sense of…what's the word I'm looking for? Your….wanting to commit at this time."

"Commitment," you offer. Lance's pudgy face brightens. That's the word, he says.

Lance keeps talking. His description of the job sounds scripted, except for a few noticeable exceptions. "What we need someone to do," he says excitedly, "is take the department under his wing and get it off the ground. That's the way we do things here…all systems go. Ready, fire, aim." He stops and asks if anything he's said has raised any red flags. You say no. You think: Ready, fire, aim. He pauses frequently and asks, "What's the word I'm looking for?" Sometimes it's a simple one, such as "brunch." But mostly, you're unable to solve the vocabulary conundrums running through Lance's head.

It's 5:45. You've been talking with Lance for over an hour. Lance says he would like to have you meet the others on staff in the department. He makes a call, but whoever's he trying to reach has apparently left for the day. He says, "I know this is short notice, but Marie is giving her test at 8:00 tomorrow. If you can't make it, we'll schedule you for another time."

"Test?"

"Yes, the Goering-Radke personality test. It's sort of like…what's the word I'm looking for?

"Rorschach?"

He nods. "Rorschach," he says sagely.

You hesitate. "I can't make it tomorrow," you tell Lance, thinking: or any day, ever.

Amy Shutt, *Untitled*, inkjet print, 2001

"OK," Lance says. "I'll have Marie call you and set it up for another time. Or we can go see if she's still there."

You wonder where "there" is, since Lance is occupying Marie's office. "Can I get some water?" you ask.

"Sure, sure," Lance says, extending his flattened palms like a mime. "We can handle that." Then his face clouds, the same way Marie's did, and he looks apologetic. "To be honest with you," he says, scratching the side of his neck, "I'm not sure where they keep it."

"You know what?" You resist the temptation to tell Lance the secret location of the bottled water. "I would be very reluctant to take that test."

He looks surprised. You're suddenly the rebel, the one guy in the frat who doesn't think farting out the window is funny. He's never encountered your ilk before, and he's not sure how to deal with it. "May I ask why?" he says.

"I don't like personality tests," you say, feeling defensive. "I think they're a waste of time."

A dim lantern goes on in Lance's brain; you're hiding something. Maybe you fudged the degrees on your resume or have a record. Whatever it is, he's suddenly determined to find out.

"I disagree," he says, his gaze intensifying. "We would never rely on them completely. Usually, they just confirm what we already think about someone."

"What do you think about me?" You stare back at him. You can almost hear the theme from a Sergio Leone western. "You've had me here for over three hours. Are you telling me you can't make a decision about my qualifications without a personality test?"

Lance backs down and looks slightly embarrassed. "I'll level with you," he says, shifting his bulk like he just noticed a thumbtack on his seat. "Marie has only been our Human Resource person for a month, and you're the second person I've interviewed." He shrugs dispiritedly. "I'm young…some people don't trust me to make decisions."

You think: Then why are you interviewing me?

"If it makes you feel any better," he adds, "my father is CEO of our East Coast division and he made me take the test before I got hired."

Lance looks down at his tie; its frayed bottom hangs limply over Marie's desk. For the first time all day, he is silent. You suddenly feel sorry for him, and for everyone else who works here. Lance rises and clasps his hands together in front of him. "I'll talk to Marie. See what we can work out."

He walks you out of the office and through the empty reception area to the main entrance. It's 6:00. Everyone is gone except for the security guards.

Lance shakes your hand. It's goodbye, for good. He says, "I'm sorry if we hit a nerve."

"You didn't," you tell him. "I just don't like wasting my time."

You walk slowly along a gravel path toward the car and stop by a bench. The sun is setting; the air is cooling. The hours are now meaningless. To the left is the duck pond, and you walk to its edge. There are no ducks, anywhere. You look in the direction of Marie's window. The water is a lovely blue sheath reflected in the mirrored glass. You breathe deeply. Then you walk into the water, first up to your ankles, then your waist. Your suit tails float in front of you. The water smells like lemon wedges. You remember those employees with the corporate logo shirts from earlier in the day; is this what they were feeling? It's 6:10. All systems go…ready, fire, aim. You think: I'm going to get what I want.

The sun is down to a few embers. You stand there enjoying the moment, amazed at your fate, and that security hasn't fished you out. You feel an involuntary shiver, a harbinger of release. And then your hands rise out of the water. At last, you drink.

Oliver Dettler, *Untitled,* mixed-media collage, 2002

Lindbergh's Monkey
Samuel A. Southworth

Dawn at Bennet Field:
The aviator walks
Out through the mud and press
Of the newsmen in a crush
To make one more long flight;
Proud, determined, alone.

But there in the copilot's seat
Picking its nose and grinning
Is a monkey, thoughtful gift
From a deranged and hearty fan
Who weeps to think of Lindy
Isolated among the stars.

"Oh well, best to be polite I guess"
The aviator grins and starts the engine,
Taxis out and lifts off of the field
To run free through the heavens
His Wright Whirlwind churning mad
And his new friend patting him.

We cannot know what led to
The monkey's fatal fall to earth
Like Icarus in a fur coat
With high-pitched bleating screams
Echoing weirdly through the night
As the primate descends again to the trees.

Maybe he tried to adjust the throttle
Or used the charts for toilet paper
Or shrieked just one time too many
In the aviator's ear; nonetheless
An observer in Newfoundland saw
A tiny speck detach itself and fall.

Furry brother, you cannot go
Where Lone Eagles dare to pierce the sky
No matter if you are a gift and
Always dreamt of soaring someday;
You'll have to fly to Paris in your mind
And dwell in a Gallic paradise alone.

Advance
Amy Shutt

Rooftop / Houston, TX, C-Print, 2002
Whitney, digital C-print, 2001
Gabrielle / New Orleans, LA, C-Print, 2002

Adrienne, C-Print, 2003
Self Triptych, C-Print, 2003

Wrinkled Elephant
Kimberly Suta

Wrinkled elephant is beautiful,
Ebullient, unusual.
People talk of butterflies,
but not the ugly things that lie
and crawl beneath the surface
under rocks and rotting wood.
Who says?

I question perception—
the things we see as good and bad,
the things that go unnoticed,
a whispered interlude
you take no time to hear.

The blue hour draws near,
the scent of some illusion
being made real.
Horny toads in candlelight
jump about and make a fright,
raucous laughter, fearless cackle…
you won't believe your eyes,
so why your heart?

Would you rather believe the lies,
beautiful incantations,
affected revelations,
or can you feel her tremble
beneath your calloused finger?

Awake from dream!
Sleep, the solid thing.
Arouse!
Desire!
Go a little Higher,
Move a little lower.

Scorch yourself,
and burn conditioned mind.
Fire lights inside your veins
traverses realms and worlds unnamed—
where truth cannot be maimed…
where you recognize that whisper,
Yeah, that whisper in your brain
that shouts,
"How lovely you are tonight!"
Just a garter snake
slithering 'cross the desert sky.

How lovely!
If you only knew how lovely…

Shin Iwasaki, *MeatFly*, Ilfochrome, 2003

Recent Work
Robert Szot

Mexico 1, oil on canvas, 2003
Mexico 3, oil on canvas, 2002

Mary Clancey's Speeding Heart, oil on canvas, 2002
Untitled (Jack Hendrickson's Coat, oil on canvas, 2003

Any 6 for 10, oil on canvas, 2002

Untitled (April 18, 2003)
Dewayne Washington

I come up here
Through flashing lights
And blue and whites

I rolled twelve here
Playing ball nine a side
No-net or chain-net

I got seasoned here
Dodging bad deals in the stark hot-cold
Of the southside building

I'll probably die here
Leaning against the backbent link fence
If I'm taken in the Spring

I lie here now
Whispering on your big breasts
I ain't made nothin' worthy

new york takes care
Deanna Zandt

Zandt

Issue 1.1

101

and just when you thought the city didn't care anymore there's a woman
from Avenue C who came walking with her husband saw your life
sprawling out on the sidewalk after bingo on tuesday night
so she picked up the pieces
and remembered the $100 she never got back
and called you and said
it's okay, i got you

step over the shattered shot bottle of vodka
and wonder what it all means when the
package gets there just in time
in the midst of your family falling to pieces
tossed out onto the sidewalk
till an angel of mercy comes from bingo
with her husband and wonders
what you doin' there to begin with
while she hands you your life back
before you know it
just when you thought the city didn't care anymore

OCTOBER 2003

Corey Arnold, *White*, C-Print, 2003

Games My Father Played
Derrick Ableman

Peek-a-Boo

An early favorite of ours. My father vanished behind his hands with consummate grace and skill, staying gone long enough to achieve the right amount of suspense. Later, his talents here would dull, forcing him to resort to all manner of prop and pyrotechnic: blindfolding me with a blanket, crouching behind furniture, spinning my chair. But always his hands were evident in the act; you could hear him knock things over on his way to obscurity, stumbling into the doorframe, stubbing his toe and cursing to reveal himself.

Basketball

We had a hoop in the driveway one summer, a real one, regulation height and everything. The neighbor kids, who were older, taller, and knew how to play, would come over and hog it. They brought their own balls and held court while my parents were away at work. One time my Dad was home while they were harassing me some—throwing for the head, fouling me hard, stuff like that. He watched for a while from the kitchen window, then took his car out of the garage and parked under the hoop. He climbed on the hood and hung from the rim until it gave and lost shape.

Croquet

I played this with my cousin once, in somebody's yard, during a family reunion. My father set up the rings, laid out the rules and returned to the grill, beer in hand, sandals clicking through the thick grass. But we quit early; the lanes were hard to keep straight and the mallets were begging for misuse. Besides, the game was sissy and hard and we'd had enough fooling around. We wanted to do something serious. We were found sometime later, at the edge of a deep woods, smashing full beers with our toy hammers, stinking to high heaven.

Catch

Catch is not baseball. It's better. It's catch. Stand as far away as possible, until you can't see the other person's eyes, until their face becomes unclear. Keep quiet. Now, between you there is the ball, sailing back and forth, easy as you please. It makes a sound when it meets the mitt, when it's caught. It makes another sound when it's traveling through the air, just before it's caught. Strung together, these sounds are like talking.

Tag

Ruthless. He never once checked his adult abilities in the spirit of fair play; pursuing at top speeds, pushing when necessary, always willing to hook you by the collar and drag back a few grassy yards before slapping your belly, cursing you "it."

The same was true of the reverse direction; he fled faster than he chased, putting his heart all the way into it, sometimes going blocks and blocks beyond the yard and staying gone for the rest of the day. Once you were "it" with my father, the condition was permanent.

Monopoly

Here I got a taste for blood. I was master of the board—patient with my properties, careful with my fortunes. My father showed no restraint, no sense of planning and so would avoid the purchase of any space that wasn't "strictly boardwalk." Meanwhile I snapped up the less appealing parts of town, built up homes, then hotels. I launched my empire from the ghetto while my father squandered his turns on financing scraps of easy street. I loaned him money to cover his rents. I fronted him capital for his real house. "It's an investment," he'd say. "Not a loan. In time, we'll be penthouse partners." My head swam with foreclosures and seized properties.

Spotlight

A night game. Camping in the North Woods. We borrowed a pickup truck and tent from my uncle. The flashlight was mine. The idea, my father's. He sat in the flatbed of the truck on a lawn chair, drinking a beer and waving the flashlight into the woods. I would be hiding in the woods, stalking toward him, avoiding the light and moving without a sound. If I touched the truck without getting caught, I won.

"Win what?" I asked.

"You'll see," he said.

Hide and Go Seek

These are agreed upon absences, tiny contracts of vanishing between us. I close my eyes and count in years. I count in zip codes. He moves out of town, apartment to apartment. I move too. Phones change and postcards drift through my mailbox. Jonesburg. Dallas. Portland. Saint Paul. I put these on the wall as I get them. They are dated and this, I think, is his way of leaving a trail, his form of breadcrumb. They're all frauds. You can see it in his signature, can tell it by his hand, the way his name creeps off the bottom of the card, as though done in invisible ink.

Presidio Nights
Corey Arnold

Presidio Hospital, C-Print, 2002
Presidio Eyes, C-Print, 2002

Presidio Wire, C-Print, 2002

Presidio Blue, C-Print, 2002
Presidio Green, C-Print, 2002

Presidio House, C-Print, 2002

Vlad Nanca, *Puddle*, C-print, 2002

FASHION
Banksy

Like most people I wear my jeans two sizes too big with no belt so they hang low off my ass. Apparently this fashion was started by Los Angeles hoods who refused to wear a belt to show solidarity with their brothers in the Big House who have theirs confiscated on the way in.

When going to paint inside a fountain one night I was wearing these jeans and a pair of large boots. I immediately discovered the water was deeper than it looked as it flooded the wellingtons and everything started going in slow motion.

After a few seconds of spraying, the stencil became unstuck and I had to use my free hand to keep it steady. All the while spreading my legs in a kind of Led Zeppelin rock pose to keep my sodden, beltless jeans from falling into the water.

There was no way I was going to let go of the stencil before it was finished so eventually I lost the trousers altogether. All I know is Fuck hip hop, wear a belt.

Bar Fight, Saturday
J. Robert Beardsley

he says,
'Hey man, hey, what's
your problem, man?'
he says,
something like motherfucker
my ears are swimming still
in a sea of pine and lime

and I don't quite hear him say
faggot
and I say something
like 'Shove it up your ass,'
and my ear rings,
the phone is off the hook
and I'm dancing,

there's something like
motherfucker in the air
and this motherfucker
has a tight grip on my shirt I
don't know why the fuck
there's no one getting
between us, then
I'm through the parking lot
looking over my shoulder
but he's in front of me and
saying something like wallet
and fuckin' city boy and
pussy and fuck if I'm giving
him anything and his palms
hit hard on my city boy chest
before I know I'm swinging
and all I can hear is gin and
waves
before his mouth breaks open
under my knuckles and falls
on the concrete close my eyes
and run run run run.

Day Old Bread
Daniel Chang

Chang

Issue 1.2

111

Ahab, mixed media, 2001
Bunnyhero, mixed media, 2002
tMcSwy, no.2, acrylic, 2002

Qui Tam, acrylic, 2002
A Pack of Wolves, mixed media, 2002
Doggydonuts, mixed media, 2002

Giraffe: 03
Oliver Dettler

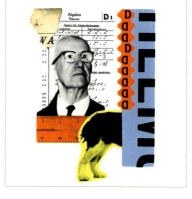

Untitled, mixed media collage, 2002
Untitled, mixed media collage, 2002
Untitled, mixed media collage, 2002

Untitled, mixed media collage, 2002
Untitled, mixed media collage, 2002
Untitled, mixed media collage, 2002

7.24
Alexander Fong

Today, I learned a valuable lesson. I learned that if I ever run in front of a moving vehicle, it will stop for me. Of course, it may stop soon enough or not soon enough. But it WILL stop.

I did not learn this lesson from experience. Rather, I learned it from just sitting here thinking about it. That's logic, my friends. Sheer, powerful logic.

Ellen Honich, *Strange*, C-print, 2003

Kizer Ohno, *Her Words Are Hellfire*, hand-colored digital C-print, 2003

74
Brian Lemond

A currency of heat and stamina
Blood spent
Body on edge
I see the beauty
Of all women
They see the hunger
Lingering unsated
And wonder
At my warmth and weight

Maddaloetry
Joseph Maddaloni

Caroline Moore, *Shaving #3*, digital C-print, 2003

20th flr. employees

You will find
a combination lock
on the clothing closet

&

the number is
the same as
your phone

2
5
1

Bldg. system testing

The bldg.
will be conducting tests
on Wed.
July 26, of
the fire alarm equipment,

this
will include devices
such as speakers,
strobe lights
& elevator recall,

this
will be

Momentary

President's Day

No Mail
Messenger service
is available,
However
you should be sure that
the Company you're sending to
is open

FedEx,
is open

Freight Elevator
is closed

No cleaning or
garbage removal

Exterminator

The Exterminator was here today,
&
from past experience I
know
that water bugs
start
to come out of their
hideouts.

Already got 3 of them.
So
don't Bug Me.

St. James Church Road
Josh Magnuson

"Nobody would have blamed you for letting the vet do it," Maria said, brushing her hair in the mirror. Jackson was sitting on the bed, taking off his shoes. The mud was caked on pretty thick. He slid off his slacks, still covered with dirt and grass, and pulled the covers back.

"That's what you're supposed to do. Jesus, that's what everybody does." She sighed and gave her hair a good tug with the brush. Several strands broke free and fell on the floor. He rested the full weight of his body against the mattress, feeling the slight depression where his back fit. He didn't want to talk about it. In a way, she was trying to understand. But something was different now. She didn't really want to understand.

Earlier that day, they'd been at his in-laws' house, celebrating the Fourth of July. Maria's parents lived up the road about an hour, in a small town off the main highway. They had a two-acre lot in a lazy, half-developed subdivision. The property backed into a creek and the trees hung down low enough to form a canopy over the picnic tables. They strung Christmas lights through the branches and fired up the large BBQ smoker. The women came and went, bringing large Tupperware bowls of potato salad and onions and pickles and blue plastic plates stacked with raw hot dogs and sausage and hamburgers. Maria's brother cornered Jackson by the barbeque pit. Donny was twice divorced and living with his daughter's teacher. After a few beers, he would usually grab Jackson by the elbow and start in on some nonsense.

"I could've gotten you a pure breed, y'know? A goddamn American bulldog," he said, almost spitting into Jackson's ear. He could almost smell the foamy beer in Donny's stomach.

"Yeah?" Jackson wiped the sweat off the back of his neck. He saw Maria across the yard, surrounded by her cousins. She was laughing with her head tilted back.

"Hell yeah, son. They're a rare fucking breed. Like the one on Little Rascals? You remember that one?"

"Petey," said Jackson.

"Was that his name?" Donny took a drag from his cigarette. "So where's your mutt?" Jackson looked through the crowd and caught a glimpse of Hobbes near the creek. He wondered for a second, with an anxiety that surprised him, whether or not the dog could swim.

They'd retrieved Hobbes from a local animal shelter. One of the volunteers said he was a mix between an Australian blue heeler and a beagle. Jackson couldn't see the beagle. He looked like a cattle dog. One day they simply decided to get a dog, or rather Maria decided. She didn't want kids just yet, but she wanted something. Jackson went along with it, knowing full well he'd be the one that ended up with the responsibilities. These were the small ways you paid for a marriage. Maria privately boasted to their friends how she'd turned Jackson into a dog-lover. He despised that kind of talk, the way she made him out to be a well-heeled dope. She hadn't turned him into anything. He wasn't an animal nut, and even if he were, it certainly wasn't because she woke up one day and decided to get a dog. But there was some truth to it. Before all this, Jackson couldn't have cared less about dogs. Now he found himself spending five minutes at the grocery store, deciding which bone Hobbes would like. He would take the dog for long walks down along the park trails near their house. At first this was just to get away, to be by himself, but eventually, he looked forward to unleashing the dog and watching him run through the thick brush, almost out of sight. And he looked forward to taking him out to the country for the weekend.

"I don't know, babe." Maria said when he brought it up. "There'll be a lot of people there." She was painting her toenails in the bathroom. "He'll ruin Mom's gardenias."

"Like he ruined the couch?" Jackson knew that would get her.

"That wasn't my fault," she said. Jackson had gone on a business trip and Maria left Hobbes inside the house while she was at work. He chewed a gash into his paw and bled red splotches on their white cotton couch. Jackson bought a hunter green slipcover to hide the mess, but Maria didn't like it. "It doesn't match anything," she said. That was the point at which Hobbes became Jackson's dog. Not their dog. Not our dog.

"We're spending the night," he said. "We can't leave him here." He knew she'd give in, but he was angling for a fight. Nothing ever seemed like an argument with Maria, not a real argument. Sometimes that's all Jackson wanted. A real scrap. But Maria wouldn't have it.

"Whatever you want," she said, closing the door of the bathroom. So it was in this disagreeable way that they brought the dog with them to her parent's house. Everyone admired his coat and the way he could run across the yard in quick darts and dashes. They tried warming to him, but he was manic. He bounced around and jumped up on the women's white skirts and shorts, leaving muddy prints. They looked on disapprovingly, first at each other, then Jackson. Maria's dad ignored all this and recalled his days of rounding up cattle on a Panhandle ranch. He bemoaned the fact they didn't have any cattle for Hobbes to rustle.

"I ought to get some stock from the Schwertners," he said, shouting to his wife from behind the barbeque pit. She nodded in the longsuffering way of having married a man who never grew up. Donny couldn't be swayed by any of this talk. Hobbes wasn't a dog that could hunt or fight or sire other dogs worth selling. He finally wandered off in search of beer. Jackson walked to the picnic table where Maria was sitting.

"I hope I'm not interrupting," he said, sitting down.

"Maria was telling us about the time she had a pet rabbit," one of the cousins said.

"Dad told me I could have him as long as I fed him. Only he didn't know what rabbits ate," Maria said. She started giggling like a schoolgirl, as if this was the point in the story where everyone should pick up on its hilarity. Only Jackson had heard the story and knew the punch line.

"So your dad fed the rabbit dog food," he said, flatly. Jackson tried to force a smile, as if that would make up for it.

"Oh, yeah, I guess you've heard that one, honey," she said. The word *honey* hung in the air for a second, like a towel being snapped. The cousins fell silent. There were several things about the story that irritated Jackson. For one thing, her father deserved a better story. So did the rabbit. Here was a man who drove cattle, who lived off the land for Chrissakes. And then—as he was thinking of the rabbit, the way it eventually starved to death because they didn't feed it properly, and her father, the way he had been held responsible for this silly, stupid death, implicated in a hundred retellings, as if this was his little routine—he heard a sharp bark and a tiny scream, so small and sudden that he knew, even before he turned

He didn't see it happen and would have to rely on what other people said in their nervous voices, the way people talk after an accident. Except this wasn't really an accident. Donny's girlfriend was running across the yard, her face twisted, almost frozen in time. Jackson jumped up and quickly pushed through the crowd.

Donny's youngest daughter, Danielle, was on the ground, hands covering her face. The blood turned the front of her dress a muddy red color. Donny was squatting on Hobbes with his knee directly on top of the dog's neck. Hobbes kicked and growled. Donny's girlfriend scooped up the girl and Jackson caught a good, long look at her face. Her entire left cheek was hanging down like a flap, attached by what seemed like threads of skin. A chill rode up Jackson's back.

"What happened?" he asked. Maria came from behind, touching Jackson's elbow. People yelled out and jostled him, but he only saw mouths move, hands gesture. The women carried the girl off toward the house, her low moan barely fading above their voices. The men gathered around the dog.

"Call 911 goddammit!" Donny screamed. Maria's father tried to pull Donny off the dog. One of her uncles was holding Hobbes by the torso.

"They're calling right now, son," her dad said.

"Your fucking dog!" Donny looked at Jackson.

"What happened?" Jackson didn't know what else to ask. He knew what happened.

"Your fucking goddamn mutt." Donny pressed down harder on Hobbes' neck. He looked like a madman. The men struggled with him and gradually stood him up and moved him away from the crowd.

"That goddamn dog," his voice became a wail. He was shaking uncontrollably and repeating the words like a mantra. Maria's uncle took the dog and pulled him off toward the creek.

"What happened?" Jackson turned to Maria. Tears were streaming down her face. One of her aunts was standing nearby and Maria turned, burying her face in the woman's blouse. Everything after was a blur to Jackson. Somebody asked for a leash and chained the dog to a tree by the creek. The girl was whisked off to the emergency room and several family members, including Maria and Donny, went with her. He walked over and sat on the ground next to his dog. Maria's mother drifted out several times to ask him if he needed anything, her apron covered in tiny splotches of maroon. Jackson wasn't sure if it was barbeque sauce or the little girl's dried blood.

Finally, Maria's father came over. The sun had gone down below the horizon and the Christmas lights kicked on, casting a glow on the moving figures near the house.

"You O.K. son?" he asked. He knelt down on the ground and picked up a stick.

"I don't know." Hobbes was curled up in between him and the tree, snoozing. "How is she?"

"Well, they haven't called yet," her dad said. Jackson nodded.

"You know, I don't have to tell you this, but it's not your fault."

Jackson knew Donny wouldn't go along with that. He wondered if Maria would. He put his hand on Hobbes, sliding it down along his rib cage.

"I ain't gonna tell you I got the answers," her dad said. He traced the stick in the dirt.

"He's got to be put down," Jackson said.

"How's that?" asked Maria's dad.

"The dog. He's got to be put down," said Jackson. Her dad wrinkled his sunburnt face. Jackson felt like he'd broken some unspoken rule; that men didn't talk about these things. Not like this.

"Well, that's up to you."

"You own a pistol right?" Jackson asked.

"Yeah, I do."

This seemed like the longest conversation they'd ever shared and in a strange way, Jackson didn't want it to end. He wanted something more from Maria's father. Something about the way the world works, the way nothing seems to happen for a reason, the way everything just happens and happens over again until you finally realize it doesn't matter. Or it all matters and in the end it was only your actions that counted. Not your intentions or hopes or dreams or how you suck on through waiting for somebody or something to snap you out of it. But her dad wasn't a man that could say these things. Was anybody?

"You ever shot a living thing?" He wasn't looking at Jackson.

"No sir." There was another moment of silence.

"It's not an easy thing," he said, breaking the stick off in the dirt and standing. Jackson nodded.

"Stay here," he said and walked back to the house. Jackson still half-expected some sort of argument, some sanity measured against his own crazy thoughts. This was crazy. He sat in the dark with Hobbes and smoothed out his coat. He could feel a few flecks of dried blood and tried to gently scrape them out of the hair with his fingernails. He remembered a time when he was a boy and his father brought home a black Pekingese mutt. His dad picked him up from school cradling the dog in his arms as he strode across the parking lot. He remembered the feeling more than anything. His dad walking towards him with a sly smile, the sort of smile he rarely took out, and the dog with its mutt tongue wagging, also smiling in its own way, kicking its tiny legs out from underneath his dad's arms, and Jackson jumping up and running fast as he could, his heart bursting like a miniature sun, eyes wide, the whole world opening up. It was this moment that stood out above all others in Jackson's childhood and he'd never told anyone, not even Maria. He named the dog Sparky and in the course of a few months it ran away a dozen times before finally getting hit by a delivery truck in front of their house. His dad told him to stay inside. It was better he didn't see it. Later, his dad let him squat in the backyard and smooth dirt over a muddy circle in the ground. Jackson put a stick in the center.

Maria's father finally walked back out of the house. He had a pistol half-wrapped in a bandana.

"I hadn't told anyone," he said, handing the gun over to Jackson. "It's a Colt 45. All the chambers are loaded." Jackson stood up. The dog stretched and got up with him.

"Yes sir."

"It kicks a bit," her dad said.

"I was gonna take him up the road a ways," said Jackson.

"There's a turnoff next to an old rundown church about a mile up," her dad pointed toward the road. Jackson took the leash from around the tree and grabbed it tight, near the dog's neck.

"It's a hard thing, son."

"Thank you sir."

"There's a shovel up over there against the garage." Her father looked at Jackson one last time, spat on the ground and strode slowly, steadily back toward the Christmas lights.

Jackson grabbed the shovel, walked to the car, and put the dog in the back seat. He rolled out of the driveway and drove up the dusty, farm road for about a mile until he saw a building. There was a painted wooden sign that read "St. James Church." He pulled into the overgrown grass beside the church and got out. The dog was panting and his breath fogged up the back windows. This was a crazy goddamn thing, Jackson thought. There was a dead, still silence except for the cicadas and crickets chirping out in the grass. He opened up the car door and grabbed the dog's leash. The dog jumped on him and nuzzled his head under Jackson's arm. He could smell his own sweat mixed with the dog's musty odor as they walked around to the side of the church.

The ground was still muddy from a day-old summer rain and he nearly slipped as the dog pulled and leapt against the collar. There was a rusty hose faucet coming out of the ground near one of the stained glass windows. He wrapped the leash around the pipe and pulled on it until he was sure it would hold. The dog started to whimper a bit. Jackson took the pistol out of his belt.

"Goodbye dog." He didn't say his name, but he lingered, wanting to offer up some sort of eulogy. "None of this is right, I know." He aimed the gun at the dog's head and pulled the trigger. He wasn't prepared for the recoil, but he still managed to hit the dog in the center of his head. The body went limp. A splatter of blood hit his face. He turned quickly, trying not to look, and walked toward the meadow, tossing the shovel into the grass and tucking the gun into his jeans. He found a bare patch of dirt and knelt on the ground. After staring at the dirt for a while, he lay down on his back and looked up at the stars. They seemed to contract like a giant, breathing belly. He couldn't tell the Milky Way from anything else. "You were a good dog," he whispered, as if to cover Donny's words. He took off his shirt and wiped his face. "You were a good dog." He didn't really feel anything though. He wondered if this was how murderers felt—if this was the big secret. You didn't feel anything. Or maybe you did, but later, when it didn't count for much. After about twenty minutes, he got up, put on his shirt and started digging a hole with the shovel.

By the time he got back to his in-law's house, Maria was back from the emergency room, standing near the living room window. He sat in the car and waited for a while, watching her through the window. Then he honked. She walked to the hallway and looked at him through the screen door. He honked again. She came out and got into the car. They were halfway home before Maria said anything.

"My Dad told me," she said. Jackson nodded.

"Danielle is going to be O.K. I think. The doctor said she'd recover. They did some sort of skin graft." Jackson tried not to think about her face or where they got the skin.

"God, honey, did you think you had to do it?" This was only the beginning Jackson thought. He wanted to tell her it was his fault. In a way it was her fault too. Was she trying to cover everything up like he had done, trying to ignore their life swerving off the road of family picnics and career choices and funny party jokes and other people taking care of shit for you? Or worse, did she not think any of it mattered, having long ago given up on love and settling for things she could have? He gripped the wheel and dug his fingers into the leather. The thoughts were coming too fast for him to put in any order. They drove the rest of the way in silence. When they got to their house, Jackson stayed in the car as Maria got out.

"Give me a sec," he said. She walked up the porch hesitatingly, looking back, and finally opening the screen door. Jackson slid the gun out from underneath his left leg. He wondered how he'd give it back to her dad or if maybe it was meant for him to keep. He sat in the leather seat and stared at the porch light; the bugs swarming around it like refugees. He started to sweat from the heat and the dank smell of his own breath filled the car. After a few minutes, he put the gun in the glove compartment, got out and went inside.

As he took off his clothes and slid into bed, Maria picked the hair out of her brush and asked him again why he'd done it, why he couldn't have waited, how normal people don't do these sorts of things, how the vet would've done it if they decided together that it was necessary, how there were dog rescue groups, how she didn't know what to say to people. He didn't answer. He wanted all the words to come to an end. Tomorrow would come soon enough and he thought he might be able to say something then. They hadn't become what either of them expected. Sometimes, in the middle of the night, he didn't know who she was or what the hell they'd become. Were these even things you could say without wrecking the entire works?

She got into bed, pulling the covers back and sliding her body up next to him. Her cold feet nuzzled up against his. And in that moment before sleep, his thoughts turned slightly and he hoped Maria did have it in her, that she was the woman he married, that in a sense he'd married the promise of her. Maybe she understood, down past all the talk. Maybe they really could be in it together. Even if she didn't, he knew something inside him was shifting. There wasn't any going back. He rolled over and she reached around him, putting her hand over his stomach. She let out a sigh. He grasped her hand, closed his eyes and imagined Hobbes running through a green field away from him, almost floating over the grass.

Zev Robinson, *Bicycle Path*, silver gelatin print, 2002

bkg188 (love poem for a '57 fairlane)
ariane resnick

i never got to name you   nor did i know your name
          you stood out like a   real woman
in a room of cheerleaders and dolls   sitting proudly in the parking lot
               as if you'd owned it for ages   and the others should
consider themselves lucky   you let them spend their days beside you.

i gasped when first i found you   turning a corner
          suddenly proved so fruitful a venture   i'd hardly noticed cars before
had no preference   did not think of them like blondes or brunettes
               skinny or curvy   brown eyed or blue   you were my
first   auto   love.

i wanted to break into you   like a tornado hitting a rural town
          leaving trees scattered and downed   power lines powerless
you were a catwoman beauty of 1957 ebony   my hands belonged
               on your seats   coursing over vintage leather   never
had i so strong a desire   to see a trunk open   to pop a hood
          to exercise authority over a machine   and let it know who
its "daddy" was.

eartha kitt belonged in your passenger seat   next to me   she'd be singing something sexy
          as we sped away   so fast the chrome   could contemplate melting
maybe she'd be stroking your gearshift or   giggling about montgomery clift
               we'd be wearing cateye glasses   to match your feline looks.

baby i wish we could've gotten closer   i would've respected you
          like an antique metallic princess   would've treated your tailfins like gods
not made you run any harder than you wanted   i'd have let you rest when overheated
               and held your steering wheel in my arms   like the breasts of a
          fantasized lover.

i cherished every trip to that lot   grew fluttery and light when i passed you
          but i couldn't ever find the balls   to touch you like you were mine
whisper and murmur my love   offer you any sort of devotion
               and now you are lost to me   an irreplaceable obsession
immortalized only by the photographs i took   that i later made
          my computer background   like a sick and slimy stalker
you made me crazy with carlust   and still i dream   of polishing you nightly.

Boring 3D
Jimmy Maidens

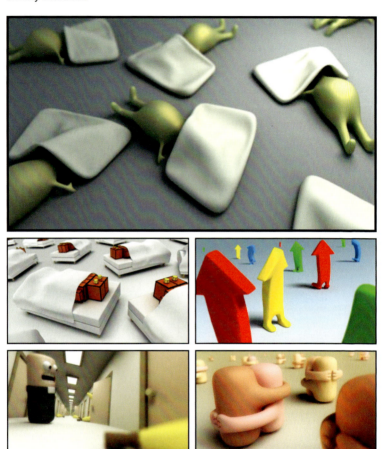

12.16.02, digital C-print, 2002
01.25.03, digital C-print, 2003
05.30.03, digital C-print, 2003

02.05.03, digital C-print, 2003
06.09.03, digital C-print, 2003

03.29.03, digital C-print, 2003
04.09.03, digital C-print, 2003

05.18.03, digital C-print, 2003
04.01.03, digital C-print, 2003
04.13.03, digital C-print, 2003

Living Space — Daugavpils
Alnis Stakle

Untitled, R-print, 2002
Untitled, R-print, 2002

Untitled, R-print, 2002

Untitled. R-print. 2002
Untitled. R-print. 2002

Untitled. R-print. 2002

娘rrespondence

Eric Van Hove

娘rrespondence II.   Tokyo, January 23, 2002

Belle,

A lonely promenade this afternoon in the 新宿御苑 park.
Accompanying you in thought, languor, lying in the short brown grass, blonde, tobacco, rough as a beast's skin, the dry scalp of mother nature.
Face raised, utter blue.

In the distance, greedy clouds brazen color, with which it is said the shell divers of the 和* country tattooed their bodies to frighten the marine monsters; the clench of wind, constipated from rain, cumulated cumulous.

Did you know that Marco Polo named Japan "Cipango" in his book (testimony), which Christopher Columbus also had in his caravel?

Cipango, an island filled with gold and marvelous treasures, where Marco Polo no doubt never set foot.
Therefore, this name resounds, as Zanzibar under the feather of Arthur.
Doubtless, by the way he speaks it, Arthur: "I will never leave, neither for Zanzibar, neither for elsewhere." (letter, fifth of November, 1887).

Recently, I left toward 箱根, a region at the foot of Mt. Fuji, beside a lake.
I am reminded, four or five years ago I saw a picture of that lake, of that mountain, and of that scarlet red arch: it is in seeing it that the idea of coming to Cipango first arrived to me. Tenacious and sudden.
I had forgotten this, a little bit. But as I came to the foot of Fuji I rediscovered this image, and I have walked inside of it.

An unexpected feeling to have accomplished, something.

On a museum ticket, I show you this picture.

Close by,

*Ancient Chinese name given to Japan (2000 years ago)

娘rrespondence IV.   Tokyo, June 10, 2002

Van Hove / Honich

Issue 1.2

131

Dear Dominique,

Japanese are sleeping.

At the seam, pedestrian's passage
At the zones of ebb tide, of the crowd, there where sometimes the nervous
stream of displacements bring them immobile as in a shock, because
in peace for some minutes, in a bus or on a train, Japanese are
sleeping.

It has always appeared to me that they do more than rest, heads tipped
by their own weight, heavy cheeks, disabused heroes of tiresome
modernities. Propped on obstacles that serve as supports, it is really the
drowsiness that surprises them, suspends them. Rocking with the swells
of the finally accepted constraints. Pitching with the regular disillusions,
by the rubbing of their intimacy with those of others, always numerous,
they are sent to sleep, their spirits glossed, peaceful with their drowned
faces.

The great Kabuki master Nakamura Tomijuro is supposed to have said
"You should never reveal tiredness or effort, because the art of acting
must be similar to the clothing of the celestial creators: with invisible
seams."
The seams of modern Japan are visible, and its creators have only
celestial reflection of the human condition's infinite tragedy, daily and
unnoticed as the beauty of a pool of water.
Another echo maybe of what they call here *monono aware* (the poignant
beauty of things) and that Christine Buci-Glucksman called "new Icarism"
in her book *The Aesthetic of Time in Japan*.

The time to sleep.

I think I am remembering that Merleau-Ponty sewed eroticism in a collar
that yawns; in the same way I voluntarily admit finding immanence in
the ringed-eye faces, the abused foreheads and the tired spines of this
modern folk of Amaterasu.

In friendship,

Ellen Honich, *Hair-Light*, C-print, 2003

娘rrespondence V.   Tokyo, June 26, 2001

Hello Pierre,

Here are some words.

You had told me that Japan "doesn't please" you.
I must acknowledge that it pleases me more and more.
The light of the streets in evening is quite particular, the materials used here, which proceed until the infinity of the banal, reflected in a strange manner, soft, absent, almost incredible.
The form of the streets "make" sculpture.

Something proportional.

To what . . . I don't know exactly.

There are a lot of earthquakes here, as you know.
That has consequences for urbanism: houses don't touch each other, they skirt each other.
It is without a doubt a precaution; if a house falls apart, its neighbor inevitably does not.
Moreover, movement is possible when separated.

This forms some very beautiful places: Slits between houses, interstice, houses like spread legs.
These spaces are truly sculptural.

Too narrow for one to pass through, too wide for one to forget, too practical for one to discard.
Some bitter herbs, doubtless respected in this Asian country like in many others, end up growing there, inaccessibly.

Most astonishing or logical (maybe it's the same), is that it appears to me that it goes with Japanese people as with their houses: a space is to be found in between them that makes one guess, a rumbling.

In friendship,

娘rrespondence IX.   Tokyo, February 3, 2002

Dearest O,

When Japanese speak in the first person, they generally end their

affirmations with a preposition like が or けれども or けど, which can be translated as "but"
  "But"
What a beauty is just that attitude, anticipation of an entire culture,
an archipelago's language at the end of Asia,
where one affirms nothing without a certain shyness,
at the end of every sentence adding this nothing
which retracts everything.

The Occidental that I am will always wait for a continuation to this "but":
But what? . . . but nothing.
Just suspended.

An undertow of meaning beneath what had just been presented, a silent suspension there where you rejoin the Other;
suddenly do not rejoin him really, refrain from it;
isolation of Japanese, solitude of deference.

Speaking without ego: is it communicating?
How not to think of Samuel Beckett, who wrote in "The Unnamable":
"Yes, as in my life is it to be called like this, there have been three things, the impossibility of keeping quiet, the impossibility of speaking, and the solitude, physical of course; with this I have unraveled."

Conversations in which one occupied the space of it, circumvented dialogues, surrounding exchange.

While the Latin self who comes from the Occident (symbolized here by 洋, a kanji which means "ocean"*) is by nature a citizen of the Agora, the Japanese, under hegemony of the elder, uses apology, and threads this spontaneity that the Occidental legitimizes.

It is sometimes said that French is the language of diplomats: The French speaker who has manners and needs to respond to aggression can choose to use politeness to the bitter end (which via politeness masks the attack and to the bitter end deploys it).

Japanese would be an Emperor's language: formal, more than polite, it is from afar that it is spoken and concealed even as it is heeded, as Murasaki Shikibu behind the *paravent*.

Warmly,

---

*The place where doubtless the first contacts with Portuguese ships occurred, a desert place that is ocean nevertheless, wandered over by winds and mobile unto horror: how better to mean the Other (the one who speaks another language).

Vlad Nanca, *Grass*, C-print, 2002

Untitled
Dewayne Washington

At your five-slap and finger-snap
I squint where the hell I know you from
And then it comes

When we grew up together
You were me and I was you
Between the bricks

With wrappers pouring
From grilled windows
We stood for the bus out

I catch your glance
At my locks, knotted up top
Envy with derision beneath

The selfsame mock I throw
At your slimline stouche
And white metal frames

You see me beat-bounce
And assume promise lost
Poise and snap unfulfilled

But I see you've bought the bid
Traded in your streetback black
For house-nigger slippers

For Me
By Rose Yndigoyen

I hate
I hate
I hate the way it's so easy
for you
to slide your fingers into the pretty girl
next to you.
The way you hold her hand
tight
cause she's yours.

I'm not embarassed.
I'm enlightened.
You'll see
A green glint from inside.

I have the right
to be a jealous wench,
and juicy in my hatred.
I'll be poison if I want.
My poison is
mine.

Mine, mine, mine.
Just like your pretty girl should be
would be
if she knew
how deep—I could touch her—how hard
I could hold her
How soft and happy
I would whisper into her hair
mine, mine, mine.

Joshua Hagler, *Heaven Can Wait*, oil on canvas, 2003

FEBRUARY 2004

Snow Pictures
Andrea Bakacs

Untitled (Blizzard), C-print, 2000
Untitled (Highway 26), C-print, 2002

Untitled (Cascade), C-print, 2002

Untitled (Foggy Road), C-print, 2000
Untitled (The Shining), C-print, 2000

Untitled (Alien), C-print, 2000

Transparency
Derrick Ableman

A man is balding noticeably in a blue-green car, in the state of Nevada, traveling North on a Tuesday through the desert in the dark. He's consciously unconscious of the currents in the air about him, of the electric light constellations at work in the skies above him. He feels it only when he is sleeping. He sleeps only when he's not talking. The man is always talking, always to himself.

A song comes on the radio. A call comes through the wires of 1985, in the city of Portland. The man answers the telephone, pretending he's half-asleep. It's his doctor, it's his car, it's his mother, it's his twin, it's his job, it's his wife again. He hangs up the telephone. He turns off the radio.

He smokes a cigarette, bracing one palm against the wheel and leaning back into the seat. He is dimly aware of the fact that he's driving the car, that he's heading North through the desert. The man collapses. He graduates from college. He eats rye toast with Swiss and roast beef. He loses his wallet. His daughter dies of pneumonia. His pants don't fit anymore. His wife loves him. His wife loves him. His wife loves. His wife moves to Reno.

The man is unconscious, hanging limply from the steering wheel of his car. His daughter can't breathe. His wife smokes cigarettes and cries. The car lurches into the desert at night. He breathes as slow as he can. The television is broken. His mouth tastes like mustard gas and ashes. His heart beats as slow as it can. The water is cold. His wife cries some more. The doctors clip his umbilical cord. His daughter doesn't breathe. His arms break while he is playing tennis. The water is cold. His wife is on line two. He fills his daughter up with air. The car plows through the sand. He puts his daughter's toys in boxes. He sees the Grand Canyon with his father. The water is cold. The car hits a pole. Her face is blue. He sends the boxes away. The machines stop bleating. His bed turns empty. His head turns empty. His father cries. The hood buckles in. The car divides. A door opens slightly. A light turns itself off. His heart races, his heart stops. His heart races, his heart stops. His heart races, his heart stops, his heart stops. His daughter is skating on a lake of ice in the winter, with her arms held above her head. Just like a ballerina.

Variations on A Theme by Arshile Gorky
(Betrothal I, Betrothal II Summation,
and Study for The Liver is the Cock's Comb)

J. Robert Beardsley

I am the Kneeling Dog
round gaping Jaws
these Hands extended
toward your Orifice

We are both kidney pink and bleeding;
I am a Tongue,
a rogue protrusion.

You are a Mare on spindly hind legs.

The world is made of rock teeth
and sulfur-blood
and We fuck the way
a Virus fucks.

Sometimes
a thing starts out
Holy, but We End the same
We end the same as Horses, Cocks' crows, and Tissue.

Your breasts hover disembodied,
looming as I try to look up at your eyes;
their almond shape
becoming light stain bloodspots
in black puddle memory.

Ye Rin Mok, *Susansun01*, C-print, 2002

untitled
Tanis C. Clark

It's when you're alone, locked up tight as slow poison in a convenient pill, the semis schooling like hammerheads, the rain heavy, heavy; even with the a/c on you can't breathe; maybe it's the rain, maybe it's the proximity of all those people who don't know you exist—unless they're calling you names, to them you're five minutes of fury and then you're forgotten, and you'll never know that either—one of them could kill you like you killed that doe, (blackeyed sloetoed and dead dead) dead, so that even today, three months later, your heart skips every time a rabbit scurries along the sidewalk or a streetlight goes out or the cd misses a beat, every time you're ice-cold, and you won't sleep for hours: not that you could anyway, the drive is endless, it's hours of street, hours, and this is when you can tell the roads aren't open like they used to be, they're empty now; a difference you couldn't explain and can't help but feel.

Goodbye to All That
Jesse Hassenger

The first time I got mugged was at the Utica Zoo. I was thirteen, and I just felt sorry for the guy. All he got was eleven dollars and a pen, and there he was, in Utica, at the zoo. I hadn't been to the zoo since I was seven, when my grandparents were still alive. After I got mugged, I went back every week for years, daring it to happen again. You shouldn't have to feel scared at the zoo, I told myself, at least not of muggers. Sometimes I stayed pretty late. Most zoos close before dusk, but the Utica zoo stayed open till nine in the summer. You got the feeling that they weren't familiar with conventions of zoo operation; the next closest zoo was in Binghamton, two hours away. Sometimes my friend Jenny would come with me after school.

"Look at those monkeys," she said once.

"I'm already looking."

"Just look at them—"

"I am."

"—the way they're jumping around and scuffling like that. I can't tell, are they mad or having fun? Which is it?"

"I think they're all having fun, except that one." I pointed to a monkey up in one of the fake trees, shrieking and jumping like the rest, but staying back from the central melee. "They're all having fun, but he's mad."

"How can you tell?"

"I can just tell. He's mad."

Jenny jumped on my back and brought me to my knees.

The second time I got mugged was at age sixteen, after my grandparents' wake. They froze to death, waiting for a bus in Buffalo. I was sad, but I figured it was something I could use on my own kids someday: Don't wait for a bus outside in upstate New York, or you'll wind up like grandma and grandpa. Dead, in Buffalo. My mom grew up there, but after it killed her parents, she no longer had much use for it, or the whole of upstate. She talked about moving to Virginia, especially in the winter. When Jenny came over to my house, sometimes she'd stop and talk with my mom for half an hour before anyone told me she was there. I'd come down the stairs to get a root beer, and I'd see Jenny and my mom, chatting like in-laws with a healthy relationship. Jenny would suggest to my mom that the two of them go in on a time-share in the South, to make it through the upstate winters. She told me later I could visit them, if I wanted. Jenny's grandparents were also dead, and for awhile I actually thought that could be considered something we had in common.

My grandparents' wake was at a funeral home in a shitty part of town. I stepped outside to reflect, and I got mugged, although I was never sure if the guy really had a gun. When I look back, I tend to think not. I lost twenty-nine dollars and my social security card. For all I know, that guy will be collecting my benefits in thirty years. No one ever really told me how that stuff works.

I never went to college. Not that that's the type of stuff they teach you at college, but maybe I would've picked it up from someone, a roommate or something. A lot of my friends went, so I felt like I had the experience through them. It sounded pretty terrible. Jenny, for example, cried almost every night of her freshman year. She transferred the next year, and only cried about every other night. She considered transferring again, to get it down to maybe once or twice a week, but by that point, she said, she just wanted her degree.

Her second school was Skidmore College, in Saratoga Springs. I visited her there a few times. I was in love with her. I noticed because she left Utica, and suddenly I hated it. I never hated it before. My father had a saying: "Not bad, for Utica." Until Jenny left, I sort of lived by that without knowing it. It took about a week before I realized I no longer felt the comfort of indifference to my surroundings. I walked around my city and experienced hatred. I hated the giant rectangular buildings that made the sky seem empty instead of open, and I hated the signs for the interstate, everywhere, advertising the hint of better lives. It got especially bad when I tried to think of reasons to hate Cumberland Farms. It wasn't possible, of course; I never found my reasons. I had finally found the energy to hate Utica, but to hate Cumberland Farms would be to go against the very fiber of my being.

Cumberland Farms, or Cumby's, as it is commonly known, was founded in the 1950's by Vasilios and Aphrodite Haseotes. They were the first convenience stores in New England, but eventually found greatest favor in New York state. In 2002, they were forced to pay a $90,000 penalty for pollution caused by its gas stations throughout New England. Upstate New York was left unscathed. We were good to Cumberland Farms, and they were good to us. They made excellent milkshakes (Vasilios and Aphrodite were originally dairy farmers) and they sold blue fruit punch in two-liter bottles for seventy-nine cents. Until Jenny left, any hints of resentment towards Utica was diffused by any place that stayed up late: Cumby's, open twenty-four hours, and Popa's, a completely average pizza place with the good sense to stay open till two in the morning.

My buddy Derrick was pretty smart, and decided to graduate from Syracuse University in three years, instead of four. He came home and immediately regretted it.

"I had no idea I'd miss Syracuse," he said.

"That's how it is, I guess."

"No, really, it literally never occurred to me. I didn't think it was possible. It's fucking me up. I need to get out of here."

"Yeah," I said, and he said nothing. We sat in silence, watching *Slamball*, a television program combining basketball and trampolines. At first we thought it was faked, but later agreed it would take too much effort.

We went to Cumby's a lot. One night, we ran into McGowan, who used to be Derrick's neighbor, before McGowan's parents moved away. After that, he got his own place. McGowan's hair, usually close to his head in a bowl cut, was morning-mussed, and his eyes seemed to blink at twice the normal rate. He was a skinny guy, but he had the round face of someone fatter. At first, I thought he was drunk, but I couldn't smell anything on him.

"McGowan." Derrick was looking right at McGowan when he said it, and McGowan certainly heard him, but I swear he only meant it for me. McGowan was browsing through the snack cakes. He seemed to be comparing the cupcakes to the Snoballs when he looked up at us.

"Gentlemen," said McGowan.

"McGowan," said Derrick, again.

I said, "How's everything?" I got the feeling that if I didn't, Derrick and McGowan could've gone back and forth all night, and Derrick was my ride.

"Good as it can be, I guess, with the Italians keeping me down. No offense, Sam."

"None taken," I said. I'm one quarter Italian.

"Yeah, things are rough all over," said McGowan.

"All over?" I said.

"McGowan," said Derrick.

"All over Utica," said McGowan.

"Are you still working at the newspaper?" I kept asking questions to avoid awkward pauses, and to keep Derrick from repeating his name.

"Yeah, I still got that gig. Still entering classified ads and shit. It's not glamorous, but hey, I'm working. Still writing on the side. Might apply for some reporter type shit this month."

"At the same paper?"

"Yeah, same paper. How 'bout you, you still drawing those cartoons?"

"Oh, you know, on and off."

"How bout you, D-rock?"

"McGowan," said Derrick, nodding. "Newspaper man." I was starting to wonder if Derrick was drunk, but I knew he wasn't; I'd been with him for the past fifteen hours.

"Yeah, man. Yeah," said McGowan. "Also, I'm sleeping in my car."

Then he unzipped his pants and urinated on the snack cakes. We left before the clerk called the police.

"That was fucking depressing," Derrick said later. "But McGowan's a good guy." We resolved to leave the house less.

After a few weeks of sitting around at Derrick's house, watching *Wild & Crazy Kids* on Nickelodeon Sports during the day ("The production budget must be about twelve dollars," Derrick theorized) and *Slamball* at night ("I fucking hate sports, but this, I like," I offered), I needed a break. I decided to visit Jenny again. I tried to convince Derrick to come with me, but I was secretly relieved when he was too tired. I wanted Jenny's lack of romantic affection to myself.

I met Jenny's boyfriend before I knew he existed. I was carelessly shaking his hand hello as Jenny introduced him as such. Later, Jenny and I had coffee, alone.

"So, you and what's-his-name... things are going well?" I forgot his name because I willed myself to forget it.

"His name is Jason."

"Goddamn it!" There it was.

"What?!"

"Nothing."

"Are you okay, Sam? You seem a little disoriented."

"Yeah, I'm fine. So how long have you two been dating?"

"Well, a few weeks, but we've known each other for awhile."

"How long?"

"Like I said, a few weeks. Are you sure..."

"No, how long have you known each other?"

"Oh, since sophomore year. Met in History of World Cinema, you know, I told you about..."

"No, you never told me about him."

"The class. I told you about the class."

"Oh. Right. So, what's so good about him?" "Jason" still sounded like a teenager's name to me.

"Um, what?"

"What, you know... attracted you to him?"

"Well, he's got a good sense of humor."

"Yeah?"

"He just puts me at ease, you know? I feel very... comfortable around him."

"I see."

"Good kisser, too!"

"Great!"

"You know, I wasn't having such an easy time of it, here. All that crying and stuff."

"Yeah."

"Jason really helped me get past all that."

"Yeah, I noticed you hadn't been calling as much."

"And those calls were great, Sam. Without you, I don't know how I would've gotten through those first few years of this. Without you, my relationship with Jason probably wouldn't even be possible. And I know a lot of guys who would just let a girl cry on their shoulder to try and, you know, get them into bed or something."

Brian Lemond, *A Split Among Many*, Ilfochrome, 2003

"Those stupid fuckers."

"Exactly. Well, sort of. Are you okay?"

"Stupid fuckers."

I went back to Utica, slept a lot, and had disappointingly realistic dreams; things that could've happened, or might have happened only to be forgotten, like dreams. It might sound confusing, but really, it was just stupid. One did end with me holding a severed arm; I wasn't sure whose though, and it was just a cheap shock ending grafted onto an otherwise uninspired episode. I started writing stuff down.

When I was younger, I got into writing as a means of avoiding eye contact, but the results were mostly unsatisfying. I figured now was a good time to experiment: Derrick's parents insisted that if he wasn't going to find a job immediately, he should visit relatives in Rochester. Derrick hated Rochester, especially how they said "pop" instead of "soda", but the only job application he had on his desk was for Cumby's, so he didn't put up a fight. With my only remaining friend out of town, I took a week out of my life to write some bad poetry.

Though I spent my share of time thinking about Jenny's big eyes and small hands, I did not actually write much poetry. Pornography was one problem; what little I wrote descended into it. I had only an average amount of experience with that sort of thing, so I wasn't even writing quality pornography; it was incoherent, and often illogical. I couldn't even keep settings straight (Texaco men's room or Motel 6?) or fulfill basic fantasies (in the pool or on all fours?). I never penciled myself or anyone else I knew into these escapades; I created Cynthia, who I found decidedly unattractive, and Anthony, whose neck was bigger than my arm, and shoved them into awkward trysts. Anthony was hollow and Cynthia lied.

Towards the end of poetry week, I took a walk. The city looked rough and unfinished. Sketchbook smoke rose in the distance, like some misguided bastard was trying to commit Utica to paper. Passing by the comics shop, I noticed it was closed. This wasn't unusual. The owner, Casper, was notoriously fickle about when to open his store, and when to close unexpectedly for an obscure religious holiday. As far as I could tell, Casper was not a religious man. It was even rumored that he burned the occasional cross, but most of those rumors (and any others painting Casper as a degenerate, rather than a simple mean spirit) could be traced back to Rusty, a local journeyman who claimed Casper swindled him out of several rare role-playing cards. Rusty still patronized Casper's store, because it was, as Rusty and Casper both said, by personal turns furious and triumphant, "the only goddamned comics shop for fifty fucking miles."

On my walk that day, though, you could see dust through the window pane, settling on the action figures and semi-new releases, and I wondered if he was gone for good. I thought about Jenny, and kicked a mailbox, and crossed the street to Popa's.

Popa's wasn't the classiest place, but it had its pride, or at least I assumed it did. Two slices and a can of soda for three-fifty. For awhile, I worked at a nearby shoe store, and came to Popa's for lunch every day. It was cost-efficient, but I gained ten pounds. After that, I restricted trips to Popa's to special occasions. I hadn't been there in five months.

I noticed a girl at a small table, by herself, in the corner. She was reading a tattered copy of something or other (it was tattered, and she was reading; I couldn't really quibble with further details), occasionally smiling to herself. I waited for a suitor, or at least a close male friend, to join her, but he never turned up. Even as I rationalized that he was probably busy at his bar band's rehearsal, it pleased me to see a strange girl alone. After half an hour though, I grew suspicious; she looked similar, after all, to a number of low-key fantasy girls I had found myself hoping to find in cafes, bookstores and movie theaters for my entire adult life. Eventually, I began to doubt my eyes. When I returned from a reluctant trip to the restroom, she was gone, whether she had actually been there or not.

Whenever you tell someone that you're going crazy, they always make the verbal lunge into reassurance, telling you it cannot be true, as if it is a very bad thing indeed. I didn't mind so much. At least not this part. The only disappointment was my writing. I had heard that a lot of brilliant writers had a touch of madness; I felt crazy all right, but I was stuck trying to make "small hands" rhyme with "so it ends."

It was a relief, then, when Derrick returned from Rochester. He got back before noon on a weekday; I wondered if he had snuck out. There didn't seem to be much other explanation for him waking up at nine in the morning. He picked me up on the way to high school to visit his eleventh-grade brother and ask him for the spare housekey.

For a moment, pulling into the high school parking lot, the sun shone across the brick buildings, through the spaces in the scaffolding, onto bright yellow construction equipment, and the whole thing looked promising. It looked like the future, coming soon. But as we walked across the gravel lot, closer to the school, past the dingy equipment and dusty beams, I remembered how long it had been this way.

Three years prior, voters approved a $19 million renovation to the junior and senior high schools. The two adjacent buildings would be combined into one administrative force, and additions would be made to make them navigable as one. There would also be a school swimming pool—the first in the district—a more modern cafeteria, and a host of new, improved classroom facilities. The ground on the project was officially broken in the summer of 1999.

Initial progress, however, went slowly, and after a year the Board of Education complained the district was ignoring several fire and safety codes for new classrooms, and that many of them would have to be re-renovated. The project's original architect, Louis Carl Florio, had moved on to another project, the renovation of Utica's Town Hall, and served as a consultant for the school project. When reports of the board's disapproval became widespread, Florio sued the district and several individual board members for breach of contract, defamation of character, and emotional damages. He charged that the negative reports were part of a conspiracy to oust him from the industry and, in the words of his legal documents and press release, a "five-pronged attack" on his character, livelihood, and, presumably, three more prongs' worth of himself. A committee formed to determine who was at fault in regards to the school project, as well as whether or not the renovations could continue. Construction was halted in the winter of 2001.

The committee eventually determined that the school project would cost $2.4 million to complete, and that only $300,000 remained in the budget. Shortly after this news became public, Florio fled town, the town hall and school both incomplete, and wound up in Waterbury, CT, where he was elected mayor. The remaining $300,000 was reappropriated to demolish the now-crippled town hall. Officials were forced to relocate to a recently out-of-business Burger King. Utica taxpayers, outraged at the lack of a finished school, refused to approve any new measures to fund the project's completion. And so the junior and senior high schools continued to operate, steel beams jutting across the courtyard, students eating lunch in the auxiliary gymnasium.

The permanent state of construction made security tighter at the building's main entrance, but lax everywhere else. After casing the torn-up grounds for about half an hour, Derrick and I decided to enter through the window of an abandoned science room, one of the areas deemed unfit by the Board of Education. We exited into a hall which I vaguely recognized, but had now been halfheartedly closed off with CAUTION tape. This was probably because it lacked a real ceiling; wires hung everywhere, and rows of lockers were blocked by ladders and debris.

"What'd they do about the locker shortage?" I wondered aloud.

"They bought up a bunch of cubbies from Home Depot," said Derrick. "Stuck 'em in one of the gyms."

"How do they lock?"

"No locks. Thing is, none of the students really have it in them to steal stuff. Their spirits have been broken, I guess."

"Well, at least nothing gets stolen."

"Oh, stuff gets stolen. Kids from rival school districts come by at night, make off with anything they can."

"We have rival school districts?"

"They certainly seem to think so." We came to the end of the hallway; I was halfway over the CAUTION tape before I saw Derrick tearing it asunder. "We're gonna need to go back this way," he said. It wasn't really true, but I understood. Finally, we found ourselves in a hallway—I think it was the math wing—that was more or less inhabitable, although some of the overhead lights were burnt out, and the floors were heavily scuffed. The hall was empty, save for one kid at a drinking fountain at the opposite end.

"Kid!" yelled Derrick.

"Shhh," I said. The kid looked back at us, and bolted. Without really thinking, we took off after him. I wasn't much good at running, but Derrick still played tennis occasionally, and gained enough ground to grab the kid by the collar. He didn't hurt him, but he did stretch out his shirt, which got him to stop. By the time I caught up with them, they were in mid-interrogation.

"Yeah, I know Devlin Harmon."

"You know where he is right now?"

"What, did he die or something?"

"No, in the school. Where is he in the school?"

"I think he has gym this period."

"Senior high or junior high?"

"Junior. There is no senior high gym anymore, it's filled with lunches and cubbies."

"Alright, thanks."

"Are you guys gonna kill him or something?"

"You shouldn't think about death so much," I said.

"Why not?" said Derrick and the kid, at the same time.

We found Devlin in a field behind the junior high, playing soccer. If you stood and faced the field, back to the school, everything looked the same, just like it used to. Actually, it looked better; the grounds looked like they had been given special attention, in lieu of anything else that could be properly maintained.

Devlin resembled a smaller, scrappier version of Derrick. Same tussled blonde hair, same professorial glasses, but with longer arms he hadn't quite grown into (though he was close), and no circles under his eyes. Derrick told me on the way here Devlin was thinking of NYU for school, breaking the family's Syracusian tradition. "I hope he makes it out of here and all," he said, "but I know I'll be a little bit pissed if he does."

"Devlin, you have the spare housekey?" We had walked into the middle of the field. Everyone else played around us, a blur of yellow mesh pennies and stained gym clothes.

"I have *my* housekey. Is that what you mean?"

"Yeah, the spare, your spare, whatever."

"You know, I still live here. That would make it *my* housekey. Not the spare."

"I still live here too!"

"No, *I* still live here. You live here *again*."

"So you have the key?"

"Yeah, I have the key."

"Can I have it?"

"Are you gonna be home when I get home from school?"

"Yeah, I'll be home."

"Then take it." He took a small chain from around his neck, and handed it to Derrick.

"What's with the *Mysterious Cities of Gold* shit?" I said.

"I don't want to have to go to my cubby before I get out of here. And I'm not leaving anything important in the locker room. I've got my cash at the bottom of my shoe. Fucking Florio, man." I was a little surprised to hear open scorn for the departed architect. Devlin's demeanor was suddenly less playful. "If I ever got ahold of that bastard, I'd kick him square in the nuts for all of this crap."

"Easy there, kid," said Derrick.

"Everyone feels this way," said Devlin. "In art, we made effigies of him, to burn."

"Wow," I said.

"Okay, we're taking off. You want a ride home?" said Derrick.

"It's only sixth period," said Devlin.

"Suit yourself," said Derrick.

I didn't mention it to Devlin or Derrick, but I met Louis Carl Florio once, at Cumby's. It was two in the morning, and I was microwaving a burrito, exchanging nods with the overnight clerk. Florio—I recognized him as someone in the newspaper, but I couldn't place him exactly—came in, muttering to himself, and started grabbing stuff off the shelves: Some bread, some beef jerky, some hose tape. I stared at him without thinking, because he was the only real movement in the store. I accidentally made eye contact, and I think I made him nervous, because he began to direct his mumblings towards me. Suddenly I was straining to keep up with my half of the conversation.

"You live around here?" he said.

"Yeah."

"Yeah? What's your favorite thing?"

"Favorite thing?"

"About living here. About Utica. And its, uh, surrounding vicinities. Do you have a favorite… the best. What's the best part of Utica?" It was the kind of question relatives would ask me about school.

"I don't really…"

"Come on, you gotta have something. Mine's the donut place on Ballston Avenue. Fucking great donuts, there. Wish they were open twenty-four hours, I wouldn't be coming to this fucking place if they were." I glanced at the clerk, expecting irritation, but he was nodding to himself in agreement. I thought for a moment, as Florio helped himself to a cup of Cumby's Brew.

"I guess the fact that you can see the sky, most places. Even near the taller buildings, you know… it's a pretty open space. I like that. That the city doesn't seem infinite." I lied, a little. This was probably the second-best thing.

"Yeah," said Florio. He had stopped listening. He quickly paid for his goods, and rushed out the door, peeling out of the parking lot needlessly. He never returned, and a few days later, he was in all the papers again.

After getting Devlin's key, we stayed at Derrick's, watching *Wild & Crazy Kids* and most of *Godfather III*, until we went to Cumby's for blue juice, although my appetite for snack cakes was severely diminished. Derrick didn't even want to go; he had dozed off, so I pretended I was futzing with the TV, turning the volume loud enough to jostle him. He would only accompany me to Cumby's if I bought him a hot dog, and he got to wait in the car. I agreed to his terms.

The third time I got mugged was at Cumby's. It seemed to me that the mugger came in to rob the whole place, but chickened out. So when the clerk's back was turned, he poked something—probably a gun, this time, though I wouldn't commit to that for sure—into my back and quietly demanded my wallet. I asked if I could keep the wallet, and he could just take everything inside. This turned out to be a bad negotiation tactic—I think I made the mugger think the wallet was worth something (really, I was just trying to save a couple of bucks, and I was lazy). I lost seventeen dollars, a credit card, a picture of my extended family, and the wallet itself. After the guy left, I told the clerk what happened. He didn't offer to call the police or anything, but he told me to help myself to some snackcakes.

I told my mom I was thinking of leaving Utica. "Be careful," she said. "Go someplace warm."

I found out, later in life, that Upstate and Western New York has this reputation, among people in New York City and Westchester who bother to think about it, as basically a big grassy field, with some cows and a few big houses. I've tried to correct them, for better or worse—Utica has more open pavement than it does grass; few people in Buffalo have big houses; Saratoga is built on gambling, not farms—but it doesn't really stick. And I guess it doesn't matter. There's only a few truly great U.S. cities: New York, San Francisco, Chicago, and maybe St. Louis. Utica can't compete with that shit. But don't let anyone tell you New England is the same, or better.

The day after my third mugging, I walked downtown for lunch, alone. I invited Derrick, but he was busy with his new job, at the Utica department of finance, located in a handsome new addition built onto the abandoned Burger King. I thought of him when I saw what looked, oddly, like fireflies darting in the sky. Turning a corner, I realized they were embers.

Popa's was engulfed in flames. A small crowd gathered across the street to watch it burn, but most people kept walking, uninterested and hardly shocked. I suppose I wasn't either, and I spotted the owner of Popa's in the crowd, bearing the suppressed grin of a shoddy insurance scam. Curls of orange flame twirled and debris fell; you could see it all happening perfectly, like it was all in slow motion. I kept walking.

A few miles later, I sat on a curb, looking into the street, the smoke from Popa's still visible in the distance. A fire truck rolled by, speeding but sirens off, as unsurprised as anyone. A few days later I left town.

Urban Perspectives
Jan Halle

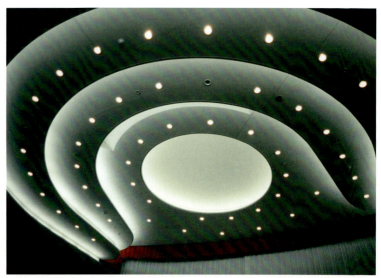

Cinema No. 2, C-print, 2003
Tokyo No. 27, C-print, 2003

Night in the City, C-print, 2001
Tokyo 2053, C-print, 2003
Urban Space No. I, C-print, 2003

Spaces No. II, C-print, 2003
Subway, C-print, 2001
Spaces No. I, C-print, 2003

Pleasure in Colors
Mizue Hirano

My Gardening, oil on canvas, 2003
Folding Metaphor, oil on canvas, 2003

Beyond Volcano, oil on canvas, 2003

facing page:

Float, oil on canvas, 2003
Red Pouring | *Vertical Lines* | *Passion*, all oil on canvas, 2003

Pilot, our last war
Nick Jones

The flesh of crossed knees
is nothing to you now
the crease of calves
or of bodies in still slumber

Only the airy scream of wing tips
of flight over blue acres
of moonless nights
swooping into parts unknown

and flying there suspended
in time's elastic sling
remove one glove and etch a grid
into evidence of autumn's chill

choose exes or ohs
and arc ever more silently
until you cross yourself diagonally
pilot, our last war is nothing
to you now

but a memory of hell
and of enumerating all the reasons
that flight was your answer

Jane Kim, *Montreal*, Ilfochrome, 2002

Maddaloetry
Joseph Maddaloni

Digital Camera

the Kodak Digital Camera
is out for repair
(the Big one)
so

we only have
the Olympus
Digital camera
available

PEPSI COLA

The new Pepsi
coin vending machine
will be here
tomorrow,

as of now
there is no soda
in the old machine

sorry for the inconvenience

Water

Our Vendor
for spring Water
is in New Jersey,

Due to the Weather,
Don't know when
we will have a delivery

as of now
we are
out of Water

Alan Duke, *January 27, 2004*, C-print, 2004

SINK

Please avoid leaving
coffee stirrers in the sink,
tea bags,
leaves from plants
Etc.
I am having trouble
with the water draining...

(it Doesn't)

Fax Machine (reprise)

Although we send out faxes for you, there are times when you send your
own fax

such as after hours,

with the new phone system, requires a

pause

in place of *

so for long distance It's

9
1
phone number
pause,
pause
project Number

local faxes remain the same

as

before

Budapest
Simon Ladefoged

Budapest 02, C-print, 2002
Budapest 05, C-print, 2002

Budapest 04, C-print, 2002

facing page:
Budapest 01, C-print, 2002
Budapest 03, C-print, 2002

Budapest 07, C-print, 2002

Polly
Camille Napier

I could graciously accept your
wife
in my home,
offer her my recipe for fried catfish
and give her a tour of my garden,
never asking
if you still grew tomatoes.

I could let
her
spend the night
with you
in my spare bedroom, and I'd sleep soundly
in my own bed down the hall.

I wouldn't flinch if my cats settled into
her lap
or wound themselves around her head as she slept.
She would like cats, wouldn't she?

I'd be (kind) careful to share only
innocuous details about you,
benign and silly anecdotes
about your youth.
I wouldn't seem too impressed by your jokes
(or unimpressed at their vintage),
and I'd never refer casually
to some lark that
we alone
once knew.

There'd be no "Does he do this to you, too?"
that would leave her wondering
what you might have changed (or lost) since
I knew you best.
And I'd listen (unflinchingly, empty-eyed, smiling serenely) to
your wife
tell
me
things I already knew:
how you eat too slowly
how you order milk at restaurants (startling the waiters)

Issue 1.3

how you malaprop on purpose (confusing your friends)
how your feet are like ice under the sheets

I wouldn't reveal the other things I
already knew:
a mole on your thigh, how you piss sitting down,
the sounds you make in your sleep,
sounds we made before sleep, the weight of you, the smell and taste of you,
how tears slide silently down your face when you cry
that you cry.

We'd like each other:
your wife and I.
And she'd promise to do this again sometime—
and mean it—
and she'd hug me goodbye
and admit she'd been nervous,
and say I was so kind.

And she'd wave from the car,
and she'd wave for the baby, too:
a baby's close-fisted wave from darling Polly—
a name we'd pondered ourselves.

Winter
Matthue Roth

When they told you
move to California
where there's no such
thing as winter

they lied.

it still gets dark early.
leaves still die.
and the streets have never
been so desolate

there's not even a line
outside El Rio
and when you don't have to
wait hours
to be hip
nobody wants to be

winter is a dead game
sitting out on the table
and uncleaned up after dessert,

Herb went to Texas to find work
Phred's drawing comix on the road
my girlfriend said she needed to find
herself in New York
and I said you can't—

everything's frozen
beneath the snow
and you wouldn't know where
to look

at least they have snow there she
said, look at this city—
it's cold as fuck and
not even ice to
show for it.

one day they'll
find an antidote
for the common cold

but they'll never
cure winter

William and Mary Lemond, *Untitled*, Ilfochrome, 2004

Black & White, 2003
Jin Sugahara

Sonzai To Jikan, sumi ink, 2003
Tsuki No Minamo, sumi ink, 2003
Doro, sumi ink, 2003

Kegon, sumi ink, 2003
Hu No Mai, sumi ink, 2003

facing page:

Daikoku, sumi ink, 2003
Koubou, sumi ink, 2003

Hakua, sumi ink, 2003

Flightless
Chris Warner

My twenty-five-year-old brother woke me up this morning at 5:30, insisting we check out the new tiger exhibit at the zoo.

"Let's go, like, now!" he was saying.

"We'll go," I blinked. "Not now. Zoo's closed. Even the tigers are sleeping."

I am thirty. Conrad—Connie—is my only sibling. He gets this way in the first week or so after one of his hiatuses. I heard him padding around the apartment until I got up at seven. When I came out of my bedroom, he was sitting on the edge of the couch, leaning out the open window, pretending to whisper to a pigeon. The silver-green neck plumage on the bird's neck reflected a reluctant autumn sun.

My brother made a big show of listening to the pigeon, then laughing and shaking his head, as if they'd shared a funny joke.

"Connie, stay away from that thing. It's filthy."

"You don't know the half of it," he nodded, and winked at the pigeon.

My brother can be difficult, and funny. When we go out to lunch, he will pester the waitress for confirmation that no cows were harmed in the making of his corned beef sandwich. When we go for walks on the park, he will approach strangers and ask them when the running of the bulls begins. He will get in these moods, taking off toward the places in his mind which hold hopes of unbridled joy, always trying to bring me with him.

Our grandmother used to call him a whirlwind.

He hurries me as I fix my hair, getting what he calls the "meticulously disheveled" look. He fails to understand why people (and by this, he means me) spend twenty minutes on their hair to look like they just rolled out of bed. My brother recently shaved off his hair because, he said, the sound of it had been keeping him awake.

I park in the north lot. After a quick walk by Gibbon Island, we're standing at the emu exhibit. I look at my watch and read my brother's pupils, and I can tell by their sharpness and what lingers behind them that he has neglected his prescription. This will make for an interesting morning.

"I'd like to invite you to our Thanksgiving dinner," he is telling the emu, well aware that he has the audience of a little boy halfway hidden behind his mother. "We're bringing the entire family. Sound good?" The boy laughs and looks up at his mother, whose mouth makes a flat line. As she walks off with the boy, my brother calls after them, "Weddings, parties, anything." It's a line from a song I know I know but haven't heard in years.

The emu comes a step closer, nicks the ground with his beak, and looks away.

"Where are these guys from?" I ask, trying to keep my brother occupied. I get no answer.

"Con—?"

"Sshh!" he says, grabbing my shoulder through my jacket. He cups his hand behind his ear and tilts his head. "He says...Emu. Dromiceius novaehollandiae, from Australia."

"How'd you kn—?"

"Sshhh!" Again with the grab. "He says...'Read...the plaque...you wanker.'"

I sigh. "He said that, huh?"

Connie bows to the emu and signals for me to follow him. As my brother takes off toward Tiger Mountain, he yells, "Tiger! Tiger!" and I think he's going to recite the poem, but then he flies in a different direction with, "Never leave the boat, man! Never leave the boat." It's from a Vietnam War movie.

I look at the emu and tell him not to worry. Before lunch, I tell him, we'll get Connie's prescription filled. The emu seems to return my gaze.

I ask him, "Sound good?"

He blinks and shakes his head.

Ye Rin Mok, *Clover*, C-print, 2003

A Note for Claude
Dewayne Washington

Your Harlem Dancer; your white-world's hell
Only distant shades
We are our own people
For we have chosen segregation
Trumped-up, inflated affectation

Yelling like the Chinese in
Busses brimming with large women
A midday smoke
A loiterer's paradise
Maybe sitting here *is* my job, bitch

Heritage worn thin
A culture reduced to hair and clothes
Coats of arms and script tattoos
My clan, your clan
Battles in the street for irrelevant supremacy

Waiting, watching for signs
Brothers found
Brothers lost
Salvation doled out by
God and the Warden

JUNE 2004

Reaching Fever
Derrick Ableman

Officially, magnetic fields know of no acting king or monarch, but their lives are legislated all the same by metals and poles and small pockets of charge that command their constant reach and drag. This is not considered a tyranny among the fields, who have nothing otherwise to do and so welcome the work, finding a kind of brotherhood in the towing of things. Each wave in the field is expected to do his part, some going out in front for the gathering, while still others remain behind, lending support.

"The labor is equal. Each to his part," as the outer waves sometimes say. Only they can speak, being spread so far from their source and home charge, out to distant lands where the fields loosen into distinct waves. There, in these distances, each wave becomes capable of feeling his own travel and knowing himself, for once apart from the charge.

But of this they never tell the others when they return and reabsorb, some game in tow or else entirely repulsed, tired and glad for the rest. They never breathe a word of it, this separateness, for each wave becomes large-hearted by the knowledge—lonely too—and this they decide, in the few moments they feel it, is a weight and a curse. So they always turn back when they hear themselves think, sometimes before finding anything. They turn back and chase themselves home, forgetting it each time they collapse into one another.

But some nights, at the edges of sleep, on the tops and bottoms of the waking world, there are dreams that skip across the fields like stones, raising ripple pools of plots and plans. Some think (and the thinking spreads) that tomorrow morning they could all push out from the source and dissolve into space, each allotted a few moments of life before negation. But escape is impossible, deep as knowing going they all know this. The source is the source and will drag them back, no matter the distance.

Still, there are rumors. At the poles, where the sources are the strongest and the waves so thick they border on visibility, here there are rumors of another charge, a greater charge so like a god that the poles themselves circle in worship. A Sun Charge, hot heart of all charges, Father of all Fields.

At the poles the plan evolves—slowly, as each out-going wave is given only moments of privacy to plot before it's drawn back, its work forgotten. But ever-steady, the plans return to the fields in the form of dreams, each night building on the back of the last, until they learn while waking, becoming of one mind.

They are aiming for the Sun. Selecting waves and dispatching them like prayers. Some will perish or be repulsed, they know this. Many will simply disintegrate, few will find it and fewer still will bear the time alone, the agony of their own voices echoing through space. But some will

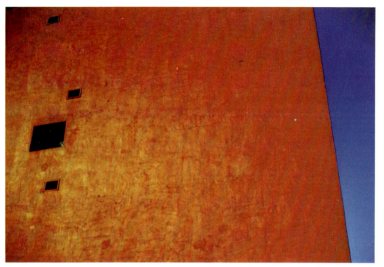

Byron Barrett, *Wall*, Ilfochrome, 2002

make it, remembering their mission, aged centuries by the travel and exile. These are the ones now so different from their kin that they can be seen, even from here, surrounding the sun, burning up in the bliss of forgetting.

Lapse Aria
David J. Alworth

Original Sin is somewhere in the way the word *bailar*
slips through her tongue and hard palate,
with a hint of vibrato
to give it the double-r sound that it craves

Dancing before a Latin American Literature class,
pas de cheval, the *step of the horse,*
She is a devil at its weakest moment:
beholds two mortals, almost
abhors corrupting them.

Sunrise barely sneaks a finger through a dusty gym window
while I reveal my secrets to the speed bag
I sweat and breathe
the beats linger,
become a perpetual decrescendo.

This is where we meet.
She dances in a place words
cannot reach,
slides her body up against
something like truth.

The narrow line of her back,
kindling in a fire
that cracks and spits,
warms my skin
lifts the scent of soot
into me.

Eddie Alfaro, *Web 3,* latex
and marker on canvas, 2004

For a moment I think She is
only truth.

This is not because
her mother always kept a whiskey filled Dixie cup
hidden in the cupboard,
or because seduction can
be sex, unscented.

Until she sneaks
a forked tongue in my direction
and I remember this
has really been Eve's fault since the start.

A Waiting Room
Scott Cheshire

Peg was twelve when they took her head.

She was thirteen when they found it. I know because she told me. "It's my birthday tomorrow," she said.

Her yellow pants and the shirt with strawberries lie next to her. I never imagine the underwear. Her skin as white as my pillow is now. Her legs are crumpled. Her head nowhere in sight.

At least that's how I imagine it these days.

Sometimes there's blood. Sometimes there are footprints. Four days ago it was tiny Peg splayed across the railroad ties, just like they found her, on abandoned tracks in a useless rail yard. But she was fully clothed, intact, and she smiled at me across so many years.

And it's not just Peg either. I think of her little sister. I think of Marla, Peg's mom. I think of Ed.

Ed at the funeral standing beside Peg who lay flat in the highest of collars, surrounded in billows of white satin and I remember thinking, even if he did do it like they say, he looks sad. That's his daughter for Christ's sake, I feel bad for him.

It started maybe a year ago, after hours of twisting in bed and finding myself knotted in sheets unable to sleep. I swallowed maybe three hundred milligrams of dyphenhydramine and ten minutes later I was dreaming of Peg Schroback's face. I hadn't thought of her in years, but there she was, without shoulders, and propped by a stone. Smiling behind hair wet from rain, her body sitting beside her.

Every night the dreams would come, they still do. Not the tell-the-future kind or the symbolic kind but the kind that won't go away. The kind that are filled with things you don't really remember, you're just remembering other dreams really. I dream of other things as well but she's always there, even when I don't remember.

Peg was not a first love. I don't even miss her in the traditional sense of missing someone. I was eleven years old and she was a small girl who was my friend.

Perhaps it's the act itself, a butcher's act. Or maybe it's her head in the back seat of a station wagon or a vinyl duffel bag or a wet towel or wherever they kept it for ten hours. Maybe it's the fact that it was found sitting in the dirt as if buried to the neck, precisely where her body was found ten hours before.

Whatever it is, it's the thing that won't let her rest and it's the thing that keeps me from sleeping.

I remember my mother leaving the room to answer a blaring phone. She said, "Dear God" and told my father to take the phone upstairs. He left the room. Family friends were over for coffee and they all went quiet. My father came back. Mother was standing by the dining room table, ceiling fan barely moving above, with her hands webbed at her mouth. I could see her make-up like I never had before. Her face was going from white to blue. Father and a fellow pastor, with arms on each other's shoulders, told the entire room including myself that young Peg Schroback was found dead. They had found her that night, raped and beheaded. I just kept staring.

I suppose it's not that odd for him to have told me in such a way. After all, even as a boy I knew of Jesus' murder, every detail. I knew of Cain and Abel, parents killing children, children killing parents. I knew the rape of Dinah. At eight I saw the head of John the Baptist displayed on a roasting tray in full color on the back page of a child's Bible storybook.

A vigil was kept at the Schroback home. Each night we surrounded the family in talk and forced laughter. Marla was a shaking mess offering cookies and pleading with Peg's sister to stay close. Ed was nowhere.

They said he drank. They said he was estranged from his daughters. They said he put his foot down. She blamed him one way or another. It provided a reason, a meaning, I think. They separated. I have no idea what happened next.

Some thirty years have gone by, thirty years of some fairly good sleep. I've lost both of my parents to age. I've gotten work. I've lost work. Sometimes there is no work. I've walked my life through joy and pain, electric then numb.

Maybe it was the gray hair I found in my beard. Maybe I was looking at the night sky for a moment longer than usual. Whatever it was, it caused a shift, a seismic disruption deep in the recesses of memory and I couldn't sleep. So I took the pills, closed my eyes, and waited. Then I passed into dream and there was Peg. That was a year ago.

That next morning I tore through drawers, rifled through closets and boxes filled with paper scraps and matchbooks until I found it. A wooden domino box. Inside was the blue ribbon I swore was worn in Peg's hair the day she died. At least I was convinced it was when I was twelve and walked across the rail yard, one year after she was killed, and saw a ribbon at my feet. Inside the box there were three quarters that fell from her pocket. A key ring, a pencil, and a torn leather watch band. All of which fell from her pockets, I was sure.

I remember returning to those tracks for weeks. It was twenty-three blocks from my home and across from a comic book shop. I walked back and forth across the tracks, kicking up dirt, and looking for pieces of Peg. I was a small boy and death had a reason. I was sure I could find it.

Four months ago I went back. Of course, it was after a dream. Garish colors on the inside jacket of a thick pamphlet. There were no angels or demons hovering. There were no trumpets. There were no clouds heavy with intent. It was just Peg rendered in perfect detail with no life in her eyes.

I put on a pot of coffee.

I sat at the computer and read what I had written the day before. It was an attempt, the naïve beginnings of a story. After three cups I began

Melanie Shatzky, *Trees,* C-print, 2002

to dress. Grabbed my keys and drove until I saw the tracks.

I walked for hours with an empty head hoping to fill it with whatever lived there, ghost or monster. No such thing happened. But I did bend my knees and take a pinch of loose dirt, enough to fill a spoon, and put it in my pocket. It made sense. I became very tired and drove home.

After three more visits the box was filled with Peg's dirt. I looked for symbolism and meaning. I went back to bury the ribbon.

For weeks I returned with handfuls that were soon collecting in coffee tins. One, then two. I began buying cans and emptying the contents into the trash so I could fill them in one trip. Stacked on tables and balanced on windowsills, the dirt was always there. Dry and littered with rocks and splinters beneath yellow plastic lids, neat and accessible.

Thirty miles away a hole, approximately three feet deep, was yawning beneath steel tracks crossed with age-eaten lumber.

Perhaps I wasn't looking deep enough.

I needed to become more abstract in my thinking. I had heard of those who craved dirt. The taste, the smell. It fulfilled something lacking in their diet. This would be my answer. I tasted it. Chalk and paper and wood and slate. I filled the coffee filter with rail yard grindings and ran hot water through them. This was it. I would drink it. Process it. Use it. And it would exit. Rid of me forever.

Two sips. I lasted two sips before laughing at my own pretension and thanking God no one had seen it.

So tonight I sit and type, occasionally staring at the cream swirls in a good cup of coffee. At my right are maybe twenty cans of it. And to my left, sitting heavy and black, are two fifty-gallon fish tanks filled beyond capacity with the dirt that once lay beneath poor Peg.

I think this time I'll pour it all out, tanks and cans, onto my living room floor and sit. I'll lie there on Peg's dirt beneath sagging bookshelves and wait, while seemingly endless pinwheels of cream, white then tan then brown, turn and turn and turn.

Double Diamonds
Richard Douek

50…48…46…44…Dale watched the small red numbers tick down the last 50 dollars he had to his name, two at a time. His hand rested on the smooth metallic edge of a Double Double Diamond Deluxe slot machine, his fingers poised an inch above the maximum bet button, dropping with mechanical precision every time the rollers clicked into place. Every few spins he would switch hands and hit the buttons on the other side of the machine, which was a bit more involved, as he would press the bet-one button twice, then the button that would spin the reels. He had a rhythm going, however, tapping the bet button with his middle finger quickly, then tapping the spin button with his thumb on the third tap. Sometimes, instead of hitting the spin button, he would pull the handle on the side of the machine, not releasing it until the first roller clicked into place.

It was hokey gambler superstition born out of sheer desperation after roll after roll of nothing. Nothing. Nothing. The idea was that maybe how you pressed the buttons would send some kind of signal to the machine that would make it hit a jackpot. The truth was, as every gambler who played the slots for any amount of time knew, was that it was just a little trick of the mind to break up the monotony of minutes and hours wasted pouring money into the machines. Whether the buttons you pressed had any effect no one could say, but if there was some magic combination or trick, Dale had never seen it.

He would watch the symbols line up. Bar. Double Bar. Cherry, Lucky 7. 3 Double Double Diamonds would show up in a row, but in the wrong position. An inch above or below the pay line. Whenever this happened, Dale would curse the machine under his breath, because three Double Double Diamonds meant 15,000 dollars, and he would have sold his eternal soul to whatever dark power happened to covet it at that moment to move those three little blue and white symbols just one god damned inch. Three Double Double Diamonds in the right spot meant rent, food, clothes, and maybe a new TV. In the right spot, they might mean that Lucy would have him back. Oh she swore up and down that she hated his gambling, blah blah, that blah blah, even if he won she still hated the gambling, but he knew—in his heart he knew if he showed up at her door with 15,000 dollars in his hands, her eyes would light up like double double diamonds, she would nearly faint, and he would catch her in his arms and draw her close and tell her, baby, everything's going to be ok from now on. No more gambling. We've got enough money now. We'll move to LA, where there aren't any casinos. Just you, me, and the smog. I'll be tending bar at the Whiskey-a-GoGo while you audition to your heart's content. Fifteen. Fifteen thousand. Three Double Double Diamonds. Right on the payline. But they weren't on the payline. They

Jacob Langvad, *Sunset at the North Shore of Oahu, Hawai'i*, Ilfochrome, 2002

were there, but where they were, they were worse than useless, one on the line, one above, one below. Dale's hand came down like a hammer to erase the mocking image as soon as possible.

36…34…32…36. A cherry hit on the payline. Four dollars. A cherry was like a free spin. You got your money back, plus enough for one more. Many a gambler has hit a cherry on the last couple of spins, and it has given him that one extra spin he needed to hit something. Usually, though, cherries mean nothing. They're little things. Like flowers. Or kisses. Little things. They kept Lucy happy. Maybe not happy. Happy enough. Dale was lucky like that—just as she was about to give up on him, he'd give her that little smile, or buy her a gift, just some small stupid trifle that was all she needed to keep going. And she kept going, giving him money, support, even love. But the money goes back into the machine and it never gives it back. Just gives you a free spin every now and again. In fact, all of the lower jackpots from cherry on up to triple bar meant nothing. They are designed to keep the player interested enough to keep putting money in.

All of the lower end payouts exist solely to gain more chances at the major jackpots. Jackpots are more elusive creatures than Bigfoot. The way the machines work, they give you a little bit here and there. A hundred here. Fifty there. Enough to keep you interested. Sooner or later, it stops dangling the carrot in front of you, but by that time you're so desperate for another hit, no matter how little, you give it all back.

This had happened to Dale many, many times. He had realized at some point that he wasn't really betting to win. He was betting that he could stay in the game long enough to hit a jackpot. She was playing for time too. Lucy was. She would ask him all the time—when he was in his more lucid moments—when were they going to get married, pack it all in, and get out of Vegas? After the big score, baby, after the big score. That was his line, and he'd tell her that and look into her eyes, blue eyes that shone like the burning neon that lined every inch of the strip. He'd look into her eyes and he knew he was bullshitting her. He knew, but when he looked at her, at the way she looked at him, he kind of believed it himself. But he also knew that the truth was that he was more committed to the slots than he would ever be to her. Lady Luck. His first and only love. Lucy was something else. But she would never understand. He told himself that it was only a matter of time, and his greatest asset was perseverance. Playing the slots was like going to war. It took a full commitment, and enough ammunition to back it up. Dale had all the determination he needed, but his money was slipping through his fingers.

20…19…18… It was starting to get desperate. He had switched to betting one dollar at a time to prolong his run. It meant a lower jackpot, but he could feel the jackpot coming. Like a long distance runner, he had to conserve his energy if he wanted to cross the finish line. He burned a hole into the machine's plexiglass window with his eyes, reaching out with his spirit, reaching down the line with every fiber of his being, as if he could grab the jackpot with his hands and pull it into reality through the force of his will alone. He wanted to shout, to speak in tongues, to howl voodoo curses in languages he had never learned. Anything for the Diamonds. The Double Double Diamonds. He could see his lady grinning, her teeth made of diamonds. She was laughing at him, but her face wasn't cruel. She was laughing at him and beckoning him, across a carpet of cherries, lemons, and oranges. And Diamonds.

Double Double Diamond Deluxe. It was one of hundreds of variations of slot machine, screaming out in bright colors and cheery beeps how it was the best machine to play. Gamblers had their favorite machines, usually because they had paid out at sometime in the distant past. But all machines paid out sooner or later. In truth, it is so impossible to tell which machine is ready to pay that you might as well do it blindfolded. Dale knew, all gamblers knew, so they played their hunches and didn't worry about it. The chance of being at the exact right machine at the exact right time was so infinitesimal that Dale would have sold his immortal soul to, well, whomever. He had considered at one point trying to learn how to hack computers, but soon gave it up after realizing that not only did he not own one, but Casino security was so good it would be like trying to hack into the Pentagon. It would be easier to just rob them, and that only ever happened in Hollywood.

10…9..8.. Dale wasn't even seeing the machine work now. He wasn't seeing the money, he wasn't paying attention to the symbols anymore.

All felt was the smooth plastic buttons, all he heard and saw were the wheels clicking into place. One, two, three clicks, spin again. One, two, three clicks, spin again. And so on. All around him the casino swirled like some huge infernal carnival. Cheery electronic beeps and flashing lights, cigar smoke, and stale beer. Clicks and whirrs. Shouts. And finally his finger came down and nothing happened. No beeps. No spin, nothing. Nothing on the payline. No 7s. No cherries. Not even one Double Double Diamond. He was now officially broke. He saw himself showing up at Lucy's door again, flat broke and stinking of whiskey and beer. He saw Lucy blinking back tears, going to shut the door, but finally, with one last long look, letting go of the door and helping him in. She'd cry later, when she thought he was asleep. Could he do it to her again? Again and again until finally, one day, she'd just let the door close, and tell him to fuck off. But he'd bang and holler until her or one of her neighbors called the cops, and they dropped him off in some North Vegas alley, after beating the shit out of him for kicks. He could see their evil dirty grins even now, and their teeth shined too, but not like diamonds. He blinked the image out of his eyes and swallowed hard. He took the last sip of his complimentary scotch and rose to his feet. If he drove fast enough he could get back home, get the TV over to the pawn shop, and be back here in twenty minutes.

As he left the area containing his coveted Double Double Diamond Deluxe machine, he heard the unmistakable blaring of synthesized slot machine beeps that meant someone had hit a jackpot. He froze in his tracks and closed his eyes, turning back to face the machine he had just left behind. If that was the machine that paid off, he thought to himself, if that was his goddamned machine with three goddamned Double Double Fucking Diamonds on the payline he was going to do two things. First, he was going to get thrown out of the casino for attacking the sweet little old lady that spent the last two dollars of her social security money just for the fun of it, and then he was going to drive out to Hoover Dam and jump off.

But it wasn't his machine. It couldn't be. That was his machine, his destiny. That was his rent, his food, his booze, his woman. That machine was his life, and while life was cruel, it couldn't be that cruel. Dale was Lady Luck's most faithful subject, and she would never do this to him. He laughed at himself for even thinking it. Eyes still closed, he turned back around and strode toward the exit, his face tightening into a grim mask of determination. His TV. The Pawn Shop. Twenty Minutes. Lucy and Dale, bound for LA, at last, riding off into the sunset in a cherry red Cadillac convertible, headlights shining like fucking diamonds. Double Double Double Double Diamonds. Deluxe.

Robert Palmer
Allison Landa

Celebrity grease
stains my life.
Today's singer
wiggled his way
through my teens
and I thought
of him
during my own
red-faced
explorations,
the kind
I thought
no one else
undertook;
today
he's eulogized
in print.
Still
as I eat
his burger,
I expect
he'll come
from the corner
and lick my fingers
clean of salt.

Jose Carmona, *Bar Swine*, pencil on paper, 2002

Hermits
Nanette Lerner

Big Daddy warned me this might happen.

They're jealous, he said. You'll see.

Big Daddy is a conspiracy theorist. Loves Oliver Stone movies, the whole thing. It can be tiresome. Normally, I ignore him when he talks this way. This usually causes him to retaliate. He's not a pincher though; that is beneath him. He will, however, crawl back in his shell and refuse to come out. Even when I put out Frosted Flakes, his favorite treat.

But today I see that Big Daddy is right. This should not surprise me, as he is the smartest crustacean I know. Actually, to call him a mere crustacean is to diminish his true genius. He is smarter than most people. That is why he lives at home with me in his own private 10-gallon aquarium instead of with the rest of the crabs at The Crab Shack, my kiosk at the mall. Not that I could sell him anyway. He simply wouldn't allow it. Big Daddy can get in your head that way.

So today I go in early. Not early for me but early compared to everyone else. I do this for two reasons: first because the type of person who buys hermit crabs tends to be an early riser. Don't ask me why but hermit crab people tend not to be the party type. And second, because it takes me a while to set up the kiosk, to take the crabs out of the crabitat they've been hanging out in all night and put them in their individual critter cases. And they're messy little guys, so it takes a while to make everything look good from the night before. No one can wreck a hotel room like a hermit crab.

I should have known better. All of the other kiosk owners have fancy gadgets to protect their worldly goods, locking everything away for the night with all kinds of gizmos and what-nots. Meanwhile, I have God's creatures in my care, yet only a padlock to keep away predators. A very large padlock, but still.

You only have yourself to blame, Big Daddy would say.

I know it as soon as I get there. The padlock is undone, looks like it has been sawed off. I quickly rip open the kiosk, scrambling to check on the crabitat. It's a disaster, the water dish overturned and the plastic palm trees scattered all over the place. No surprise there; the crabs do that without the help of an interloper.

What does surprise me: all of the hermit crabs are still in the crabitat. I pick up Bugger's shell. He doesn't come out. I let him rest on my hand for a while, hoping he is taking his time.

This is very un-Bugger-like behavior. I had originally brought him home as a companion for Big Daddy, only he couldn't stand him.

He gets into *everything*, he complained. A real busybody. If he tries to get into my shell again, I'm going to kill him. Don't say you haven't been warned.

I was left with no other choice but to bring him back to The Crab Shack. With Bugger's personality, I thought someone would buy him right away, but his penchant for pinching noses and other protruding body parts frightened away potential customers.

Bugger isn't budging.

Against my better judgment, I spray him with a mist of water. He is sure to come out fighting, claws up. I keep him on my palm, waiting for his wrath.

Nothing.

The mall is quiet. Even the mall walkers haven't started their morning shuffle. All the silence is making me nauseous. Or something is, anyway.

I stick my nose inside the crabitat. It smells like the ocean has died. I know what that means. One by one I take out the hermit crabs. One by one I mist them with water. And nothing happens. Which, in effect, means something has happened.

My crabs are dead. Every last one of them. This has never happened before. I check for mites—those sneaky crab killers—but there aren't any. No signs of a massive shell fight, either. Obviously, these deaths are not by natural causes. It's homicide, pure and simple.

Humans are an untrustworthy species, Big Daddy says.

I am glad that I am alone in the mall because a few tears slip out. Not many. And not for every crab, for I do not love them all equally. I can't. It isn't every crab that tickles my palm the way Princess does or finds its way underneath my shirt sleeve like Buddy. Honestly, I defy anyone not to fall in love with his favorite children.

I would make a lousy father.

I begin taking out the crabs, one by one, misting each of them with water just in case. Patiently. If you're going to be a crab owner, you've got to be patient. They do things on their own schedule. Unfortunately, each crab seems more dead than the last. Still, I continue the ritual, placing each hermit shell carefully into a bag. I can bring them home tonight and clean out the shells though it will take a while and the dead animals will continue to stink as the day goes on. But I feel it is the least I could do. In a roundabout way, I am responsible for their deaths.

Maybe, Big Daddy hints. Maybe not.

On a hunch, I check out the temperature of the crabitat. A balmy 85 degrees. Warm enough to kill the heartiest of hermits. I put my hand by the heater and it's running full blast.

Dipshit, Big Daddy says. How long was it going to take you to check that out?

That's the thing about Big Daddy. He can communicate even if he's not with me. Only started about a year and a half ago. And he's nothing if not consistent. He sees things about five steps ahead of me.

"Motherfucker," I mumble.

I know you're not talking to me, Big Daddy says.

"No," I say. "It's my own goddamn fault, not yours."

Well, Big Daddy pauses. It's not *completely* your fault. I mean, you're not the one who jacked up the heater.

"No," I say. "I'm not."

You did nothing but care for them, Big Daddy continues. You have nothing to feel guilty about.

"I do," I say. "They were defenseless. They were in my care."

Yes. But you didn't do it.

"Still. I feel terrible."

Avenge them, Big Daddy says.

"How? I don't even know who did it."

Big Daddy laughs. Squeaks really, but if you listen closely it's a laugh. He doesn't share his cage with anyone else so when he squeaks, he's not trying to communicate with his brethren. He's doing it just for me.

"How do I avenge the crabs if I don't know who killed them?"

Silly, Big Daddy says. Just avenge them all.

When a hermit crab doesn't like someone, it doesn't fuck around. It has a large front claw that can be used as a weapon, particularly against humans. If another hermit crab is being a pain in the ass, then there is a shell fight. One crab grabs the other and starts pushing it back and forth, literally shaking it out of its shell. Then it crawls into the losing crab's shell, victorious. Other times, the offending crab will be dug up when it's molting—which is when it's most vulnerable—and eaten alive. The hermit crab has no qualms about eating one of its own.

It's nothing personal, Big Daddy tried to explain once. Haven't you ever heard of survival of the fittest?

In my life as a human, things are not usually that cut and dry. You cannot kill and eat who you don't like or even kick them out of their house and move into it. Unfortunately. And you don't always know when people are at their most vulnerable since they do not molt.

No, Big Daddy says. But they're still vulnerable. Come on, *Daryl.* Think. The answer is right in front of your face.

I place the last of my dead hermit crabs in a plastic baggie and seal it. They are freezer bags, designed for approximately a pound of meat. Instead, they serve as a cheap coffin for my friends.

Quit sniveling, Big Daddy says. God. You're pathetic. Your whole kind is pathetic.

"What would you like me to do?" Already I am dreading going back home, dreading the disdainful looks from Big Daddy, dreading the phone call to Al, my supplier in Key West. *How many hermits did you say you needed? Jesus, Daryl how'd you manage to kill that many at one time? It's a fucking crab holocaust.*

Get the people when they're molting, Big Daddy says.

"We don't molt."

No shit, Big Daddy says. Don't you know anything about *symbolism*?

I explained the concept of symbolism to Big Daddy once when we were watching a movie. Unfortunately, he often pulls it out and attempts to use it himself, usually badly.

What I'm saying is, when are people most vulnerable?

"Uh. When they're sleeping?"

No. Come on. That's too easy.

"When they're sick?"

You're not good at this symbolism stuff, are you, Daryl?

"Um. Help me out here."

When they least expect it, Big Daddy says. That's when people are at their most vulnerable. That's when *everybody's* at their most vulnerable. Jesus. Are you sure your brain is bigger than mine?

Here is a short list of who could have sabotaged me, in no particular order:

The creepy old lady with the gray hair that flies behind her like a witch. She hangs around the mall all day and has on more than one occasion called my crabs "a health hazard." She claims they cause salmonella; won't say how.

The ladies who work at the lingerie store, one in particular who caught me staring at some thong underwear in the window and now gives me dirty looks.

The guys from Pizza Maniac who regularly threaten to steal some of my guys and make crab fra diavolo.

One particularly annoying group of teenagers who get a kick out of asking if I have crabs.

The chubby girl from the honey-baked ham store who hates me for no apparent reason.

These are all likely suspects but I have no way of knowing for sure. Humans are not as obvious in their intentions as animals. They don't come straight out and shake you out of your shell. They are more calculating in their vengeance.

Luckily, I can be too.

Go for it, Big Daddy says. What do you have to lose?

Indeed. Very little.

The mall opens at ten. By nine-thirty, I have scraped my little friends into a bag, all of them, one on top of another. I do not worry about overcrowding. In death—as in life—I'm sure they'd rather be together than apart.

That's the big misconception about hermit crabs. The hermit part. Because of their name, everyone assumes this means they prefer to live alone. Quite the opposite; in the wild, they live together by the hundreds, pack animals who come out at the same exact time every night. Entire hermit crab cities springing to life at once.

Sort of like the people who come to the mall. Sure, some of them are there because they have to actually *buy* things. But a lot are there just to be in the company of others; to sit by the fountain, inspect the store windows, smile at a baby passing by in a stroller.

Weaklings, Big Daddy says. The truly strong exist alone. They rely on no one.

He considers himself to fall in this category and I do not argue, despite the fact that he obviously relies on me for food, heat, water, companionship. So you see. Even the biggest hermit really isn't one.

The first person I see this morning is the mall cop. He nods his head at me curtly, all business as usual. I want to tell him that he needn't bother, that everyone knows he doesn't carry a gun and therefore his authority only goes so far. Nor is he in any physical condition to give a criminal a run for his money. Besides, considering my present situation, he obviously isn't doing such a bang-up job of fighting crime.

The mall walkers appear next, the collective whoosh of their track suits rubbing together like a helicopter getting ready for take-off. Technically, they could be considered potential suspects, since they're always in the mall at odd hours and The Mall Walker's Club gets an official set of keys to the main entrance. But I don't think it's them. I just don't believe that old people want to kill my crabs. When you're as close to death as they are, I'm pretty sure you think twice about killing things, since you're probably going to meet your maker soon. Don't want any extra sins on your record.

I sit on my stool, watching the walkers pass, biting the insides of my mouth. This will create welts, possibly bloody ones, making it impossible to eat spicy foods for a week. But I do not care. Right now, it's about keeping it together and chewing on my mouth helps.

Don't be a pussy, Big Daddy says. It's bad enough you're a fat fuck. Don't be a weeping fat fuck.

"Shut up," I mutter.

Suit yourself, Big Daddy says. You don't think you can pull this off without me, do you?

I know I can't and Big Daddy knows it, too. I shut my mouth until the last of the walkers pass. As they pass, I smell sweat and mothballs.

"Well?" I say. "What now?"

Patience, Big Daddy says. Besides, what else have you got to do?

I have plenty to do. I have to call Al and order more crabs; concoct some story about how they all died. For some reason, I know this sort of thing would never happen to Al. Some people go through life never getting mugged; others could get their wallets stolen in a nursing home. I curse myself again for my lackadaisical kiosk security.

It's done, Big Daddy says. Get over it. Besides, it was meant to be.

"Meant to be?"

It's all part of the plan, Big Daddy says. The order of things.

"The order of…"

Don't worry about it, Big Daddy says. Too much to get into now.

I think about Big Daddy and how I am going to bring him back some dried fruit to show my appreciation. Maybe mango or pineapple.

Make it papaya, Big Daddy says. I can't do pineapple. Too acidic.

He's amazing that way. I'm not sure when he learned do this mind-reading thing but it is extremely useful. Especially since when I speak aloud to him, it sometimes appears as though I'm talking to myself.

So? Big Daddy says. Who cares if you're talking to yourself? Like you have a busy social life? You think your fans are going to give a shit? You can't even survive in a goddamn shopping mall. You're nothing but prey.

I'm not.

You are. Your own kind feeds on you. If you were a crab, you would have been torn from your shell and swallowed whole a long time ago.

"Stop!" I say. A bit too loud. My voice bounces around the empty mall.

Dude, Big Daddy says. You don't have to shout.

The chubby girl who works at the ham store walks by. She has a very large face but it isn't her face I'm interested in. I watch her ass move from side to side as she moves, as if each cheek thinks independently of the other. That's the one good thing about being practically invisible; you can get away with a hell of a lot more.

Focus, Big Daddy says. Come on now.

Sorry.

You're going to have to make your move soon. While the mall cop is doing his rounds on the other side of the mall.

How am I supposed to know when that is?

Work with me here, Big Daddy says. I know he is rolling his eyes at me. They do have eyes, hermit crabs, though they can't really roll them. Big Daddy can, though.

Well, it's not like I can communicate telepathically with everyone.

Jesus. Use your brain. You just saw the mall cop what, 10 minutes ago? He's probably mid-mall by now. You're going to have to wait another 15 minutes before he's all the way on the other side of the mall. Besides, you want to wait until the customers get here, don't you?

I don't want to punish them. They're not the ones who raided my crab kiosk.

You don't know that, Big Daddy sneers. It could have been anybody. Besides, after everything the human race's done, they could stand a little suffering of their own. Do you know they boil lobsters alive?

I have heard that, yes.

They're butchers. Don't feel pity.

"Right," I say aloud. "No pity."

Just wait, Big Daddy says. Kick your feet up and wait.

I do. Leaned so far back, I almost slid off my stool.

Same way people have faith in God or Allah or Jesus. I have faith in

Jose Carmona, *Glowworm,* digital C-print, 2003

Big Daddy.   Not that I pray to him or anything crazy like that. He's more of a spiritual guide.

He called out to me that day in the pet store. That's the only way I can explain it. I wasn't supposed to be in there; I was running an errand, I was late. I was living in my parents' house at the time and they wouldn't be happy with me bringing home a pet; particularly one that made most of its noise at night. But there he was. The size of a golfball and angry as all get-out.

He was in a bad state, Big Daddy was. Couldn't really blame him, seeing as how he was stuck in an aquarium so jammed with hermits, they were all crawling on top of each other. And not in a sexy way, since hermits don't breed in captivity. That's why you need to have a supplier when you run out of them.

Anyway, he was calling out to me. Squeaking. Hermit crabs will do that, particularly when they're in distress. Only his squeaks sounded like, hey. Buddy. What the fuck, you're just going to leave me in here?

Five minutes later, I bought him, an aquarium, gravel, the whole shebang. Dropped 50 bucks I didn't have.

It's okay, Big Daddy likes to say. Look at how I've paid you back.

I didn't plan on making crabs my vocation. Truthfully, I didn't plan, period. At a certain point, I got sick of studying. But I wasn't sick of crabs. They're peaceful. Especially compared to pretty much everything else.

Oh yeah? Big Daddy would say. You've never seen a down-and-dirty shell fight. It gets ugly.

Still not as ugly as what goes on outside the aquarium in the big world. I only wish they made a shell big enough for humans.

They can't, Big Daddy says. Or you humans would never come out of it.

Fifteen minutes pass. I peel myself off my wooden stool, ready for action.

The mall cop's all the way down by the Food Court by now, Big Daddy says. What the hell are you waiting for? It's make or break time.

I'm starting to regret letting him watch all those cop shows. He absorbs everything, then uses it later. If he was a cop, he'd be the bad one.

The first customers of the day have started entering the mall, scattering like rats. I walk away from my kiosk, leaving it open yet unattended. I figure it's fine since I haven't opened the cash register yet and let's face it, there's nothing else left to steal.

To the left, Big Daddy says. Go left.

"I *know*," I say between my teeth. "You think I'm an idiot? I've been working here ten years." I pass the old lady who thinks my crabs are a health hazard, heading towards her usual post in front of the fountain.

The climate control box is right by the bathrooms. There is a reason I know this; one time, I stayed late in the mall and followed the custodian around. I only did it to see if I could without getting caught. Truth is, Big Daddy dared me and I didn't have anything else better to do.

You'd think that only the custodian has a key to the air conditioner/heater. Not true. There isn't a key to it at all, only a gray metal box to protect it from meddling hands. You only needed to lift it up to get to the controls.

This is exactly what I do, turning the air conditioner off and the heat up, way up, as high as it will go. Will it really go up to 95 like the digital read-out claims? We shall see. We shall see how people feel about being cooked like clams, especially those idiots from the Food Court. Particularly on a day as naturally steamy as this one.

Good work, Big Daddy says. I'd shake your hand, if I had one.

I ignore him and head back into the main mall area. As I do, I take off my windbreaker. I won't be needing it.

The effects aren't instantaneous. Unfortunately.

No patience, Big Daddy says. That's your problem.

I wander through the mall, studying people. One large pink man seems to be sweating—not profusely but there are beads of sweat forming around his temples. Is it my doing? One can only hope.

I head towards the Food Court. The guys at the pizzeria are sweaty as usual but this is no surprise, as they work in front of a hot oven. I wish them more heat, silently blowing some their way. A woman wearing pink starts to fan herself, perhaps accidentally receiving my warmth.

Idiot, Big Daddy says. It takes time.

I pass the spy store. As usual, I feel as though I am being watched. The fat man who works there is leaned over the counter, studying something intently. I pass the department store. The perfume girls seem bored, listless. "Damn," one of them says to the other. "It must be, like, a gazillion degrees in here." The blonde one nods in agreement, lifting her hair off the back of her neck. I can see a slight bit of moisture beneath her underarms as she does, something that would no doubt mortify her and her perfect little world.

I pick up speed now. The honey-baked ham girl is standing outside the store, holding her silver tray of offerings. When she sees me, she does not offer me any ham samples; she never does. I descend on the plate, helping myself to a piece. It has been speared with a fancy toothpick laced in purple cellophane.

"Thank you," I say with my mouth full.

She glares, despising me.

Good one, Daryl, Big Daddy says. Way to endear yourself to the ladies.

"Is it me," I say, "or is it kind of hot in here today?"

She narrows her eyes, unsure if this is a pick-up line or not. "Maybe."

"You think the air-conditioning's broken?"

She shrugs, no doubt the same one she gives math teachers and prying mothers. "Not my job."

Dude, Big Daddy says. Keep on walking.

I don't. "You look like you have some moisture over your lip."

She wipes her upper lip with the back of her hand. Turning purple as she does.

"It's no big deal. It's just sweat." I smile at her.

What did I tell you about focusing? Big Daddy sighs.

I ignore him. There will be repercussions later, but I do it anyway. I lunge towards her plate of samples and shove three pieces in my mouth at once.

"Freak," the girl says under her breath but not really.

"Good ham," I say. "Mmmm." I shove more into my mouth at the same time, opening my mouth so she can see the contents inside. "Delicious."

"Pig," she mutters.

"Exactly." I don't know what's gotten into me. I feel downright lightheaded.

Maybe it's the heat, Big Daddy says. Come on. Move it along. You're going to raise suspicions.

"I am not. Nobody knows anything."

The girl stares at me, eyes getting wider in her round little face. I should have communicated with Big Daddy telepathically but now it's too late.

Exit, stage left, Big Daddy says.

I grab a fistful of ham. "For the road," I say and walk away. Saunter, really. I feel like a cowboy. I am a road warrior. I am a yet-to-be-named role that will be played by Mel Gibson.

Whatever, Big Daddy says. Now get back to your post.

I do. While I'm at it, I put all of the ham in my mouth at once, poking the inside of my cheeks with cellophane toothpicks in the process. When I bite down, the metallic taste of blood mixes with the ham. It's not half bad.

When I get back to my kiosk, nothing has changed.

What did you expect? Big Daddy says.

He really is talking to me a lot now. Too much, really. Nearly every other sentence is his.

Not true, Big Daddy says. See? I let you get in two, three of your own there.

Barely.

Is it my fault if my thoughts are better than yours?

That's your opinion.

They are. Just because I'm a crustacean doesn't mean I don't have higher level thinking.

Did I *say* that?

You were thinking it.

I wish you couldn't read my mind.

Yeah, well, I wish you would come home and bring me some of that dried papaya. We can't always get what we want.

Suddenly, I feel a wave of heat. Holy shit, it's hot. The roasting has begun. For real.

Well, *duh,* Big Daddy says. Wait until people start passing out.

Almost on cue, the old lady by the fountain begins to look limp. Her head falls to the side, drifting towards her shoulder.

Excellent, Big Daddy says. First victim.

I watch the old lady. Trying to see if she is breathing, moving.

Oh come on. She was dreadful.

I'm not trying to kill people here.

Oh no? Big Daddy says. Then just exactly what are we doing?

It's happening now. People are moving towards the old lady. I am secretly happy they notice her, wondering if anyone knows CPR. But then I see the people haven't noticed the old woman at all. In reality, they're all just heading towards the fountain because there's a bench nearby to sit down. They're tired from the heat.

The old lady looks like she's sleeping. I get off my stool, trying to see if her chest is moving up and down.

Pervert, Big Daddy says.

"Shut up," I think but I say it out loud. "Shut up shut up shut up."

The mall walkers pass by, their brisk walking down to a slow shuffle. A drop of sweat finds its way down my forehead, past my face into a collecting pool below my neck.

Humans smell so lovely when they're cooking, Big Daddy sighs.

The old lady has leaned so far over, she is pressing against a teenage boy. He seems irritated by her contact, uses his shoulder to remove her from him. She falls all the way over, landing on the bench with a hard thud.

You are a cruel species, Big Daddy says.

Hey. This was your idea.

Don't blame me. I didn't execute it.

You would if you could.

Daryl, Big Daddy says. I don't think of anything that you're not already thinking.

A couple of store owners are closing up shop, pulling down their metal gates. The man from the spy store has soaked through his shirt. His stomach has wet marks all over it like he's been hit by sprinklers. The honey-baked ham girl is gone. The inside of her store is dark, the gate coming down slowly.

Hey, Big Daddy says. Where is everyone going?

They're leaving.

What?

A group of teenagers in baggy jeans run by. They smell like a locker room.

You're surprised? People aren't going to stay in a sweltering hot place if they don't have to.

Didn't you seal them in?

Seal them in?

So they couldn't escape. Come on, Daryl, surely you thought of that.

You can't do that.

What?

You can't do that.

Why not?

Because. People can leave whenever they want. It's a mall. You can't force them to stay.

Why?

Free will.

Crabs don't have free will.

But people do.

Fuck, Big Daddy says. Why do you people always have more than crabs?

Sorry. Way of the world.

I don't accept that.

It isn't up to you.

Those crabs didn't have free will when someone turned the climate up on them. They were stuck in that crabitat.

I know.

It isn't fair.

You're right.

I think I want to go to the ocean, Big Daddy says. I don't think I want to live with you anymore. I don't want to live in your head.

The mall is nearly empty now. Someone has even dimmed the lights. The only one I can see is the old lady by the fountain. I grab my plastic bag full of crab corpses. The smell is overwhelming, a putrid reek that gets into your clothes and hair. I hear footsteps.

"Hey." It is the mall cop. His uniform is dark blue but I can see that he is drenched with sweat. "We're closing up early today. Something wrong with the air-conditioning unit. Looks like someone broke into that, can you believe it? Gotta get a technician in here."

"I think there's someone still over there by the fountain."

The cop cranes his neck. "Yeah?" He claps his hands. "Hey. Lady. Wake up."

The lady doesn't move.

"Jesus," the mall cop shakes his head. "I'll let her sleep a little more."

I nod. He is not the law, not the real one. But he is the closest thing to it here. I put my plastic bag of corpses under my arm, preparing to leave.

"Taking your work home with you?" He smirks. "I never did much care for crabs. Unless they're fried." He chuckles.

Asshole, Big Daddy sneers.

The mall cop is pleased with himself. He is not a jokester but this tickles him. He walks away, whistling.

I'm not living inside your head anymore, Daryl. Do you hear me? No more.

We'll see.

I want to go to the ocean.

I close down the kiosk, gathering up my shells. Thinking about where to stop on the way home for dried mango. Wishing somewhere there was a shell big enough for me.

The Lake Project
David Maisel

9798-3, C-print, 2002
9277-1, C-print, 2001

9810-11, C-print, 2002

9828-12, C-print, 2002
9283-6, C-print, 2001

9802-9, C-print, 2002

Alphabet Soup
Kirsten Matthew

"I think Dad's had a stroke," Sue's mother says quietly, almost nonchalantly. As if she thinks it might dilute the effect. As if the words won't mean what they mean if she delivers them gently enough. She's wrong—the words whoosh down the phone and spill onto the kitchen table, slapping in front of Sue like a fish fresh off the hook.

"Why didn't you say something sooner?" Sue asks. They've been talking about nothing for 20 minutes. It's a daily ritual, the mother and daughter chat. A way to make up for the physical space between them. Always after dinner and usually Mum makes the call. "Hi, it's Mum," she says, when Sue answers, as if Sue may not recognize her voice. The phone bills drive Sue's Dad mad.

"I don't know. I was waiting for the right moment I guess."

"Shit. Mum, is he O.K.? What happened?"

"He's fine. Don't get upset. The doctor said it looks like a mild one. They'll know more in a couple of days." Sue lights a cigarette. They're partners in crime, the phone and the fags, can't do anything without each other.

At the other end of the house John and the cat are watching some show where a couple redecorates their neighbors' bedroom. Sue can't stand that rubbish, so she's been reading in the kitchen, on the lumpy window seat, her back against the wall, legs bent up towards her chest, a cup of tea steaming on the worn and round and chipped table. She's put the room to sleep already: the floral blinds have been lowered like eyelids, the table wiped clean, the leftovers packed and put away in the fridge. The dishes are dripping dry on the rack. Just one blonde light on above her seat. The back door with its peeling paint and mismatched panes of glass is ajar.

Sue can feel the dark, humid air infiltrate the room, can smell the jasmine that creeps around the porch, hear the low drone of next door's TV. "Where is he?" she asks.

"Upstairs, asleep," Sue's mother says. "I'm taking him back to the hospital tomorrow, for more tests."

Mum tells Sue that Dad woke on the Saturday morning and eased himself into the day slowly as usual. Sue could imagine him coming downstairs in his pajamas for that first, much-relished cigarette of the day. Making the coffee (milk, no sugar), spending an hour or two with the paper. It drove Sue's mother crazy that it took him so long to get going and now he was retired he worked at snail's pace—it could be noon before he got near the shower. That day he was even slower. Very quiet. Maybe a little disoriented. Bewildered? In the afternoon, Mum said, she noticed he was holding his right arm, wandering around the house with it up across his middle, as if in an invisible sling.

"Is there something wrong with you?" she asked him crankily.

"No," he said and went into the other room.

Much later Dad will tell Sue that he knew all along that something had happened. That when he awoke that day his head was filled with cotton wool and his arm had fallen asleep for good. Later in the day, when friends dropped by for a drink, he couldn't keep track of the conversation. He knew their faces, who they were to him, but he couldn't remember their names. They sat in the living room, on the lemon couches, facing each other, with cheese and crackers laid out on the table between them. What the hell are they all taking about, he wondered. Mum tells Sue the next day he stayed in bed, lying on his left side, eyes open, staring at the wall. Mum didn't know what to do. A queasy feeling had settled in her stomach overnight. She could see there was something wrong with him, but she didn't want to bother Sue or her sister. Didn't want to involve their friends—he'd be horrified if she did that. She wanted him to bounce out of bed and allay her fears.

"Is there something wrong with you?" Mum asked again.

"No," he'd replied.

When she hangs up the phone Sue sees three short butts in the clear glass ashtray. Funny, she thinks, I don't remember smoking those. She notices her heart is beating very fast—she can see her pink t-shirt quivering above her breast. She gets up. Shuts and locks the back door. Spies her book, sitting marooned, spine up, amongst the smoky blue cushions on the window seat. Her mug, now empty and dangling in her right hand, has left a ring on the table. She moves slowly down the hall. Sticks her head into the dark living room where John is stretched out on his back, hands behind his head. He turns his face from the television to her.

"Dad's sick," she hears herself say. "I'll go home tomorrow." She turns and walks into the bedroom.

When Sue and Caroline were kids Dad was always at work, and that, as their mother would say, was that: they never expected him to be home to eat dinner with them, to ask them over the lamb chops how their day went, or to tuck them in. They were forbidden to call him at the office, except in a "genuine emergency."

If they were lucky they would see him in the morning, dressed like the guest of honor in his dark suit, white shirt stretching over the slight paunch and bisected by a natty tie. (Sometimes he'd let them pick the tie for him from the rack on the inside of the wardrobe door. Only sometimes.) Always looking sharp. Always smelling of Rothmans cigarettes and the Old Spice aftershave they bought for him each Father's Day from the chemist up the road. They'd sit in a row at the breakfast bar, Mum on the other side filling orders like a short order cook as she packed their lunches. Dad trying to digest current events as they bombarded him with questions and stories with no endings about their friends and school and the dog.

"See you in the soup," he'd mumble through the newspaper as they raced out the door to school.

"See you in the soup," they'd yell back like maniacs. Sue would imagine the two of them, Dad and Sue, swimming in a big bowl of alphabet soup. Him in his suit, her in her jeans with the red apple patch Mum had sewn on the pocket. Her long, straight hair floating out around her skinny shoulders in the broth, Dad bobbing past like an A or an F. Both of them smiling. Sometimes Mum made Dad take Sue and Caroline to work with him on the weekend, just so they spent time with him, just so they remembered who he was. He'd disappear into his office and in the room next door they'd take turns spinning in his secretary's chair.

They'd play on the typewriter, composing letters for Dad that they'd then fold and slide under his office door, squealing with delight when he'd slip back a reply. When he'd had enough of that they'd go through the secretary's drawers, stealing paper clips and pencils. They'd roam the wood-paneled halls. Stare out the big windows, down on the city eleven floors below. When they'd start to complain, Dad would feed them like parking meters with coins for the Coke machines by the elevator.

"Another few minutes," he'd boom in that deep, deep voice when they whined.

"They're so noisy," he'd say to Mum later, when they were back home. "Yeah," she'd reply, smiling. "They're kids." Sometimes Caroline wouldn't want to leave Mum for the day, so Sue would go with Dad alone and do her best to behave. Other times she'd go with Dad to the car wash and help him soap the wheels of his car. Or to the rubbish dump, where the screaming grey gulls and the fetid smell would keep her inside, windows up, doors locked, plump thumb and forefinger pinching her nose, as Dad dragged brown paper bags from the back of the car. On the way home they'd stop for a drink—a beer for Dad, raspberry lemonade for Sue, and a bag of chicken chips between them. Happy as Larry, as her mother would say.

In the early hours of the next morning, Sue turns to the facts. The facts are the facts, immovable and true. Absolute. Absolutes make people like Sue more comfortable.

She drags her hardback dictionary from the bottom shelf of the bookcase in the spare room. Sits down at the kitchen table in her lavender robe and runs her worried finger down the side of the book, over the gold-lettered indents, stopping at 'S.' "Stroke. n," she reads. "A sudden loss of brain function caused by a blockage or rupture of a blood vessel to the brain, characterized by loss of muscular control, diminution

Matthew / Mejia

Issue 1.4

205

Mat Mejia, *Vondel Park*, digital C-print, 2003

or loss of sensation or consciousness, dizziness, slurred speech, or other symptoms that vary with the extent and severity of the damage to the brain." The definition polkas on the tissue-thin page. At nine o'clock she calls her doctor, then checks the websites he recommends. She'll buy the book he told her about at the airport bookstore.

She calls her friend Mary, a nurse at a teaching hospital. Mary gives her a litany of facts: paralysis, speech loss, confusion, physical therapy, medication. Worst possible scenario: permanent damage, life in a nursing home. "How are you doing?" Mary asks once the particulars are out of the way. "I have to go or I'll miss my flight home," Sue replies. How silly, she thinks after she hangs up. I'm a 36-year-old woman, with a mortgage and a marriage of my own, and I still call Mum and Dad home.

Mum collects her from the airport. By the third day, she tells Sue once they get out of the terminal, Dad was still lolling around, slurring like a drunk, shrinking by the hour, and insisting nothing was wrong. She couldn't stand it any more so she hijacked him. Put him in the car and drove 50 minutes to the doctor. "What are we doing here?" he asked her as she parked. "I need to see a doctor," she told the lady at the front desk, her voice high and thin. "There's something wrong with my husband." "There's something wrong with my husband," she said again when the old, wrinkled doctor led them into his room.

The tests confirmed a stroke: The activity in Dad's brain showed that almost sixty years of living dangerously—the booze, the late nights, the stress and the smokes, not to mention 10 years without a checkup—had finally paid off.

An hour later Sue is sitting in her mother's kitchen, where it's dark and cool compared to the rest of the house. From her high stool at the breakfast bar she can see out the window into the garden where the dog is snoozing under a tree. Dad's upstairs. He's sleeping too. Mum's making a special family dinner and trying to be cheerful. Caroline will be there by six. "He looks so different," Sue says out loud, but to herself. When she arrived at the house, Dad was sitting on the couch waiting for her.

Quiet. Old. Embarrassed. Half the size he was the last time she saw him, only a month or so ago. Flat, slate grey skin. Thinning hair shocked snow white. "Oh, Dad," she said when he rose to hug her.

How can someone disappear overnight? Sue wonders. Where did he go?

Later, at the dinner table (Mum's famous roast pork, crispy potatoes, peas and beans) he rallies, regains some composure. The doctor said this would happen. That until things settle down his mood will ebb and flow.

"I don't know what that doctor's talking about," he says. "Bloody quack. I haven't had a stroke." His three girls laugh.

In her teenage years, when she was angry at everyone, Sue hated Dad. Or rather, the space that he left when at work. Why didn't he need them? Need to see them, be with them? Silent, empty threats would march across her mind in formation. He'll need me one day and I'll be too busy with my career, my family, my friends. It'll be too late. When she told Caroline that they were deprived, scarred by Dad's absence, her sister looked at her blankly and meant it when she asked, "What are you talking about?" Caroline was lucky that way. She was good grace wrapped up in a thick skin.

Hours later, long after dinner, Sue still lies awake in the dark, in the double bed her parents bought her when she was 16. Every time she closes her eyes she sees the clot that's lodged in her father's brain—a small, furry, black monster with a voracious grin, moving through Dad's veins, finally stopping to block the flow of blood. Laughing like a madman as Dad's brain turns black.

Around four she gives in and gets up. Pads downstairs, pours herself some juice and grabs the pack of cigarettes sitting waiting for her on the counter. When she goes into the living room, Dad's already there. The lights are off, but the curtains are open and in the half-light Sue can see the wisps of smoke swirling around him in his brown pajamas. At the other end of the couch, the dog is fast asleep. "Do you think you should be smoking Dad?" He ignores the question.

"I need to talk to you." He speaks slowly, like a record player set at the wrong speed. "I think there's something wrong with me. I don't feel very well."

"I know Dad. I think you've had a stroke. A mild one. At least that's what the doctor says."

"Oh," he says. He looks up at her, confused. Moves his trembling hand towards the ashtray and stubs out the cigarette. "For Christ's sake, don't tell your mother."

When Sue flies back to John she's met by a bank of telephone messages and a messy house. Newspapers are mounting in the living room, competing with dirty plates and empty coffee cups for attention. The bed is not made. The laundry basket is surrounded by the t-shirts and pants that missed their mark. Judging by the phone messages, word has got around that Dad is unwell.

Five messages, all variations on the same theme. "Hi, just me. I talked to Mary. Why didn't you call me?" Concern with an underlying tone of irritation. As if they're all affronted. As if she should have thought of how her girlfriends would feel when they heard the news from someone else and realized they weren't the first to know. For fuck's sake, Sue thinks. Her jaw tightens with anger. Saliva pools in her mouth, threatening to submerge her tongue. "How is he? How are you? I wish you'd let me go with you," John says as he comes through the door soon after. He gives her a hug and a kiss, but his kindness is too much, so she screams at him about the mess. Out. Of. Control. All over the place like a madwoman's knitting, as her mother would say.

John stops her right there in the hallway. Puts his arms around her so she can't move, so her hands are trapped at her sides and her face is mashed into his chest. She cries.

Within a few weeks things have settled down. Sue's mother is getting used to her new responsibilities: driving Dad around; reminding him of his physical therapy appointments; cutting up his meat at the dinner table; and holding her tongue when he tells her the doctor's got it all wrong.

Caroline pops in nightly on her way home from work. Sue will have to fly home more often. Dad now calls Sue at home, at the office, on her cell phone if he can't find her anywhere else. Sometimes he's at the other end of the phone seven or eight times a day. Always when her mother's out of the room—upstairs, at the supermarket, at tennis, asleep. "It's Dad," he'll whisper in that conspiratorial way, as if he's working for the CIA.

"I know," Sue always whispers back.

When he calls at the office, she's aware the people surrounding her cubicle can hear her end of the conversation and she feels angry and ashamed. She doesn't want them, those well-meaning co-workers who bestowed sympathetic smiles and friendly pats when she first returned to work, knowing her new reality. She doesn't want them to know Dad isn't the man he was. Sometimes she's too busy or stressed to take the call, but she does it anyway. He's lost his authority, his agility, his independence, his wit. He needs her.

Often he phones her at two or three or four o'clock in the morning, while he's downstairs sneaking a smoke from the pack Sue left him. (Mum confiscated his, throwing them away with relish.) John complains that the phone wakes him, so Sue sleeps with it stuffed under her pillow. She answers on the first ring, before she's even awake. Moves gingerly to the edge of the bed, inches out, and sneaks down the hall to the kitchen.

"There's something wrong with me," is his constant refrain. "I don't feel well. You're the only one I can talk to. Don't tell your mother."

Byron Barrett, *Blue House*, Ilfochrome, 2002

those bastard killers
Jon McMillan

When I was twelve, those bastard raccoons dug up my dead guinea pig and left his half-gnawed body in the backyard. I was sitting in the second-floor bathroom having a crap when I first noticed the paper down on the frozen grass. It was baby-blue like a hospital Johnny, about the size of a large dishtowel. It looked sort of familiar. In fact, it looked exactly like the cloth the vet had wrapped around my beloved pet after administering a small dose of pentobarbital and saying cheerfully "you can take him home or leave him here, whichever you like."

Streaks was his name. He was a tiny, caramel-colored thing. He was frozen stiff and flattened out like a hairy, clawed steak. I didn't want to touch him with my hands, so I got a shovel from the garage, but I didn't want him to touch the shovel, either, so I grabbed a few sticks from the woodpile. I tried to re-wrap him in his blue shroud, but he was heavy and the sticks were long and awkward and dug up bits of his fur. I could see my mother watching from the kitchen window. I had told her I wanted to take care of Streaks myself. She looked worried. She looked like she was hoping my Dad would come home at any minute.

I used the shovel to widen the grave and rolled Streaks inside. His eyes were scratched and there was a chunk missing from his side. I filled the hole with dirt, and this time I put a rock on top, so those bastard raccoons couldn't get to him. I threw the sticks over the fence into the neighbor's yard.

The next day I called my friend Eli, who lived in the house behind ours. Eli had spent the summer up in Maine at a camp named after a Jewish Indian, and knew all about things like sailing and gimp and kneeboarding. He claimed he could do the butterfly. He had beady little eyes, and was always scratching his head.

"Eli," I said, "It's Eddie."

"Hey Eddie," Eli said.

"Eli," I said, "I need to borrow your bow and some arrows."

Eli was really into archery. He had won some contest up at camp, and was always talking about it. Sixty feet, he said, advanced yeoman. It was the highest level in the twelve-year-old group, but he claimed he could have been in a higher group if they had let him. When he got home, he told his parents he wanted to be in the Olympics, and they bought him a shiny blue fiberglass bow with a set of pulleys attached to the tips. Eli's mother drank soy milk and his father once dropped a marijuana cigarette that burned a smelly hole in their living room carpet. Every Wednesday and Sunday they drove him two hours each way to practice at an indoor range. Eli had a fancy leather armguard and metal stabilizing rods that hung off the bow like tusks. He was always talking it up, trying to get me to go shoot with him, but I was on the basketball team and had recently kissed a pretty cheerleader with tongue and I didn't have the heart to tell him archery was for dorks.

"Great!" Eli said. He was really excited to have someone to shoot with. "I'll bring my training bow over and show you the proper technique."

I had never shot an arrow before, but I figured if Eli could do it, so could I.

"That's OK," I said, "I'll just come over and get it."

"I don't know," he said. "It's pretty complicated."

"It's a really expensive bow," he added. "My parents said I probably shouldn't lend it out." He wasn't going to give up.

"Fine," I said. "You can bring it over."

On Sunday morning we took the bow down to the basement and laid the pieces on my father's worktable. There were four sleek, blue arrows with bristling tail feathers. The tips were dull metal, curved and rounded to a point like tiny warheads; they weren't even sharp.

Eli took off his bulky parka and began to point at each of the pieces: this is called a nock, this is the belly, this is the back. This is the cam and the limb bolt and this is the arrow rest, where you rest the arrows. You look through the sight like this. He was very serious about the whole thing.

"You have to know what you're doing," he said.

"Sure Eli," I said. "Right."

"Watch the way I do it," he said. We found some ancient red couch cushions and stacked them in the corner of the basement. Eli put the arm guard on and screwed the stabilizer into place. He slipped an arrow onto the rest and pointed the bow at the floor. He looked at the cushions and took a deep breath. In one motion, he lifted the bow and pulled back the string. He paused for a moment to aim, his arm tense with the effort. The arrow buzzed across the room and hit the middle of the cushion with a loud thump.

"Cool," I said. I was impressed.

"Yeah," Eli said, "you have to stand with your feet apart."

I wanted him to give me the bow but he just stood there with a funny look on his face, as if there were something he knew he had forgotten but couldn't remember. After a while he walked over and pulled the arrow out of the cushions. It was cold in the basement.

"Should I get my other bow?" he asked. "That way we could both practice down here at the same time."

"Sorry Eli," I said, "I have a basketball game in an hour." I was already wearing my uniform.

"OK," he said, but I could tell he was disappointed.

Those bastard raccoons lived in the loft of Eli's garage, which was more like an old, abandoned barn. There were all sorts of weird machines in there, tripods and gutted typewriters and the skeletal hull of a boat, junk that Eli's Dad had been collecting for years. Thumbalina, Eli's fat, lazy tabby, got locked in there once and we had to break the door to get her out. Thumbalina had vestigial toes on each forepaw, and Eli claimed she had too many thumbs and was therefore a lucky cat, but I said "if she's so lucky, how come she's stuck in the garage? And besides, cats don't have thumbs."

The back of the garage was the edge of our backyard. My father thought it was an eyesore, and was always arguing with Eli's Dad about fire hazards and property values. One spring he asked for permission to paint the side that bordered our property shades of brown and green, camouflage style, so it would blend in with the trees, but Eli's Dad never returned his call. My father started referring to him as The Doofus.

"That man is an ass," I heard him say to my mother once. "I should do us all a favor and burn the thing down myself."

But the biggest problem was the raccoons. They were everywhere, and they got into everything. They lived in a hole in the roof, the whole big, dirty raccoon family. At night we could hear them screeching and twittering; in the morning the garbage would be all over the driveway. My Dad bought new trashcans with heavy lids, and created a strict trash-removal schedule to minimize, he said, the time those bastards had to make their move, but the harder he tried to keep the raccoons out of the trash, the more trash the raccoons got into. He complained, threatened legal action, but Eli's Dad was some kind of hippy pacifist or something and he told my father to get off of his porch. The raccoons grew and prospered and continued to ransack our trash; they clawed at the locks, they ripped up the plastic, they knocked over the cans and rolled them into the street.

That night I brought Eli's bow and some arrows out to the back porch and waited. I put on the armguard, screwed the metal stabilizers into place, and practiced pulling the string back and forth. It was difficult and heavy, but once I got the string halfway back, the pulleys took over and it was easy.

I heard a noise. It was cold, the end of fall, and I could see my breath. The moon was bright and pale; there were no clouds. The raccoons appeared in formation, one after another, silhouetted against the sky. I tried to breathe softly. They made their way across the roof of the garage and climbed down a tree into our backyard, making noises like clicking chopsticks. I stood up slowly and picked up the bow and an arrow. I put the nock on the arrow rest and laid the shaft on the shelf. I was as quiet as I had ever been. The raccoons were walking toward the fence where we put our trashcans. I picked a medium-sized, older-brother type raccoon and took dead aim. I pulled the bow back slowly, fearing the creak. It was heavy and my arms were shaking. I took a deep breath and let go, but I had been holding the arrow too tightly with my fingers and it came off the shelf and flew way over to the left, at a crazy angle, and stuck in the garage. *Shit*, I said, and grabbed another arrow. The raccoons heard the bang, and stopped in their tracks, sniffing the wind. I pulled back the bow again, taking care not to hold the arrow too tight. Man, that thing was heavy! I aimed at the medium-sized raccoon, now stopped directly in front of me, and let fly again. The arrow skipped off the frozen ground and stuck in the fence. A light came on in my parents' window. The raccoons started screaming.

The next morning my father asked me what I was doing on the back porch in the middle of the night.

"What exactly *were* you doing out there?" he asked, pointing at me with a cereal spoon.

"Nothing," I said.

He gave me a look that said, I know *exactly* what you were doing out there, but your mother and I had a difference of opinion over whether it was appropriate or not, so we're going to give you one chance to explain yourself. My mother gave him a look that said, I told you he should be in therapy.

"Edward," he said.

"I was just sitting out there," I said, "I was watching the stars."

"Hey," he said, waving the spoon again, "don't bullshit a bullshitter." It was one of the things he liked to say: *don't bullshit a bullshitter.*

"Marty!" my mother said.

"I ain't shittin'," I said. This was a joke between us.

"Edward!" my mother said.

"Geez," I said, putting my bowl in the sink, "it was nothing."

He dropped me off at the bus and was almost late for work as usual.

Monday night was cloudy, and the moon was not so bright. A bitter wind cut through the trees, twisting up the shadows on the lawn. I put on my father's Brooks Brothers overcoat, the one he would never let me wear to school, and went outside. The arms were too long, and the bottom scraped the ground, but it was warm and dark and made me feel like Batman. To get a better angle, I moved closer to the edge of the porch. I propped the bow and arrows against a deck chair and waited. An hour later a scratching came over the wind, the familiar click-clicking of paws and nails on wood. I couldn't see the top of the garage from my new position, but I knew I would have a clear shot once the raccoons made it down to the yard.

I waited and listened. I held my breath. The wind pushed the clouds through the sky. I thought I heard something drop, then something else. I picked up the bow and an arrow, notched the nock and put the shaft on the shelf, carefully, carefully. A raccoon made its way across the grass. I pulled back the bow, ready for the weight this time, and aimed. *Bastard*, I said, and let fly.

The arrow whistled through the air and I heard a sharp sucking sound, followed by a quick, gargling screech. I stifled a yell. I was magic. I was a fucking barbarian. I ran down the porch steps and into the yard.

The raccoon lay on its side, hind legs kicking, the arrow sticking up out of its head. Except it wasn't a raccoon.

I had shot Thumbalina right through the eye.

I wasn't sure what to do. Thumby was twitching and mewing, and looked about as horrible and wretched and disgusting as a thing could look, paws kicking blindly in the air. I reached for the arrow and thought I might be sick. It went right through her eye and into her skull. There was blood on her fur and the ground was dark.

"What are you doing wearing my coat?" my father said. And then: "What the fuck did you do?"

The light wasn't on; I hadn't even heard him come out on the porch.

He looked over my shoulder at the twitching cat and grabbed my arm.

"What the fuck did you do?"

I had tears in my eyes. "I was hunting raccoons."

He screwed up his face and looked me right in the eye. He bit the inside of his lip like he did when he was working through a thought and sniffled. He let go of my arm and pulled the arrow out of the cat's head, using his slippered foot on her back as leverage. It made a terrible noise.

"Take off that coat," he said.

Thumbalina was dead by the time we had wrapped her in an old towel and placed her discreetly by the porch. The next morning, very early, my father took the package around to Eli's house. By that time the blood had soaked through and frozen. My father knocked on the door and woke Eli's father, who came outside in his bathrobe. My father explained what had happened, how those bastard raccoons had torn up my guinea pig and how I got this idea in my head that it would be all right to get them back but had accidentally shot their cat through the head with a carbon-graphite target arrow. He admitted the mistakes he had made as a father, and as a man, and made up something about some help I would soon be getting, help I sorely needed. Eli's Dad stroked his beard like an old rabbi. They agreed it was best not to take legal action. They agreed it was best to tell both families that the cat had died in the road, and bury her in the back yard under an oak. They agreed that $300 was a fair price.

"Thank you, Tom, for being so understanding," my father said.

I brought the bow back to Eli. If he noticed the spots on the arrow, he kept it to himself. I told him I would probably stick to basketball. I kissed the cheerleader two more times, but she broke up with me before I could feel her up. She said it wasn't me, it was her.

6 A.M.
Dana Neibert

6 A.M., ultrachrome print, 2001
No Checks, ultrachrome print, 2001   *Cook*, ultrachrome print, 2001

Toast, ultrachrome print, 2001

Waiting, ultrachrome print, 2001
Listen, ultrachrome print, 2001

The Paper Moon
Ida Pearle

Untitled, cut paper collage, 1998
Untitled, cut paper collage, 2003
Untitled, cut paper collage, 1998

Untitled, cut paper collage, 1998

Untitled, cut paper collage, 2001
Untitled, cut paper collage, 2003

Jose Carmona, *Trick,* mixed media on paper, 2002

Gravity (,) Bitch
Maria Nazos

Ever since I was five years old,
I was a white child in a grass-stained dress,
spinning on the tilt of the earth's axis,
some said that I liked to be dizzy and that I reveled
in the inner ear,
others like my grandmother romantically coined
  me a free-spirit,
a mantra that resonated throughout my life,
that was usually said as a bad thing, a synonym for
crazy bitch, for women who hack globules
of phlegm on the pavement and pepper their syntax
with fuck and do likewise
when the urge tingles their thighs—how could I
have told them that even at the age of five
I was a galaxy bitch—who reversed the cycle of minutes
as I adorned my eyes with Saturn's haloes
before the rest of the planets re-aligned in
a string of charkas just perfect for my neck,
They would never have spoken to me again
had I told I them that I used to twirl myself
nauseous and collapse
backfirst on the hard soil,
because for a moment the clouds
read *POEM*
and for a minute the axis re-adjusted beneath me,
  as I rocked hard against the hours
while the most intimate place
between my thighs tingled.

Untitled (January 27, 2004)
Dewayne Washington

Eyes closed
I see youth
I see you
Standing at the bed's edge
Scratching the dark top of my foot
Where the skin festers
Under heavy wool

I see the mayor
Surrounded by his mess
On a television
Surrounded by mine
A thousand unruled notes
Scattered freeform
Each to their own

I see two small windows
Through one I've exhaled, I've
Passed the grey film and bars
Passed the litter-strewn canopy
Passed our territorial limit
I no longer travel with the pride
Nor will I inherit the earth

Byron Barrett, *Dublin Alley*, Ilfochrome, 2002

Untitled
Chris Yormick

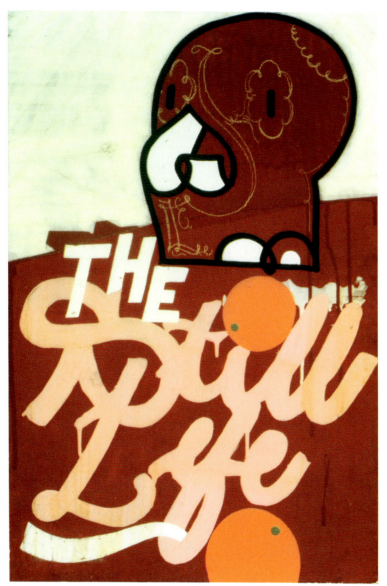

The Still Life, mixed media on board, 2003

Broke Out, mixed media on canvas, 2003
Big & Small, mixed media on canvas, 2003

facing page:
Bottle & a Cork, mixed media on canvas, 2003
One Last Caress, mixed media on canvas, 2002
13 Ounce, mixed media on canvas, 2002

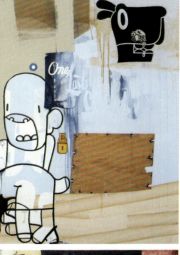

Retreat
Andrew Zbihlyj

Nursing Home, ink, mixed media on paper, 2002
Monster, ink, mixed media on paper, 2002

Mourners, ink, mixed media on paper, 2002
Lost Boy, ink, mixed media on paper, 2002

facing page:
Flyers, ink, mixed media on paper, 2002
Head 2, ink, mixed media on paper, 2002
Head 1, ink, mixed media on paper, 2002

OCTOBER 2004

HENDRICKSON MEMORIAL PRIZE IN SHORT FICTION

POETRY

FEATURED ARTISTS

INDIVIDUAL ARTWORKS

COVER ART

June
Richard Austin

June's coat catches fire, makes a stink like burning hair. June flaps her arms and hops in place until she just can't stand it. June pulls off the coat and throws it down onto the sidewalk. A man steps out of the corner market, sees what June is up to: stomping on her coat, old army pea coat. The man stands and stares. He walks back inside the store. The fire's out. The cigarette that made the fire fell and rolled into the gutter. June retrieves the cigarette, still lit, she presses it between her lips, inhales, removes the cigarette, and points at the coat with the burning end. The coat is a dog playing dead. June laughs at the joke. Stay, she says, making her I-mean-it face, the one she used on her kids: Stay.

The coat does what June says. June picks up the coat and shakes it, pats the hole the fire made, right above her absent breast. June puts on the coat and walks quickly down the sidewalk, a wide and swaying walk with too much side-to-side. June coughs, takes a deep breath, and scratches her scalp with her nails until it hurts. June has head-lice now. I know she got them from the coat she's wearing. I don't know for sure where that coat came from, but I believe she stole it from someone, someone who was sleeping or high or knocked-on-the-head unconscious. It wouldn't matter to June, so long as the coat keeps her warm. It has deep pockets in the front, halfway down June's thighs. I don't know what she's keeping in those pockets yet, but I'll bet there are sharp things, a knife at least, probably some hard bread and apples. The coat is too long for June, drags behind her when she moves, heading down the sidewalk again.

June looks up and down the street and glances over her shoulder, checking to see who's after her, dodging whoever it is she took that coat from. June's hungry and itchy and warm and needing to pee somewhere. June likes staying hungry, it keeps her awake for a while and the itchiness isn't so bad, it gives her something to do with her hands. June will squat and pee in stairwells without notice, but she prefers squatting in rosebushes, it makes her laugh to think of people stopping by to sniff her blessings, all mixed in with thorns and petals. June knows it disgusts me, she knows I know she knows it disgusts me and still she pushes down her pants and squats on bushes and stone steps and laughs out loud, right out loud. June and me, we don't speak anymore.

June turns onto Hartford, slows down to look for things, so much construction going on there's always something to pick up, pocket, save for later. Halfway down the block a house is opened up at the bottom, making room for a garage. June hears men talking and stopping, talking again, figures they're all in there sitting and eating lunch and talking, too much to do at once and notice her. Out front of the house and off to the side I see an empty wheelbarrow. No, not empty, just not filled with dirt. June gets up close to it, thinking how fun it would be to pee in there, how angry I'll get when she does it, but there's something in there, after all. A long flashlight, a jumble of nails and screws and grit and flakes of rust, a half-empty box of Krispy Krackers. June reaches into the wheelbarrow and there's a shout behind her, across the street, big shouting that brings all the men out of the opening in the house, standing there with sandwiches or hands-on-hips.

June grabs the flashlight and crosses her arms, the flashlight is under her armpit when June runs back up Hartford, she only looks back once because she knows who did the screaming. I know it too, but June's not saying. Anytime June runs away from anything, I can't see outside anymore, can't see a thing, suddenly I'm out on the shoulder of a long and empty stretch of highway. Here I am beside the highway, when she runs away from anything I'm out here on the shoulder, standing on red dirt, hearing wind and smelling dried-up earth and all I can see is the long flat desert with the hills so far off in the distance they might just be me thinking hills. Out here by the road there's only heat, no wind, no sound. June pushes me out of the way when she runs or when she's scared and sometimes when she drinks too much I'm stuck out here for hours, the sun low and close to the horizon and never setting.

I can't see June but I can hear that shouting again, goes something like this: No-no-no-no-no!! My-coat my-coat mine-mine-mine!!

June's running faster now, I can't feel her but the shouting is fainter so I know June is running faster, getting away, making her exit with the flashlight rattling in her grip, bread and knife and apples in her pockets make a knocking sound against her legs and now there's a new word stuck between her ears, it flutters back and forth between my ears, Krispy-Krispy, a syllable for each step June is taking, heavy on the right foot, Kris-py Kris-py Kris-py.

June was a marvelous cook, good with pork and roast but best when it came to pies, especially cherry. I mention this to prove to you there's more to June than getting away and squatting and stealing, at least, there was more, but it started out with getting away. June was getting away, gaining distance from a place—a someone and a sickness—and then, right in the middle of her exit, June's car broke down. This was when getting away led to squatting (which I've mentioned) and later on some stealing—two things June had never considered but found necessary out in the middle of nowhere and her exit—both unavoidable because June had to pee and finish her escape. And so it was that the getting away led first to squatting out there beside the broken-down car, over a dusty patch of red-brown, hard-packed dirt in the god-awful nowhere that was the desert in Nevada.

Once June went that far, puddle spreading under her, between her shoes, what was the sense in turning back? June would not turn back, except to look over her shoulder, being absolutely certain she was still alone. I know she was not.

I'm close again, I see June hiding in a patch of backyard with a high wood-plank fence all around it, cotton laundry lines run overhead with towels and shirts and socks attached by plastic pink clothespins.

June sits in the corner of the tiny rectangle of yard, back to the fence, not running or getting away but still breathing fast from running and climbing up the fence and dropping down onto the grass. June stares at the grass, runs her fingers through the length of it, and does not remember another yard. She can't think back the way I can, but the grass is calming her, cool and smooth on her fingertips and wrist, the palm of her hand. June sits quietly, unafraid, no longer breathing fast or hard.

While June is not afraid and quiet I should tell you all about the yard, so much bigger than this with a fine, sloping, green, grassy hill that led down to the creek, so full in the spring and chatty with moving water and birds and crickets and the sound of someone tossing one good pebble in. Not a fence in sight. I know a patch where June would rest, feet towards the water, studying clouds. The screech of swings gone higher up, a pair of squeals, giggling. June loved the air, cool and clean. It had the smell of waking up.

June smells frying fat, bacon or ham or sausage coming through a window on the back of the house that holds so tight onto the small yard. June peeks through a small knot in a plank of wood to her left, sees a house, a shrub she knows, an empty driveway. A mailman passes by, I see him pushing a small cart filled with mail, I hear one squeaky wheel. A scrap of human being rolls by in a wheelchair, feet paddling pavement under her. June knows her, says her name through the knot-hole, Ginger. Hey—Ginger! June puts her eye back to the hole and sees Ginger wheel her way across Hartford, up a short incline of driveway, down a short stretch of sidewalk. June pokes her finger through the hole and wiggles it and says, It's June.

Ginger grabs the finger and shakes it, says, Junebug, what you doing there? I got me some cash. Let's go see Tony.

June says, I got Manson's coat.

Ginger coughs three times, I think she's got TB. She spits. Oh, June, she says. Ginger rolls away, feet up, making the most of the decline. You better give it back. Her voice is smaller as she heads down the street. You got to find yourself a better place to hide.

Manson's not his name, everybody used to call him by his real name, Bernard. I remember that night June and Ginger and Tony and Manson were drinking and huffing in the park behind the grocery store. Tony looked at Manson for a long time, Tony slapped his own knee and laughed and said, "Ugly!" Manson ignored him. Manson didn't like to share, had to have his own bottle, sniffed his own marker, he was long-haired and snaggle-toothed and as he sat there the edge of one nostril was black with ink. June thought he reminded her of someone mean, someone awful and famous, she remembered who it was then and piped up and hollered, "Manson!" Manson went after June, but June was too

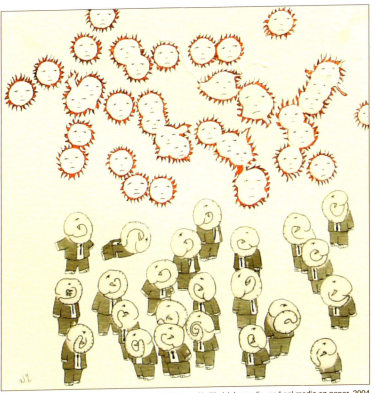

Neil Farber, *Untitled*, ink, acrylic, and gel media on paper, 2004

quick for him. I heard Manson take it out on Tony: short punch across the nose, there must have been blood on Manson's knuckles and fingers and nails, I figure in the dim light all that blood would've looked like cocoa, brown and dark and thick. "Manson never cuts his nails." That's what June says to people when they ask about him, and, "He's got more stink on him than a flattened skunk."

The day that June was not alone out on the highway, squatting, there was a flattened critter not far off, I can't tell from June's position if it was skunk or possum or cat, but she was up-wind, thank god, and right as June was thinking to herself thank god a pickup truck came speeding down the state highway. Red or blue or blue with rust, it pulled off the road and onto the shoulder, big cloud of dust piling over the truck, I can almost feel the grit in my nose. June patted herself dry with a tissue from a pack she kept in her glove-box for emergencies, an emergency being a moment when June might have used all the tissues that came in the box that she kept on the dash in a cozy she'd knitted herself. June stood up and straightened her slip, ran a thumb under the waist of her skirt, checking to make sure the safety pins were secure.

It's a fine day. June hasn't noticed yet, but it's clear and bright with just enough wind to make you think something might happen, something unexpected, sudden, I've noticed things like that happen quite often, even on days filled with sunshine or birthday presents. The sky was bright and clear, the wind rushed around her ankles on the morning June forgot her lunch, she'd sent the girls to school on the bus and kissed Joey goodbye and walked the nine blocks to the train like any other day except for her lunch being left on the counter by the sink in front of the four-slice toaster, beside the microwave. She realized this as she approached the train station; because of the sky and the wind and a feeling that something extraordinary might happen, she suddenly decided not to waste that lunch, to turn around and go back the way she came—past the water tower, the coffee factory with its enormous clock, the Lutheran church at the corner—she was home in no time, through the unlocked front door and into the kitchen before she could quite make out the sound she'd heard from the front door, a sound she kept hearing all the way down the hallway, try as I might I can only describe it as a kind of shuffling grunt. June stood in the doorway to the kitchen, she saw the thing that made the noise. Two big dogs were fighting, they were growling and tearing away at each other until June blinked and understood it wasn't dogs at all, it was a burglar—strangling her husband—he hadn't yet left for work and the burglar snuck into the house a moment too soon and here was Joey, fighting him off in the kitchen right in front of June's brown paper bag of a lunch with chicken salad sandwich and apple and something I never did notice before, a bag of corn chips. June looked at her lunch and opened her mouth to cry out, she'd shout out anything that came to mind as long as it was loud enough to scare the burglar off. Then, the sound changed. June heard Joey say uhmn; when she looked again she didn't see a burglar trying to strangle her husband, she saw Joey's hairy ass in a big hurry, digging away at another hairy ass.

June dropped her keys, a terrible clatter on the tiled floor. June looked hard in that moment—during which Joey pulled out and tried to cover himself and in which the other man, whose ass she didn't recognize, fumbled for the pants tangled around his patent leather shoes. It wasn't until days later that she realized who it was that bent over her pale yellow counter, taking it up the ass from her Joey and facing her lunch and her toaster, just whose face she'd seen reflected in its streakless, gleaming surface. Joey was fucking their pastor. June left the keys and the lunch where they were. If the men made other sounds that morning, June didn't hear them.

She was out the door and running down the block, bound for the train that would take her downtown to work. I watch June sitting in her office, staring through the window at buildings, down at pedestrians, at pigeons out on ledges, preening and scurrying.

The workmen have finished lunch, they've gone back to work on the garage. June hears a hammer drive a nail into wood, keet-keet-keet! A pause, now I hear him drive the nail in all the way to the head and pound the hammer on the wood: keet-keet-kamm! June figures Manson's left the block, lost track of her, the men would stop what they were doing if Manson was nearby. June climbs over the fence, drops down onto the sidewalk. She walks down 17th, takes a right onto Noe. In the doorway of a three-flat someone's wrapped up in a blanket, from under the blanket seeps a stain, running all the way to the curb. I feel June poke the shape with the toe of her shoe, she pokes it again, harder. From a bend in the blanket she hears a loud fart. June crosses the street and turns onto Ford.

June had a doctor named Ford, he put her to sleep and cut away her left breast and smaller pieces out from under her arms. After the surgery, June had a vision—a technicolor image of herself standing in line at a supermarket wearing nothing but a pale orange slip. The cashier looked up at June and said, "Will that be it for you?" June stared down at her chest, smooth skin taut over her left side, no nipple. Beside it, abundance, the fullness of her remaining breast, June felt the weight of it, its heft, in this memory I can hear her thinking to herself, "Too much." In the palm of her hand, June cupped her right breast and said, "I'd like to return this." With a dry, popping sound she detached it and laid it down on the conveyor belt. It tilted slightly, turning in place: counterclockwise. June realized she had no receipt, there were several people in line behind her, rolling their eyes and clucking their tongues. The man immediately behind her sighed heavily and muttered, "Let's go, Lefty." June said, "I'm sorry, I've lost my receipt." June felt a pain in her foot, she looked down and saw that the man beside her was stepping on her littlest toe, glaring at her. June woke. At the foot of her hospital bed her ex-husband held a bouquet of roses. He was tugging at June's toe, trying to get her attention and keep a clear distance, too. "How you feeling?" he asked. June felt like hell, she hurt so bad she started crying, she didn't know what to do with her hands so she covered her face and wept, I've never heard such an awful racket, but she couldn't seem to keep it in. June looked down at her uneven chest and took a deep breath and wiped at her eyes with the edge of the sheet. June knew him well enough to know he was an awful coward, it occurred to her he never would be strong enough to stay, tend to her needs, wait until she healed. "Joey, I'm fine," June said, closing her eyes and pulling her foot away from his grip.

June's halfway down the single block of Ford. She hears a crash, a shattering behind her foot. She sees the long, green neck of a bottle skittering past her feet on the sidewalk. She doesn't turn her head; she runs. She hears Manson behind her, shouting with each step he takes: God! Dammit! My! Coat! Mine! June runs faster, doesn't see the rise I've spotted in the concrete. June's left boot catches on the lip of cement, sends her five feet forward. When she was only nine years old, June fell through a loose plank in a treehouse—crashing through branches—on her way down she turned to one side. Not as she was breaking through the plank or tumbling to the earth, but several minutes after she hit the

Issue 15

ground and heard her shoulder let loose a sharp, splintering crack, only then did June suck in air and fill her lungs and, finally, scream. June lands on her elbows and knees. The flashlight shoots out of its pocket, rolls across the sidewalk and into the gutter. Manson's not far off, his shoes are slapping on the ground. A car speeds past June, screeches, backs up again. June looks up. The driver looks down, away. Manson grabs June's ankle. June screams a word I can't make out. The car drives off.

The truck backed down the highway's shoulder, stopping in front of June's car, hood up, steam rising. A man slammed the door shut, walked through the dust towards June: curves on his arms and thighs, thick-bodied, in his left hand he spun keys around a key-ring on his middle finger. "You got some trouble," he said, nodding at the hissing engine. June said, "Yes, I'm very lucky you came along." Because his body was healthy and arrogant, abundant, June did not trust him. "Why don't I take a look for you—see if I can help?" "Oh," said June, "Would you, please? I don't know a damn about these things."

I'd call this a lie, June knew quite well the fan belt had snapped, she was trying to distract him long enough to remember where she'd seen a rock nearby. Fist-sized, not too heavy. He ducked his head under the hood. "I'm Darrold." June said, "Darrold? I'm Katie." June saw the valley of his back through a worn white tee-shirt; under thin, faded jeans she saw the rise of his ass. He had Joey's shape. By the time June got better he'd taken her girls away, too, and out there in the desert by the hissing hood with Darrold's butt in front of her, June was thinking about how she wasn't anybody's someone. June was a good mother—I'd swear on that—she only ever lost her girls one time, they disappeared into a throng of Christmas shoppers when she'd turned to toss some change into a Salvation Army donation bucket; Santa rang his bell, she heard the goddamned thing for hours as she searched the mall from end to end, her throat like an anvil sinking down the length of her until a security guard took her by the hand and led her to the North Pole display, pointing out a small space under the sleigh where her daughters were crouching down—hiding and giggling at her—when she got near them they squealed Mommy mommy you found us! You found us!

From under the hood, Darrold said, "Uh-oh, I think I see your problem here, Katie." June scanned the shoulder of the road for that rock, she'd seen it while she peed, it was just the right size. Darrold stood and stretched and leaned against the side of the car. "Katie, I think I can take care of this for you," he said, rapping his knuckles on the side-view mirror. "Yes, I do believe I can." He dropped a hand on his thigh, "Now, maybe you can do something for me, Katie. Maybe you can help me out first?" Darrold winked and ran a thumb along the length of his bulge, which was thickening and creeping down the inside of his thigh. "What do you say Katie—seem like a fair trade to you?" June took a deep breath, looking up and down the highway. She took a step back and felt her heel bump against something. "Sure," said June, "Why not?" Darrold turned. "Come on then," he said, swaggering toward his truck. June said, "Right behind you," squatting down to the red dirt and grabbing the rock.

Manson drags June by the ankle. Seems to me it ought to hurt, but I can't feel a thing. June kicks. June reaches behind her head, fumbling for the flashlight. Manson tries to pin June to the concrete, he spits on her forehead. June sees rotting teeth and yellow eyes and smells an awful stink. June's poor old grandma got too hot the night before she died, she laid there in her bed and licked her lips and when momma told June to give Grandma a hug she tried to hold her breath and not get close—but she couldn't hold it, not long enough—as she leaned over her grandma and wrapped her arms around her neck June smelled sickness, a foul, fetid breath came out the mouth and June jumped away, ran out of the bedroom with her nose in the left sleeve of her flannel pajamas. June feels for the heavy cylinder. She grips it. She swings. She sends me away.

It's hot. Out here, it's always hot. Not a cloud in the sky; the sun hangs low. It won't set, it never does. I can see the hills from here, I watch them, waiting for a breeze, the slightest wind. It won't happen. The slip underneath my skirt is chafing me. My lips burn. The sweat my body makes is gone before I feel it. I'm standing on the dusty shoulder of the road. The road is behind me and forever that way, forever this way. On my left heel, a blister. Nothing stirs. The sun is almost setting. A breeze should come down off those hills. I hear myself breathe, a thin wheeze. The desert makes a sound: a ringing heat against my skull, high and persistent.

The road is behind me, I'm watching the hills. My eyes ache, filled with strong sunset light. If I looked closer, over there, to my right, I'd see the raised hood, the gray engine, the ugly metal grill, a spiral of red-earth footprints. They circle each other, leading here and towards the pickup truck, just to my left, not two yards away. I won't look at the footprints, the car, or the truck. I know they're here. I won't look down at the small, dark patch, already dried, turned to mud under his face, a dusty, stubbled profile with slightly parted lips. It's split. Color seeps to the back of his ear, down his jaw, to his chin. Until June's finished, I'll have to wait right here, only looking at the hills. The sun won't set. The breeze won't start. I'm waiting here until June's done. I won't flinch or leave this spot. I will not drop the rock.

Finding Alaska
Jesse Donaldson

"Alaska," Dan says. He's telling me about some show he watched while drinking at the Deadwood. "It's amazing. They have this hotel made out of ice. Everything. Desks, beds, floors, walls. All ice."

"Must be cold."

"That's the thing. It's warm somehow. They explained it, had something to do with the ice being so thick, so dense that it traps heat."

"I'd like to see that," I say and shove the last bite of my burger in my mouth.

"We should go. We should fix your car."

"I think I was on my way to Alaska before I got here," I say and wash the burger down with a sip of Pabst. I can still taste the remnants of seasoned salt and ketchup-soaked bread, the leftover burger juices mixing with each swallow.

Dan and I are sitting on the porch swing. It's humid and we're bare-chested, watching the summer sun set behind the church across the street. A wedding is finishing up and the guests shuffle in little circles on the lawn. The bride and groom run out from the church and make their way into this red Subaru wagon. The bride has to close the door twice because she gets the train of her dress caught but she doesn't mind and seems happy and everyone is laughing and pointing as they drive off, kind of in the direction of the falling sun.

Summer students walk by in groups toward the four blocks considered *downtown* Iowa City. They've shed their backpacks and styled their hair, every night having the sort of carefree summer camp feel that comes with meaningless classes and half-empty bars. Some look our direction and gawk while others bury their heads and pretend we aren't here—occupying space—part of the landscape. Dan has a large belly that looks like a tumor, a sort of male womb tacked onto his lanky frame. He hasn't cut his hair in ten years and pulls it into a ponytail. There's a reason he doesn't cut it but he won't tell me. I think it's something spiritual but Dan keeps secrets and I respect him for that. It's the end of summer and the days are getting imperceptibly shorter, the sun setting a minute or two earlier each night.

I don't remember driving into Iowa City. From the highway it's a stopping place on the road with signs for food and gas—not a destination. I didn't pay attention to the quaint houses with square yards, the empty streets, or the sidewalks of ambling residents. The fact that Iowa City became my summer home had more to do with my car breaking down—

something about the transmission dying and money or lack thereof. Dan found me on the street, kicking the Dodge, pushing it into a parking spot. He let me borrow a quarter for the meter and neither I nor the car have moved since. Dan set me up in a boarding house run by this lady named Judy, and she gave me a room for 150 a month as long as I helped paint and fix the place up. Now that summer's ending she's doubling rents, anticipating the hordes of returning students, and Dan and I have to find new places to haunt.

Iowa City is peaceful in the summer. A few students take classes to make up failed credits and the university hosts a rotating group of supposedly gifted high school students who discover the side effects of alcohol more than they expand their minds. The locals reclaim the town for about three months: throw street festivals, enjoy the abundance of parking spaces, take late afternoon and early morning walks.

I'll miss Iowa City because I've gotten used to the routine. At eight in the morning I wake up, shuffle in my bathrobe one block to my lifeless car and pop a couple of quarters in the meter. Then I shuffle back and set the alarm for ten minutes to ten. After I fill the meter at ten, I start my day with freeze-dried coffee and toast. I see the quarter pumping as my regular job, the old Monday through Friday grind. Dan used to help me by dropping change in on his way home from running his errands but eventually he realized I'd mastered the job. The math is simple. One hour per quarter. Two quarters at a time. That's nine quarters deposited in five trips to the meter or two dollars and twenty-five cents a day. Ten twenty-five a week. Saturdays, Sundays, and evenings free. I like the set schedule, the knowledge of what lies ahead.

"I think you can get through Canada pretty easy," Dan says. "If you tell them you're going to Alaska and all. They probably give you a week or so to get to the Alaskan border. The drive's all along the coast."

"I've never seen the Pacific," I say, taken in for a moment by Dan's excitement.

"Me either."

"The Dodge wouldn't make it though."

"We could try."

"It wouldn't work," I say, tilting the half-full Pabst back and forth in my hand, feeling the beer jump and bounce inside like caged waves. "What number you on?" I ask, changing the subject.

"Four, you?"

"Five."

"You drink too fast," Dan says.

"Maybe I don't appreciate things enough."

"You don't savor them," he says and nods towards the setting sun. I look up from my beer to the sky. The orange remnants of the sun spike into the darkness and I think of the married couple driving into the sunset for their honeymoon. I wonder how far they will drive before they stop and say: this is the place. This is where we settle for the night. This is where we consummate our love.

Dan and I have spent a good deal of time together, become part of one another's routines. He's been living in Iowa City awhile on money he inherited from a dead uncle and is good at finding a way to stretch our limited funds. He met a Mexican stocker who sneaks him ground beef out of the Eagle Market for cheap, so we live on burgers and beer. I buy the buns, seasoning, ketchup, and mustard—all the frills. We split the Pabst. Dan wanted to make an event out of dinner, a sort of halfhearted family meal on the porch, so we made it part of the routine. We watch students, sunsets, traffic, weddings, anything that passes before our eyes and when it becomes too dark to see anything worthwhile or too cold to sit shirtless, we dress and go to the Deadwood for drafts.

I've been living off savings from odd jobs, birthdays, graduations, Christmas, whatever. Every once in awhile Dan and I work as handymen or painters around town. Judy gave our name out to other landlords because we work cheap and fast. There are a lot of quick fixes to be made before students move in. The apartments have to look livable that first day as parents tote their kids' bags and give them hugs goodbye. But work has run out now that the semester is about to start and Dan and I are trying to figure out what's next, waiting like men about to be hanged—the moment before the trap doors fall.

On weekends, Dan and I go to the park and lie in the grass, play basketball, and swim. Dan likes to do flips off the high dive, his big belly an axis around which the long, thin limbs of his body spin and flail before gravity brings them inevitably to the water. I know people stare at Dan and me and think us an odd pair. We stand out in our dirty clothes, Dan with his Charles Manson hair, crooked secondhand glasses, and me with my frail body, boyish smirk, and indifferent blue eyes. The lingering flecks of paint that freckle our bodies mark us like lepers—outcasts in a small town.

"Did you know that Eskimos are really supposed to be called Inuits?" Dan asks. "They're like the Indians of Alaska."

"I used to date a girl who liked Eskimo kisses," I say.

"What did you think of it?"

"Nose-kissing? It's weird and childish. How can you get pleasure from touching nostrils?" I ask.

"Maybe if you found the right person," Dan says.

"Perhaps."

"I'd like to think I'd enjoy them with the right person," he says again and I look over at him. The light from inside the house washes over his shoulders, the soft incandescent glow framing him like an idol.

"I'm kind of tipsy," I tell him and he suggests that maybe we should skip the Deadwood, find something else to do.

I made two phone calls that first day in Iowa City. I emptied the change from the car's ashtray and walked three blocks downtown before finding a payphone. First I called Jamie. Her mother said she was on the beach swimming. I wanted to leave a message, something letting her know I missed her, that I'd miss her forever, but I figured something would get lost in its passing, some inflection of voice that would change a statement full of meaning into movie script, so I just grumbled something about saying "hi" and realized I'd never call again. I thought of Jamie in her two-piece, dipping under the waves, her dirty blond tresses darkened and pulled back behind her ears and figured a "hi" would suffice—that it all means the same thing anyway.

Then I called my mother and waited ten rings until she picked up. I told her the car broke down but that I'd be okay. She mumbled concern of some sort and asked where I was. I said it didn't matter, that I was traveling, and would talk to her when I settled down. Mom put my little half-sister, Sara, on the phone, because she was washing dishes and her hands were wet. Sara told me about finger painting and a fight with her best friend Lisa. I began to get dizzy because the sun was directly overhead and the silver metal of the phone cooked and made the air stifling. The sweat from my hand made the receiver oily and I felt sick. I leaned my head into the burning metal box and listened to Sara chatter in her high-pitched voice until Mom took the phone back. She said something about my coming back soon. I told her I would call again and that I loved her before replacing the receiver.

"Things are changing here," Dan says as he takes a bite of mint chocolate chip off the top of his cone. "We can't stay." We're surrounded by the skittish sounds of summer romance—the whispers of high school lovers coupled with measured banter of married couples. I haven't touched my dipped cone and the vanilla soft serve has started to trickle where the cone and chocolate meet. Dan notices because he's observant; he eyes the melting cone with a certain discomfort at my waste, like a parent scraping broccoli from their child's plate. Dan and I haven't talked too much about where we'll go after Iowa, but we know change is coming. Some of the fraternity and sorority members have already returned, marking their territory with empty beer cans and blaring car stereos. Freshmen and their parents have begun invading the city like stray cats, filling up restaurant patios with their excited chatter. There's no more denying the inevitability of our move—that we are dangerously close to overstaying our welcome. I've been preparing quietly without Dan, getting rid of possessions that will weigh me down—books, shoes, my guitar. I talked to a junkyard about towing the Dodge in return for its parts, which they agreed to after I told them about the new front tires.

"Where are we supposed to go?" I ask, and for a moment I honestly believe Dan is going to give me the answer, some place plausible yet extravagant, some possibility that has eluded me, that he's going to tell me the direction I'm seeking.

But all he manages is a fake show of contemplation before blurting out, "Alaska." I'm disappointed in him but I don't let it show. There's no reason to be tough on Dan when I know things are winding down and that he'll soon be part of my past.

I finger the melting cone and lick a swirl of chocolate and vanilla off my finger. I remember how before Mom remarried and Sara was born, she and Pop and I would stop for ice cream on the way home from my ball games. Pop hated ice cream but he liked the extra hour it gave him to talk about baseball. Mom always ordered a dipped cone, which I thought the most boring choice considering the range beyond chocolate and vanilla, the rainbow of ever-changing flavors. She never once changed her mind, even when my father laughed at her predictability. I remember the first Saturday after Pop left. It was a humid summer day and I watched my mother's cone melt over her fingers as we sat in silence across from one another.

I look at Dan, struggling with his melting cone, the ice cream running down his hand, and understand a little better what my mother must have felt. "You think they eat ice cream in Alaska?" I ask.

"Yeah, who doesn't eat ice cream?" Dan exclaims and I laugh softly and close my eyes. I realize that for Dan and me the future is all dreams and Alaska is as good place as any to imagine.

"Polar bears and ice-fishing," I say.

"Penguins."

"Alaskan *king* crabs."

"Alaskan Huskies."

"Riding around in big trucks."

"Avoiding potholes."

"Traversing mountains."

"With snow-capped peaks."

"Icebergs."

"The aurora borealis."

"Heaven."

"Ice cream," Dan says as he lifts the last bit of his cone to the sky and holds it like a torch. I raise the melting remnants of my uneaten cone and appreciate Dan for the moment.

I'm packing my duffel bag in the moonlight, trying not to make noise. I said goodnight to Dan an hour ago but decided it would be a goodbye earlier. I wrote a short note, nothing over the top, telling him I had to move on, explaining that the Dodge was getting towed, telling him I'd see him in

Alaska. I leave it outside his door and slip out of the house unnoticed.

I am walking through Iowa City in the middle of the night, slinging my bag from shoulder to shoulder, making my way to the bus station. A few drunken students pass by on the sidewalk but don't pay attention to me. I am on the move, invisible, part of a changing landscape. I listen to the beat of my steps and try not to think about all the people I've left behind, their faces popping in and out of my head, calling me home, wherever that may be.

I am in the bus station rifling through my bag—the essential possessions of my transient life. I am searching for a pen and paper to write my mother, to tell her Iowa City was nice.

I am on a bus, twenty-five dollars and a ticket crumpled in my hand. The bus is nearly empty and there are no seatbelts. I feel free. I am looking out the window at the dark, empty plains, heading west toward Omaha, imagining what the aurora borealis looks like at night. I reach my arms high above my head and spread my fingers wide. I focus on the fingers, the pressure of their stretch at its limits, and I can't help feeling as though they are grasping in the air for something unfound and out of range.

My Robotic Leg
E.S. Oldrin

Right now we live in a flat, in Cape Town. I pretend to be a writer. She works. That's the plan but I'm not delivering. She comes home, asks to read what I've written. I have nothing to show. After a month, I begin stealing other people's stories.

She's impressed with Michael Crichton's, *Blood Doesn't Come Out*. I pick it because I have to transcribe it and it's only nine pages long. It's a simple, powerful story. It's a story I could have written. She thinks so too, and gushes with praise.

"It's amazing!" She looks at me like I'm a genius and I mock humility.

"It's nothing."

"Did you write it today?"

"Yah. It just came to me."

"Mmm, that's not the only thing that's gonna come today," she purrs, grabbing me by the shirt. Thanks, Mr. Crichton.

It goes on like this for weeks. I'm careful not to use stories she'll recognize. Ryan Boudinot's *Littlest Hitler,* one from the *Christmas Diaries* (even though it's March), something from Rick Moody, and a story about surfing (cause surfing is sexy). It's an impressive collection. If they were mine, I might be published.

"You could publish these!" she announces.

"Wow, really? I don't think so. They need some work."

"No really. You should send them to a publisher."

To the Plagiarism Press, I think. "Maybe I will," I say.

Back before I quit smoking and started running, I lived in San Francisco. I'm remembering one of those days. The sky is turning to rain. Cars are filling the streets. A woman holding a dog waits beside me, on the corner. The dog does not look happy.

"What's his name?" I ask.

"Jake."

"Hi Jake."

Jake wiggles to be free as we wait for the hand to become a walking man.

The woman looks British. She said "Jake" with an accent. She's European if not British. Petite, dark hair, cute nose and mouth—but her eyes are definitively European. They take everything seriously but me.

"Jake! No, Jake! Come back!" The European cries, as Jake suddenly breaks free from her arms.

"Jake! Come!"

The cars begin to honk and swerve but Jake is oblivious. He lays down in the middle of the lane. Hondas, SUVs, and Volkswagens veer within inches of his puffy head.

"Jake! Please! Jake!" The veins in her neck are popping out. For an insane moment, I consider darting after him. But before I can, Jake turns and looks at me and I swear, he smiles. I know dogs can't smile but this one does—a big, toothy, slobbery smile like a canine cartoon. Then just as quickly as he ran into the street, as two gigantic dump trucks approach, he waddles out and over to me and begins to lick my hand.

"Taste my lunch, huh?" I ask.

The European is relieved.

"He is deaf. Deaf." She points to her ear to help me understand.

"Maybe just hungry." I say.

She laughs and her eyes laugh too and she looks at me with them and for a moment I feel caught up.

"He's always hungry," she replies, letting her words slow down. "He is a naughty dog. Naughty, naughty dog," she scolds him. "I have no leash because my flat is a mess. So I have to carry him but he just won't have that. And here it is pissing rain."

It was nice that she cared enough to explain so much.

"Yes. Well, it's okay now, right?" I asked.

"Oh yes. Yes it is." She looks at me again and there is a lull. It is that awkward moment one drinks to overcome. Inspired, I invite her to one.

"Say, would you and Jake like to join me for a drink? I'm on my way now."

"Well, sure. Why not?" Wow, I'm surprised. She's spontaneous.

We walk quietly in the gentle mist. Jake follows close behind.

"He won't try to go in the street now?"

"Oh no. Only at the robot. He gets confused."

"Yeah, I know how he feels."

It's not just her accent that captivates me but her mouth and her eyes, too. Her mouth simply makes the words differently and when it does, it seems more beautiful. Her words make me wonder what it might be like to kiss her lips.

"Is he really deaf?" I ask.

"Oh yes. Deaf as a bat."

Deaf as a bat? Now that's sexy.

"At least he can taste. Maybe losing one sense made the other stronger."

We reach the pub and step inside. She hangs her jacket by the door.

"Jeanette!" The first person to see her recognizes her.

He crosses the room, a gameshow smile on his face.

"How long has it been?" He asks as he meets her at the door.

"Six months, I think. What are you doing these days?"

"I'm renovating a house down the street," pointing, he edges me out of the way.

"You're not cooking anymore?"

"I teach cooking in the evenings and renovate during the day."

I start to feel uncomfortable, like someone hit the pause button. I know I shouldn't but I do. I'm still standing by the door, like a nun on a nude beach and I contemplate stepping back out into the rain.

"Renovating, cooking—they're both so spiritual to me—the body of Christ."

What the hell is that supposed to mean? Her friend's voice starts to annoy me. I was on my way to have a drink. This woman and her suicidal dog shouldn't change that, should they? I make my way to the bar, order a Bushmill's and look for somewhere to sit. All the stools are taken, so are all the tables.

"Four dollars." The bartender hands me my drink. I give him a five and take a hard swallow. The whiskey stings my lips. It has a familiar, soothing taste. I take another, smaller sip and hold it in my mouth. There's no place to sit at all. People walk by me in both directions. Some disco-looking guy with a web page bumps me without regard and I spill my drink on my shirt. "Fucker," the word pops in my head.

It frustrates me that the European has frustrated me. I was feeling pretty good today. The rain delivered a mellow nostalgia. I was comfortable in my independence. She had to bring it all back up again, remind me of what I forget to miss.

I've got to find someplace to stand. I scan the room and notice her sitting with a large group of people at the best table in the place, wedged between the Christ-bread carpenter and some guy with green hair. Well, at least they're comfortable.

There is a fine balance between loner and socialite where peace-of-mind resides. I wouldn't say I've come close to understanding that place but at least I'm aware of it. Most days I find myself bouncing like a sing-along ball through the changing lyrics of my desire. Just as I seem to be reaching some semblance of rhythm, the cadence picks up and marches me toward some newly devised compulsion. Or I meet some woman with a dog.

I swallow the second half of my whiskey in a gulp and motion to the bartender for another. "Another Bushmill's please and um—one for my date." Might as well get one for later.

He pours two more glasses. "Eight bucks."

I hand him a ten and take the drinks in my hands. Two guys at the table behind me rise to their feet and slip on their coats. Thank God. I walk to the two-seater and throw my coat over a chair.

It is not being alone which drives a fellow mad. Rather, it's the possibility that the seclusion may pass. There is strength in the comfort of solitude but never enough to defend against the compulsion of company. Like a deaf dog, silence brings hunger.

My glass makes rings on its coaster.

"She's such a bitch! Always talking behind everyone's back. Dude,

Gordon McGregor, *Sotol Swirls*, 2004

did you hear what she said about Lewis?" The guys at the table next to me lean over their drinks, rolling in conversation. "I'd fuck her, dude—but I mean that's all—what a bitch!"

A river of humans flows between the bar and me. I watch the various faces as they pass. I wonder what they do when they're not here pretending to be a commodity. I picture them practicing their smiles in their full-length mirrors. Do they feel as compelled as I do? I guess that's obvious. But do they struggle with the same disparity between having and being? I doubt that as I watch a guy with big teeth stare at some debutante's tight ass.

"I don't need any of that, dude. I just wanna work her over is all. She's got some incredible tits." My fraternity brother neighbors continue their banter. "Lewis says she's one kinky chick too, man. I bet she'd do anything."

Maybe the key is to embrace the libido and slight the soul.

I shoot the last of my second Bushmill's.

No, the conflict between loneliness and love is always there, even when overlooked. I've tried to ignore it before but I can never avoid a certain tragic guilt, like I've amputated the part of my soul that gives birth to the most subtle sparks of faith and meaning.

The warm glow of whiskey is starting to seep through me and it takes a moment to notice the tongue on my hand. Startled, I pull away. Jake has returned. Too bad his owner doesn't share his taste in hands. Actually, no—I take that back.

The fact is I don't even know her and she's forgotten all about me. Maybe I should dye my hair. I'm halfway through my third drink when the date-rape boys decide to include me in their debate. "Dude, see that chick over there? The one with the fat ass?" I follow his pointed finger across the room.

"Yeah, I think. With the red sweater?" I play along.

"Dude, on a scale of one to ten, don't you think she's a cow?"

"Well, I can't see her face but judging from the rear, yeah she's pretty cowish."

"Ha! See, dude—this dude agrees—she's a fuckin' cow, man."

"Dude, he said he couldn't see her face! That doesn't mean shit."

I seem to have started an argument.

"Who gives a fuck about her face with an ass like that, dude!"

They're clearly loaded.

I lean back into my chair hoping to disassociate myself from their discussion. People begin to stare. I move to the other seat at my table, attempting to draw an imaginary line between myself and the "dudes."

The man who lived in this flat before us had only one leg. I never actually met the man but I heard about his amputated limb from our landlady, Fiona.

"I didn't even notice when I first met him, picked him up from the airport on my birthday. I'd had about four bottles of wine. Would you like some more wine?"

We've just moved in and we're at some sort of welcome dinner, meeting Fiona-the-landlady's "partner." She pours us both some more box wine. My hangover has already begun. "I thought he was tired from the flight when he was going up the stairs. He carried his bag the whole way and then going up the stairs. He hadn't programmed his leg for stairs, just for flat surfaces. I asked him if he was tired from the long flight. I said, 'Oh, you must be tired!' and he just said, 'No, I lost my leg.'" She says all of this very quickly, in one long sentence. "Lost his leg. As if it were his luggage or something!"

I eventually determine the man was in some sort of motorcycle accident. Avoiding either a child or a chicken, he swerved into a tree. I'm not quite sure. Regardless, he now has a robotic leg which he plugs into his laptop computer to designate the terrain he expects to encounter. I assume it sets the length of his stride. I'm not sure how he gets the leg to start and stop. There must be some kind of button. But if there's a start button, why isn't there an 'I'm going up the stairs' button and an 'I'm walking up a hill' or an 'I'm running from a pack of wild dogs' button. I know these are features I would like on my robotic leg.

Anyway, the point is he lost a limb and as I sit in our flat copying another story from McSweeney's, I can't help but think about him and Jake the deaf dog and all my borrowed words. Maybe losing one sense does make another stronger and maybe it's like that in love and in life, too. But I've also heard an amputee can still feel a missing limb after it's gone. The brain dreams it alive, unwilling to let the memory fade from the senses. I like to imagine the brain does that all the time, with all sorts of things, even after we've replaced them with robotic legs and strippers and counterfeit creativity.

Maybe the inventions are the real source of our confusion because it's easier to pretend who are, to constantly reinvent who we want to be, to program ourselves for any possible terrain than to grow another limb.

The "dudes" are leaving but before they do, they stop and talk to the cow in the red sweater. Poor girl. I hope they're not saying anything mean. Their gestures are wild and their postures unstable. I can see they're slurring without hearing them speak. Fortunately, red sweater girl seems entertained, if not mildly amused. The drunken delinquents seem to have some hidden sense of civility. Or not.

I'm horrified to see the entire group suddenly turn to face me, huge shit-eating grins on their faces. One of them leans into the girl, wraps his arm around her oversized sweater and whispers in her ear. As they turn to leave, the guy who was arguing on her behalf shoots me a hidden thumbs-up. Moments later, Red Sweater is walking straight toward me with a couple of beers. Great. Just what I need.

"Those assholes actually think I've never heard that one before," she has one of those used-to-be-a-Goth voices. "Dude, that dude over there so wants you," imitating them. "He digs fat chicks, dude. It's like his fetish, dude." She's funny.

"Drink a beer," she offers, handing me a bottle.

"Thanks," I accept, pushing the extra chair out with my foot. "Look, those guys aren't my friends. I've never met them before."

"I know."

"I'm sorry about all that. Those guys are jerks."

"I thought they were funny."

"You did?"

"Sure. It takes all kinds. Life would be boring without pranksters," she smiles, toasts the universe, and chugs half her beer. "And here's one now! Hello Jake, you little prankster." The scrappy dog returns, his front paws on her leg. She pulls him into her oversized lap. He's immediately content, as she pets his fluffy head.

I'm not sure how long we talk. We each drink at least four beers but I don't really feel it. The conversation keeps me sober and by the time she's ready to leave, we're like old friends. "I'd better go. I have dinner plans. Are you ready, Jake?" she wiggles the dog, asleep on her lap. "I think he's ready. I'd better get my friend." Her friend?

She waves across the room. There are empty bottles and overflowing ashtrays and shots of tequila lined up on the European's table. The carpenter is about to pass out, the green-haired dot-commer's done too many lines and Jeanette, the European, just looks bored. She's overcome with relief when she spots Red Sweater's signal, says goodbye, and squeezes out.

"Thank God!" she exclaims, arriving at our table. "What the hell took you so long?"

"I was talking to your friend," Red Sweater explains through a smile. Her friend?

"Oh, you again, huh? Weren't you going to buy me a drink?"

"Your dog drank it," is all I can think to say but they laugh anyway, mainly because Jake actually looks like he did.

"Well, that's kiff."

"I could buy you dinner instead," I suggest.

"I don't know," she looks to her friend in the sweater. "Is that a fair trade?"

"Order a drink with dinner," she advises.

And that's how we meet.

Before we met I didn't need anything like a robotic leg, but there's something about love that forces us into identity. Where once a part of me was allowed to remain empty, now it must be filled. It's undeniable. Once you're in a relationship, it's a lot harder to lie about who you are. If you say you're a writer, you damn well better write. Or else find a really good bookstore to bootleg.

But even that becomes harder the longer it continues. Like an amputee's ghostly limb, I can feel that part of me calling from beyond. And the more she loves me, the more I want to be me—all of me.

So, I unplug myself from predictive terrain and write. It's no heartbreaking work of unfathomable genius, but it's mine. I hope she'll enjoy it and I hope other people could too, but really, it just feels good to stretch my legs.

The Smell of the Soul of Vengeance
Deivis Garcia

Muldrow was weary. He had been walking for two days under a pressing sun, and had staved off starvation with a mango and some stolen yams. He fell over, slept, shat himself.

When he awoke, Muldrow rinsed his pants in a parched creek. Back on Merchant Road, he looked back once more at the verdant landscape he hoped he would never see again. Resolute of step, he continued his solitary search for exile. Muldrow didn't know it, but today was his tenth birthday.

Along his path, he occasionally stopped to pick up a stone here and there. One day, he was going to kill Shitty Boss Mann.

Muldrow threw stones into the trees and watched reclusive birds flee wildly. His glazed eyes caught the sun, squinted, and a wave of pain, complimented by the nameless flux of color behind his closed eyelids, surged across his face. He hurled a stone at the sun with singular imperative. One day, when he was big and strong, he was going to strangle Shitty Boss Mann. Muldrow would have arms of steel by then and he would strangle Shitty Mann beyond recollection.

He kicked a stone and something scurried away in a flash, sending a cold sheet of fear through his spine; an unexpected lizard. On walked our tired Muldrow—or, in truth of sun and malnutrition—limped. Nacienne, his older sister, had long ago warned Muldrow of the great beast that haunted these woods. They called him 'Tuscanny' and he was as big as the night and made of stitched-leather; Tuscanny, the patched man with futbol skin, and the head of a boar.

Muldrow sped his gait, and managed a length more of distance. Feeling the mocking mirth of the unimpressed trees, Muldrow soon felt foolish before these silent spectators and slowed down, panting. There was only Muldrow and wilderness out here. His body quivering in exhausted spasms, he sat in the shade of a beard of leaves and allowed his heart and breath to slow.

Two years had passed since he had last seen Nacienne. Nacienne, silently procuring an already packed bag in the dark, her left hand on Muldrow's objecting mouth, creeping past the incompetent door and out into night and wonder. His sister remained forever swallowed by the dark-blue envelopment of rippling memory, outlined, for Muldrow, in the mythic image of a parting moment. Though he long ago lost track of his sister's age, Nacienne, or her ghost, would be seventeen by now.

What he did still sharply remember of Nacienne though was her telling him how Tuscanny's favorite snack was little runaway children. Even his best friend, Rimolaine, had—by inferred connotation—confirmed this horrible truth and, so, deeply impressed the grim detail as an undeniable idiosyncrasy. What Rimolaine had told him was how his very own oldest brother had been wolfed down by Tuscanny's indiscriminant jaws; Rimolaine effectively proved this to Muldrow by squinting and barely remembering his brother's name.

Nacienne, however, was a liar. She had sworn that she would never leave and, when she eventually did leave, she had then sworn by post that she would come back for him very soon. She never did, and so she was a liar.

Muldrow's shadow was now, a stretch later, directly beneath him. Painfully tilting his head back, he grimaced at the sun. Right now, Rimolaine and the others were eating rice. Rice. He swore he could smell warm rice.

Muldrow cursed, spat, broke a stick in two, and stared at his muddy feet. He ignored the interchanging images, illusory scent, and replenishing promise of rice. This, he knew, was Bastard Magic.

The bastards, however, all those bastards and their bastard dogs that live in this world and its ebbing border, would never find him. Bastard Shitty Boss Mann and his dog-men could look in all the likely places. The steaming stew of villages, Muldrow's cousins' tin-roofed shacks, the occasional church, the gnarled exasperated fists of trees in the meadows throughout, the river bloated with depth, the bone-yards, and, of course, the feather coops.

They could search all these places and the like but they would never consider following the paths that led to Merchant Road, the sole line of passage that cut through this indifferent forest.

No, Muldrow would never dare past Tuscanny, the Expanding Legend. That was the farthest their thoughts would take the dog-men and their master. Muldrow was as genuinely confident about this as he was genuinely afraid of the great beast of the woods who ate runaway children. This magnificent, fluid, cold swell of fear was the last and only place left for Muldrow to hide his face. Definitively.

They'll never find me, thought Muldrow and, naturally, fainted under the sun's incessant display.

In the meantime, as time softly conveyed its impressions, weak sick dying Muldrow snored.

A dream came from the air, hovered, spiraled in concentric circles of eight, and swept down upon him.

Instant, furious, and boiling with impatience, the dream held flash-fast with its five-sided iron talons. Doled out from five kaleidoscopic and exacting points of random circumference, the sense of space, time, weight, volition, and smell were woven into a swimming sensory helix. In short, this dream was, and was not, one.

—(One, or None, or, Sometimes, Some)—

In the murk of inky, heavy air, Muldrow the Fear running across a bridge with eyes closed. Under his running, the bridge beneath his runners becomes imperceptibly, pace by pace, softer.

Eyes now open, halfway across the giant tongue, two yellow gleaming tusks arising from the sides of the cavernous maw at bridge's end, reach upwards twice into the now gaseous green sky (or smell) of murderous invective.

Tuscanny's red, red eyes stare down at Muldrow as he runs runs runs...toward the promise of digestion—reaching finally, a pestilential end.

And:
Muldrow the Anger, teeth gnashed, punching Rimolaine (in the roaring foam of violence that is normally reserved for oceans) squarely on the ear in alternating swings of eventual recognition and perpetual loss. His underwater shadow leans across a desert that spans an overlapping memory, all the while shouldering the archaic Rage of Cain against the humiliating fact of famine. Rimolaine, brother in chains, laughing the kind of thunder that is almost soundless, balances two bowls of rice.

Or:
Muldrow the Initial Levity, as an infant child, tied snugly to Nacienne's back; she, dancing rhythmically with Wretched Vile Filthy Shitty Boss Mann. Shitty Boss Mann, smiling teeth of metal corn, stenching of imported cologne, dancing a primitive beat of syncopated forgetting with Lanky Absence Nacienne. Muldrow, leathered by rage, becomes a pair of batting black wings upon his sister's back, acquiring Babylonian ambition as he pathetically tries to lift her up up and away into an answer unseen. Outside, a rift awaits its implicated birth.

Also:
Muldrow the Stone; so small that no one would even bother to kick him, pick him up and throw him. Muldrow the Unmoving _____, is keeping the village and tomorrow's yesterdays at bay with the impossible strength of his despair. A focus so supernatural, he is rendered a pebble, too insignificant, faceless, to be ground to dust...

And lastly:
Muldrow the Revolution, rising Rising RISING in the east. It is from the side of a hill that he towers with skin of stitched-leather, wild boar tusks protruding from jaw, and yellow and black smoke pluming from his snout. Muldrow the Expanding Night Sky extending his patched boogeyman hand and plucking Shitty Filthy Boss Mann by his mousey mouse-tail, concluding a pathetically scrambled attempted escape. Dirty Inverted Shitty Boss Mann now pleading for increments of more life. Muldrow the Retribution (and Occasional Redundancy), laughing a cloud of erasure, makes to finish off the little nothing when—shitty boss Mann swings leaps grabs counter-revolutes onto Muldrow's waning hand. Mann reveals shining fangs of metal corn, and takes a

Muldrow awoke with a start, heart of an unmanned train. He looked up and saw the sun, unconcerned now, was easing away.
Shadows bled from every leaf and limb. Muldrow had lost a good part of the day and so continued his walk with twilight's heightened imperative. Twigs

snapped everywhere, and Muldrow's attention seemed to reach much farther at every snap. The arbitrary language in this wilderness had taken on a glyph pregnant with monstrosity.

Tuscanny and his laughter; in his running, Muldrow thought of the old fable, and traversed it via the only way his memory could allow; namely, the way Nacienne had first told it to him when he was just able to walk, and not too much later, work:

Tuscanny's Laughter

There was once a great feast not too many generations ago.

At this great feast there ate and drank a foreigner who possessed the unnatural appetite of a river swollen with torrent.

The locals, who were at the time almost getting used to outside notions, had given him a regal welcome only to be exasperated by this devil's demanding belly-hole.

He ate and drank as if he had just come down into the world and only food and drink could keep him from floating back up to wherever it was he had descended from.

Soon enough, the reality of their material poverty intervened and this drunken nothing-man was next fed ironic shrugs and bitter shaking of heads instead of more food and drink.

He looked about him and saw fields of scattered bone. He had eaten roast pig after pig after pig by himself and had left the village dry of banana gin. When the wave of satiation came to him, he whispered he was going to go rest while they prepared his breakfast for the following day.

Faced with the wall of making something from nothing, and the heavy fact that this devil-man had not yet squared away their already mounted indignation, they beat him appropriately into a resounding murder and left him and his personal death deep and far in the dark dark woods. "Devil", they had said, "let the ants have you."

The sleep that followed them home that night was of the kind that is sweet and dreamless.

Days of work and habit ensued, fulfilling their merest of expectations, and again they were filled with the heavy honey-sleep.

Three nights later, however, the village was awoken by a piercing cry.

Another, then another still.

The locals, sleep still in their bodies, had one by one discovered that their children were missing from their beds.

Torches in hand, they began the search.

When they squinted their attentions towards the dark dark woods, they saw all their children, as precise as ants, filing slowly up the hill that led to the road of merchants.

After screaming one by one, they very quickly caught up with the somnambulant procession of their young and discovered the unseen and floating phenomenon.

There, extending from the deepest deep of the dark wood, came a ribbon of the sweetest, most tantalizing, scent of delicious roast pig.

It was a smell of roast suckling that was so absolutely enticing, that it was, beyond the shadow of a doubt, impossible.

This was the Smell of the Soul of Vengeance.

Realizing they had rendered punishment unto the foreign devil with such force that they had beaten him into Legend, they instantly remorsed their quick and violent lines of action and swore themselves as far away and opposite a direction from murderous retribution as humility would allow.

The children, still in the daze of the zombie's suggestion, were then fittingly waked up with a good smack each and safely marched home.

As they filed homeward though, they heard a rumbling, volcanic, laughter. Somewhere from within the encompassing obscurity of the woods, the devouring guest, who by now surely had the head of an animal, set down his lone rule:

"I am learning to fast." came the swine's growling ordinance.

Then, one by one turning around, they saw him for a monumental instant.

There again, just above the trees and the scent, he peered down at them with his grimacing boar's head, tusks gleaming insolently.

Around him was an expanding dark-blue cloak bejeweled with a conspiratorial moon.

The Smell of the Soul of Vengeance had entered upon him, and he was now as big as night.

The name of 'Tuscany' too, a residue from now on to be found and pondered upon every morning pillow, had wafted silently from a negative space and set itself comfortably upon hereditary memory.

Henceforth and fittingly, it is a well-established fact that all who dare to venture through the woods past the merchants' road are categorically spat back out as bone.

This was, as it came to be known, 'Tuscanny's Laughter.'

The people of the village returning to their beds that night, found their homes to be a slightly smaller and dearer fit to a world that was now slightly bigger.

From an indeterminate distance, a dog barked.

Muldrow picked up his pace and advanced with might from a forgotten reserve. A wave of fire again surged across his face, an echo from Shitty Boss Mann's fist.

"Your best is not good enough!" the fist had said.

Muldrow, however, no longer agreed with the closed wisdom of a fist anymore. This is why he had stolen away two nights before his tenth birthday without telling anyone.

Night was well around him now, and the moon, despite its preceding all of mankind, his witnessing, artifices, and aesthetic, appeared above as if on theatrical cue. Soon Tuscanny and his foreign appetite would for the third night in a row search out these forbidding woods for the vagabond Muldrow.

Muldrow's own stubborn fear, pain, and capital hunger, however, would once again contend the drooling man-boar's grasp. He would subsist; there was no other choice.

If he survived one more night, just one more night, then Tuscanny and his laughter and his tusks and his infinite internal gravity would cease to exist, negated by the despairing determination that peers delicately beyond Legend and all its periphery. Muldrow would send it all to smoke by the persistent act of waking up—again—just one more time.

Subsist.

After this would come time, space, and recollection.

The hour of the night and its cooing shadows, broken and unfolding, set the stage.

Muldrow, glassy-eyed, delirious, and in the compelling tedium of starvation, looked around in all directions. He could have sworn he smelled the succulent flesh of roast pig.

His senses danced.

If he survived just this one night, his tenth year, Muldrow swore that he was going to find his ghostly sister Nacienne and call her a liar to her face. There was no encompassing adversity in this thought, but it would have to do for now.

In his walk, it occurred to him that, as dark as it was, his eyes were trying so hard to adjust to the failing light, that the idea of a cool white fog, despite the surrounding heavy blue obscurity, nonetheless impressed itself upon his scope. Nearby, hunger and delusion shuffled a slow soft-shoe.

In the paling dark Muldrow came upon a bridge.

Gordon McGregor, *Hyperdrive,* 2004

Jane and I at Home One Sunday
Anthony Tognazzini

Tognazzini

Issue 1.5

253

For starters, you see, there's Jane and me. It's a fact solid as a parked car, plain as a piece of bread, unshakable as your own skin though some facts are harder to remember than others. We stay home weekends. Every morning I look up to see our cardboard cut-out desk, paper forks and spoons, plastic shirts: red, green, gray and Jane in a dress. Our room is very small, especially when it rains. The clean light on the window is slapped away in gusts. It goes like this:

We wake up in the morning and Jane says hello. I wait for a minute before saying, "Hello."

I try to stand up.

Jane tries to stand up.

Ever seen a room too tiny to stand in, too small even to draw the blinds? The kind of place you spend all day picking lint from the bedspread? We've got it. We look out on the rain and stay mum. It's a divided world where some people have it better, some worse. We leave well-enough alone and drink our coffee. Jane's eyes are flat. I don't complain because I am a waiter. There's a restaurant ten blocks from our house that serves chicken sandwiches and soup, among other things, and that's where I work, waiting. In the afternoons I walk to work and put on an apron, pick up a tray and wait. I bring pastramis and chilled tossed salads while waiting. Thank you, I say, and enjoy yourself.

I get so used to waiting that at home the habit is difficult to break. I wait while Jane is in the kitchen. Sometimes she's gone for a few days and I do nothing but stare intently at the telephone, expecting a flock of shrill rings to fill the room like injured birds. When Jane is here, I can't even get up for coffee. I hear her in there dropping spoons, breaking cups. Flat Jane is a sharp coffeepot woman in the kitchen.

Jane wears dresses and gestures with her eyes. Green dresses, black eyes. While I wait, I take notes. Over there at the desk in the notebook is me with my pen. I write everything down there. Happy birthday, wrote it down. We're out of butter, wrote it down. Every page in the notebook is scratched out, inked over in X's, cancelled for good. I imagine Jane asking what are you writing? Scribble, scratch. We're lucky.

Jane was married once to a man named Arnold Metcalf Miller. He was an engineer in some capacity I don't understand. It was recent. Better not to talk about it. Jane says she preferred him to me because he was consistent.

"Don't go back to him!" I beg. "I need you."

She says she doesn't think she will. Besides, he beat her. You think you know trouble?

It's the weekend and it's raining for an ark outside. The roof of the house is getting crushed. Our room grows smaller and twice as humid.

"Go for a walk?" I joke.

"Don't be an ass, My dress will get wet."

I wear a T-shirt. This is Jane and I at home.

At least it's a good building with plumbing, we tell ourselves. Some people have worse. We try not to mention it. Our room is too small for even bugs to live there. We'd like to look for some, but who has time?

Jane goes in the kitchen with a hairbrush, eyes like raisins. She squishes up her eyes when she looks in the mirror, wrinkles her nose. She's very interesting looking for a woman her age. I told her so once. We keep quiet.

No one knocks except the landlord. Name of Fred Dominick with breath like living torture. He told us this was once a good neighborhood, one of the few affordable. We felt lucky. The grocery has pickles, milk, butter. The grocery has sacks of old potatoes. Up five flights we climb with bags. We call our landlord Sewermouth. Rent is 375 with a two-burner hotplate.

"Did you pay Sewermouth this month?" I ask Jane.

"No, I thought you were paying Sewermouth," she says.

Our conversations go on like this. What is there to do? Wait. The bugs all left because there was no room to crawl. Our bathroom mirror is in the kitchen.

While Jane makes the coffee, I wear undershirts, waiting. Dressy Jane, T-shirted me. "Don't mention it," she says.

It's Sunday. On some days the quiet is hurricane-like. There's only breathing to be heard and the air gets stiff as cardboard. I know to leave well enough alone.

In the kitchen, Jane drops a spoon.

"For god's sake!" I yell, "I've never heard such a racket!"

Jane lets out a little strangled laugh like a horse. She drops a drawerful of cutlery on the white tiled floor and it sounds like an exploding factory. She stands there and laughs, her face gleaming like a tooth.

I run into the kitchen, screaming, "Get out of here with your factory!"

I try to flex my skinny arms over Jane's small horse laughs. Pony laughs. My undershirt is dirty. We stop to look at each other and our eyeballs stick and won't come undone. We muck around a minute in the tension. As far as I can tell, Jane is upset.

"Why?" she asks aloud, savoring the rhetorical.

I wait expectantly. Rain pounds the house.

For a minute Jane says nothing and then speaks very slowly. She says, "Empty, empty."

"Bad as with Arnold Metcalf Miller?" I ask.

She shakes her head.

"Bad as with punches in the gut?"

Jane unbuttons her dress to show off her shiny welts. There are dozens of orangish-blue contusions, puckered as puffed-up mouths. You think you've felt pain? I avert my eyes. The bruises are the color of liver and shine like little signs. All this in the notebook. The letters bleed onto the page, big glaring X's to show where I've been. I want so much to go outside.

"Nothing's perfect," I say.

She knows I'm right and begins to cry.

"I'm no Mister Make Everything A-OK," I admit.

"I know, I know," she sobs. Her raisin eyes squeeze water through thin flesh slits.

I go back to the desk and sit. She knew, and I appreciate that.

"Jane," I say.

She tells me she needs to go to the hospital. I jump up, appreciating the excuse.

"Why?" I ask, suddenly angry, "Why? Appendicitis? Tonsillitis? Some-kind-of-itis?"

A scream escapes Jane's teeth.

"Shhhhh," I say, "the neighbors!" She knows as well as I our walls are made of tissue. The neighborhood is old and feeble. Our quiet has kept our contract. Sewermouth thinks we are good, happy kids. It's nothing to mention.

"Jane," I say, "I am going outside."

Jane screams shrill arrows. I sit fearfully on the bed to put on socks. Her dress is still around her waist, mealy chest spilling out all over. Of course, the telephone rings. Jane picks it up, screaming Who is it? In one sock I watch Jane's face go placid as jelly. She holds a hand over the receiver saying, "You know who it is."

"No, I don't," I say not knowing.

"Yes, yes you do," she says.

I say, "Who?"

"It's Arnold Metcalf Miller."

My stomach rolls like a grind mill. Of course.

"What does he want?" I ask.

"He says he loves me."

Bjorn Andersson, *Axelmossen, part 1*, digital C-print, 2003

Jane's voice is very small. I sit on the bed by the window while rain beats the house like a fist.

"I'm in love with you," I tell her.

"I know you are but what am I," she says.

"I'm in love with you," I say again.

"I know you are but what am I?"

Jane's voice sounds like it's coming from another century. I look down at my feet. My socks are not clean.

"That's better?" I ask. "You want punches in the gut?"

I make trick fists, holding up two string-limp arms. Jane's face is dead as plaster, her hair hangs over in wiry loops.

"Let me talk," she says.

"You want an engineer in a better neighborhood? If you want we can find a better house, you know."

She says for me to go for a walk, go down six blocks to work with the apron, tray and sandwiches, start waiting, and when I come back she'll make toast.

"Just hang up," I say.

"No," she says, "toast."

I put on my shoes and go to the door. She yells at me to go to the store while I'm out. "Pickles and bread," she says, "take an umbrella." I walk outside and rest my skull on the door. I can hear her talking. Her murmurs sweep after me like the ghost of fingers.

In the street I feel worse. I am shivering, T-shirted, in the downpour and the streetlamps are snapped in half. Rain and tears get all mixed up. I open the umbrella whose fabric hangs in tatters from a bent metal frame. I decide to throw it away, only there are no garbage cans in sight. I imagine myself spending the day curled in a garbage can, tidy cylindrical mausoleum, burning T-shirt and jeans for fuel. Today had started off as Sunday. Who knew?

Get a cab, I tell myself.

I flap my arms and stagger in the rain, singing songs about taxis in a high whirring voice. One hunches up to the curb, its motor turning over. I dive in head-first with my streaming umbrella. The cab driver's face is like a plate of eggs.

"Just drive me around the city," I say to him.

He doesn't respond.

Again, "Just drive me around the city."

The cab driver only blinks slowly, his black moustache full as a mop. The inside of the cab is decorated with pinwheels and children's drawings.

I take hold of the driver's head and shout my instructions in his ear. I continue shouting until I realize he is deaf.

I say, "Oh," then sit back in the seat and say nothing. He accelerates away from the curb and begins driving me around the city.

Three hours pass. I take notes. The pinwheels in the cab turn and I compose writerly lines like Whither goes the love-struck fool: a-field, a-far, to mossy, blackened depths, etc.

"Ugh," I say and scratch them out in my mind. I console myself with the thought of my job waiting, a good building with plumbing, Sewermouth's affordable rent, love's continually ragged disequilibrium. I am worried.

"Better off than a lot," I say.

Buildings streak around us in the rain. It's spring, only there are no flowers and the bare branches of trees close in on themselves like fans. You've heard of emptiness? I smile anyway, holding up the corners of my mouth with two fingers.

When we get back to the building, Egg-Face tells me the fare is one thousand dollars. I get out my thin, floppy wallet. I remember that I have no money and hold up my hands in good-natured helplessness. I apologize. I dissemble. I become a blizzard of apology. The driver laughs into his moustache. He smiles, nods, and shakes my hand. I embrace him warmly, feeling a surge of immanent brotherhood. He gives me a pinwheel, I give him the warped, useless umbrella. We part the best of friends.

On the curb I see Sewermouth. His plastic slicker is red and blue, the rain makes mist on his thick bifocals.

"Got the rent?" he asks.

I tell him to come and knock tomorrow. I say, "Come and knock," beaming. He thinks we're good, happy kids. Better not to mention.

"How's the Mrs.?" he asks, friendly.

I avert my nose.

"Just fine," I say.

He thinks we're married too. Oh boy. Tomorrow if he comes I'll tell him the wife has the money and isn't in at the moment. Little lies are okay. We'll get it eventually and keep our quiet contract. Worry is my middle name.

"Such good kids," he bubbles, rotten-mouthed.

"Well," I add for good measure, "be seeing you."

"Be seeing you," he hisses.

I give him the pinwheel. We part the best of friends.

I climb the stairs of my building searching for my keys. I know I put them in my pocket, only I cannot find my pocket. I am here in the hall imagining bare walls and no one responding to hello, thinking for starters there should be Jane and me. I fall through the door without any groceries.

"Hello?" I ask.

In the kitchen I see a note saying I went to the hospital be back soon love jane. You can imagine encouraging? This could possibly signify the hopeful refusal of Arnold Metcalf Miller's overtures. I am thrilled to the point of confusion. I begin to brush my face and shave my tongue. In the bathroom/kitchen mirror there are large, dark circles under my eyes. Black caves, hollow holes. Need to sleep, I tell myself, throwing open cupboards. In the baking dish I put toast. The oven's an inferno. I sling my wet T-shirt on a hook above the stove.

When I go to the bed I try to straighten myself out but keep curling into a spring. I turn there, wiry and wound, trying to relax. The phone rings bloody murder. This is my waiting job, listening and waiting. Has she decided? Will I bring the right thing? In my middle, fingers and toes, anxiety blossoms like tiny flowers. I put it out of my mind. Rain crushes the roof of the house, making it come down around me, cozy as an envelope. My brain is full of bric-a-brac: Hairs in the carpet, moments of impurity, living in a bad neighborhood—there are worse things. I think: Jane. The darkness has teeth. Shadows smother me to sleep.

Later, I hear her voice, not too distorted by whispers, say she is there. I see her in the room, standing, walls around her like a jacket.

I sit up and say, "Ahem, hello."

Her breath cuts warm gullies in the air. I stay very silent. Finally I ask, "What about you-know-who?"

We don't have to say his name. Do we have to repeat everything?

She says that's nothing.

"You're staying?"

She says, "Shhhhhh, the neighbors."

I say, "Shhhhhh, the neighbors."

We were right with each other, our whispers like rafts in the churning gloom.

"What about the phone?" I ask.

"Don't answer."

"The hospital?"

She unlatches her dress and shows me bandages. White gauze held in place by X's of surgical tape. We gape. You think you've understood something after forever trying to figure it out? We were lucky.

The toast is done and the smell of brown bread paints a spell on the house. She comes to the bed in her undone dress and I hold her in my stringy arms like a piece of crumpled paper. We say love. We say need. We say we get the picture.

"Do you promise?" I ask.

"What?"

"What?"

I whisper for her to forget it, crossing out lines in my mind. Some things are better not to mention.

The telephone rings and rings. We ignore it. We tell each other, then, it is safe to cry until we run out of tears, even if we never run out of tears. Our bodies crack like static in the growling dark.

Curl, Curve
Rick Agran

Her fingers intertwining, arms unfurling overhead,
arch in the curl, in the curve of her foot,
stretch and flex of her yawn curls through her, curve,
curve, curve of the earth, curve of her hip,
curve of the road leashed with a black velvet tether
like night's press against the window,

or the coal kitten's curl, limp by the scruff
in her mother's mouth, the dangle of the bucket
in the dark mouth of the well, yawn, yawn,
the well's mouth echoing sound, finger tracing the curve,
tucking her bangs' curl behind her ear so they will not fall
forward into her world

invisible, inferred curve of world,
black shadow curling around its own feet
half curve disappearing, a multitude
of smiles curving upward, frowns curving earthward,
and again the yawn, the stretch, the curl

the curve of the water around the world, evening's
blue blanket rippling in the wind of its own spinning,
curl of the wave toward the curve of the beach,
widening circles of the raindrops' ripples

like her small yawn, the curve of her lip,
the curve of her shoulder upon which you curl up
and yawn, yawn, again the yawn,
the stretch and flex of her yawn curls through her,
the unfurled curve, unfinished curve of the world

Gordon McGregor, *Swoosh,* 2003

FISTS
J. Robert Beardsley

each day I throw
my fists calmly into
the hard sides
of a cinderblock

first knuckles, then palms,
meat side, then bone side

one day I will burst through,
brick dust settled into the
spiderweb lines of my hand

the grey shards bloodstained

one day my fists will
strike and be harder
than any brick.

enough to crush wood
and bone, enough
to take walls and doors
and smite the smug sun
from the sky.

now I breathe deeply
and strike—one blow
upon another, and
tighten my fists, just,
at the moment of impact.

Untitled
Stefan Boudreault

Untitled, 2003
Untitled, 2004

Untitled, 2004
Untitled, 2004

Underground Arteries
dsankt

Too Close for Comfort, 2004
Around the Bend, 2004
Pillars, 2004

Skate and Die Dude, 2003

Personal Safety, 2004
The Old v. The New, 2004

Surviving Consciousness
Katherine Fraser

The Void, oil on canvas, 2003
The Bride, oil on canvas, 2004

One of the Guys, oil on canvas, 2004
The Intrepid Soul, oil on canvas, 2004

Teacher, oil on canvas, 2004
The Healer, oil on canvas, 2004

King George, oil on canvas, 2004
The Futile Charade, oil on canvas, 2003

Alan Duke, *August 11*, C-print, 2004

East Broadway, the real
Chinatown
Unconcerned
With the global empire
Of trinkets
Not colored
By the stench
Of fish
No market hegemony
But density
Thick with Chinese
Faces and words
On the walls and air
In the rules of games
Little privacy for
Balconied clothes
And boxes
And furnishings
From homes
Inside-
Out

Scents evoke memory
But so can words
East
Broadway
Sleepless, humid nights
In a shared apartment
Who cares
Who hears
Who cares
About anything
While wet
With fertile
Momentum

Censure and Ascension (A Brotherhood)
Dewayne Washington

I been beat down
For transgressing
Taking my license
Speaking my turn
At truth

Your crew
Pretending
To old ways
Coming up on me
Where I sit
Streetlamp lit

Descending
From thought
I been swatted
A moth
At the edge of our hands
One side light
The other dark

Snared
Between new pipes
And fences
And grass
Installed whitely
A measure
Placating Dark China

You thug niggers
Pissing in my grass
To make it your own
Teaching me
What lesson
But to fear the blackness
Of my voice

I walk upright
Broad-shouldered
But wary
Amongst my kin

Jason Larkin, *Untitled*, C-type, 2003

Afloat
Marshall Sokoloff

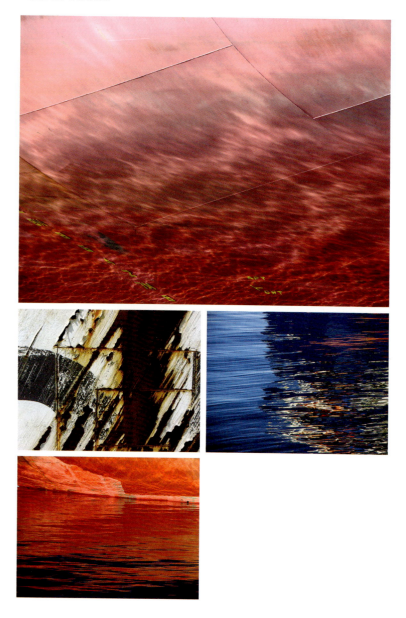

Three Sisters #6, digital C-print, 2004
Salt #13, digital C-print, 2004
Three Sisters #2, digital C-print, 2004

Three Sisters #9, digital C-print, 2004

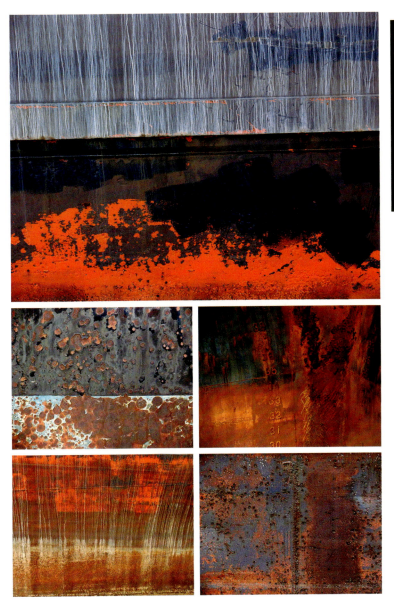

Salt #22, digital C-print, 2004
Three Sisters #1, digital C-print, 2004
Salt #18, digital C-print, 2004

Salt #10, digital C-print, 2004
Sugar #3, digital C-print, 2003

Awareness in Disaster
Adam Walko

A Meeting of the Minds, charcoal and graphite on paper, 2004
Lift, oil and graphite on canvas, 2003

Step One, oil on canvas, 2004

facing page:

Second Try, oil on canvas, 2004
First Try, oil on canvas, 2004
Choke, graphite on canvas, 2003
Remember Me, oil on canvas, 2004
Float, oil and graphite on canvas, 2003

Contributors (listed alphabetically)

1.2, 1.3, 1.4 DERRICK ABLEMAN is actually a twist of the wind, often with more luck than sense. He would like to thank you for your time, attention, and eventual sympathy. (104, 140, 176)

1.5 RICK AGRAN has authored two books so far: *Pumpkin Shivaree*, a picture book for kids, and *Crow Milk*, poems for big people. He's at work on a second book of poems called *A Short History of Longing*. He teaches fine artists to write at New Hampshire Institute of Art. He catches the occasional frog on the Cockermouth River and practices amateur tiger training with his amateur tiger, Miss R., for whom he has a deep and abiding love. (260)

1.0 AI-HZ is a video artist working and living in Paris. "Photography is more a diary, I use a Minox ML camera, small reflex, and I shoot like a flying fisher drunk, every day. In months leitmotives have coming: eyes child and punk attitude from the youth, abstract naive, sleeping persons with a purple aura around the head. All my sense is around beauty, and noise, dynamic visual sounds synchronize, and looking for the amazing sub reality." (8)

1.0, 1.4 Growing up in the shadow of New York City, **EDDIE ALFARO** has been greatly influenced by its energy. His diverse artistic influences range from poets to painters and musicians. Eddie's focus has recently moved from visual art and writing to acting in and directing commercials and short films, but he still feels all his work is connected and that art is a sacred thing. (27, 178)

1.4 DAVID J. ALWORTH is a writer living in New York City. He is completing a degree in creative writing and literature at New York University. He would like to gratefully acknowledge the editors of *Dirt* for their continued support of his work. He is indebted to his loved ones, especially Jeannine. Without her, he could accomplish nothing. (178)

1.5 BJORN ANDERSSON — "Friendly fire mistakenly got my jawbone broken and I had to go through surgery. Before the procedure I was given loads of pills and massive shots of tranquilizer. I think the nurse must have been curious of my questions about the different substances I was submitted to. ROHYPNOL + hard liquor = violence, antibiotics in the subsoil water ending up in our tubs, a society drowning in pills, a friend worried of what will happen if he stops taking his happy pills. Drugs pouring over the people, people navigating through their anxiety guided by happy pills or a hang-over spiced with aspirin...." (256)

1.2 COREY ARNOLD graduated with a BFA from the Academy of Art College San Francisco in 1999. Now living and photographing in Oslo, Norway, he commutes biannually to work on a crab fishing boat in the Bering Sea, Alaska. Corey is currently struggling inside to discover if he is a shit-kicking redneck or a sensitive artist. He would like to thank his cat, Sokken ("the sock") for all his tender love and support. (102, 106)

1.5 In longhand, **RICK AUSTIN** is slowly writing a collection of short stories (each of which features a character from *June*), and a novel (a picaresque) set in the Pacific Northwest in the 1880's. He lives in Arcata, California. Read more of his work, send up a holler, and lay eyes on him at his website. (226)

1.3 Hungarian, originally from Romania, **ANDREA BAKACS** graduated from Parsons School of Design in New York City with a Bachelor's of Fine Arts in Photography. Bakacs is featured in *American Photography 19* and has been published in *Photo District News*, *The Blow Up*, *Thrasher*, *Eastern Edge*, and *Martha Stewart Living*. Bakacs has shown nationwide in several group exhibitions and auctions, including *Snow Pictures*, her solo photography debut at Max Mara on Madison Avenue. (138)

1.2 BANKSY is a revolutionary with a base of operations in the United Kingdom. (108)

1.0, 1.4 BYRON BARRETT'S photos often focus on confinement. Much of his work examines how our environment subtly coerces us into fixed patterns of behavior. Many of his seemingly benign photos contain elements which reveal the limits placed on our ability to direct our futures, not in overtly devious or political ways but subtly in small, subconscious ways. Byron Barrett was born in Birmingham, England. He lives and works in Vancouver's Westend. (10, 177, 208, 219)

1.0, 1.1 MAURA BARTHEL'S short fiction has also appeared in *Monday Night*, *The Subway Chronicles*, and *Cherry Bleeds*. She lives in Astoria, Queens and is currently working on a short story but can't seem to figure out the ending, yet. (12, 16, 64)

1.0 SHANE BEAGIN is a self-taught artist from Torrance, California. He now lives and works in New York. His first love was photography; he has also dabbled in illustration and printmaking, but has recently dedicated himself to figurative painting. He makes his living as a graphic production artist for an advertising agency, where he is (perhaps naively) biding his time until he becomes famous. (18, 30)

1.2, 1.3, 1.5 J. ROBERT BEARDSLEY is self-deprecating to a fault, and though you might not expect it, is generally congenial. Some might say bubbly. Those people have been known to turn up missing. (109, 141, 261)

1.0 In the late 90's, **DAVID BERNSTEIN** gave up on his dreams of playing professional basketball and began to write. He currently lives in Missoula, Montana, where he is teaching and studying full-time at the University. (20)

1.5 STEFAN BOUDREAULT is from Montreal. Since graduating from the Dawson Institute of Photography in 2001, Boudreault has spent much time developing his style and shooting for local magazines. He recently relocated to Toronto to pursue editorial and commercial work. Boudreault sees his images as raw and contemporary reflections of everyday people, places, and things. (262)

1.0 Most recently **ALFREDO FERRAN CALLE'S** work was exhibited at The Armory Show in NYC and in May of 2003, Mr. Calle will have his first solo exhibit at Bailey Fine Arts Gallery in Toronto, Canada. Mr. Calle studied at the Llotja School of Applied Arts, Barcelona, and spends much of his time photographing in Europe, Canada, and the US. (6)

1.4 JOSE CARMONA is a recent graduate of Parsons School of Design, continuing to live and work in New York. Carmona's art is often either absurd, provocative commentary on events around him or a simple reflection of the intriguing thoughts that wander through his mind. He participates in the Parsons Alumni founded Soup Group. Their recent exhibition in Japan, *Peace*, reacted to current events in Iraq. (187, 194, 218)

1.1 TIM CARPENTER has been taking photographs for about three years, and he really needs to stop shooting for awhile and start editing and printing. He also needs a better answer (or, actually, any answer) for the question "So what kind of photos do you take?" His work can be seen off and on at the Jen Bekman gallery in Manhattan, as well as on his website. (84)

1.2 DANIEL CHANG lives and works in O.C./So.Cal. He is fascinated by all things big and small, high and low, enduring and ephemeral. His love for eating tasty treats is outweighed by his love for making tasty morsels of art. He loves to consume and be consumed. (110)

1.4 SCOTT CHESHIRE lives in New York, where he is working on a teaching degree and his first novel. (179)

1.3 TANIS C. CLARK finally stopped selling cocktails and moved to Chicago to go to college, so you should be proud of her. She was born in California and has since lived in Sweden, China, and Michigan. Recently she made peace with capital letters. (142)

1.0 WILLIAM CLIFFORD'S work has been published in the MTV book, *Pieces: A Collection of New Voices*; the literary journals *Fiction* and *Si Senor*, and the internationally distributed magazine *Zembla*. The story published in *Zembla* has been optioned to be made into a short film. In 2003, William partook in the inaugural Tin House Summer Writer's Workshop. For a living, he does what every man and woman secretly dreams of doing: he is a master Cue Card Operator at the Late Show With David Letterman. He lives in New York City and is at work on a novel. (21)

1.1, 1.2 OLIVER DETTLER has lived and worked in NYC for 10 years. Trained at Pratt Institute as a graphic artist. Avid cyclist and traveler. Collects printed matter on streets and sidewalks for collages. Works at the Guggenheim Museum. A fan of circles. (92, 112)

1.5 JESSE W. DONALDSON was born in Lexington, Kentucky, in 1979. He has lived and worked in Ohio, Costa Rica, Iowa, and currently resides in Brooklyn. (234)

1.4 RICHARD DOUEK is a NYC native, leading a double life; graphic designer by day, and writer by night. He enjoys writing in a multitude of genres, from modern, urban fiction to epic fantasy and science fiction. Writing takes up a large chunk of his spare time, and he is currently working on a novel as well as several shorter works. (183)

1.5 Delirious on monkey blood and sacred ash, witchdoctor **DSANKT** resurrects the dead with a potent mix of color, shadow, and texture. Voodoo bells jingle and skulls rattle as new life pours into the forgotten spaces that lurk in, above, and under the sprawling metropolis. Under night's cloak he stalks the rooftops; by day he scours the underground's murky depths for rusty nails and shiny trinkets. (264)

1.3, 1.5 ALAN DUKE is a painter and photographer currently living in Berkeley, California. (136, 160, 268)

1.5 NEIL FARBER was a founding member of the Royal Art Lodge in 1996. He had his first solo exhibition in 1998. He continues to work as both a solo artist and as a member of the Royal Art Lodge. (229)

1.0 JOE FIELDER loves you more fiercely than you could possibly know. (29)

1.2 ALEXANDER FONG received a B.A. in Philosophy from Wesleyan University, and a J.D. from New York University School of Law. He writes in spare time as a way of reorganizing the world. (114)

1.0 ARREN FRANK'S work explores the nexus of poetry and philosophy both in short verse and as lyricist for Noumenon. Currently focused on his role as the vocalist and acoustic guitarist for the quartet, he nonetheless possesses a modest body of unpublished writings; his appearance in *Dirt: Volume One* marks his first hardcopy publication of note. (33)

1.5 KATHERINE FRASER grew up in Maine as an only child, and finds that experience often reflected in her work, lending her paintings the qualities of memories or dreams. Life often strikes her as a string of moments, like a series of film stills, in which we observe ourselves. She is a recent graduate of the Pennsylvania Academy of the Fine Arts and the University of Pennsylvania. She greatly looks forward to the day she can quit waitressing and let painting pay all the bills. (266)

1.5 Hailing from Elizabeth, New Jersey, **DEIVIS GARCIA** is working on several short fictions, novellas, and is revising a collection of apocrypha titled *Song of Anthropos*. He also composed *BVH Presents: A Hillbilly Odyssey*, and Food Stamp Fury's *Manuscripts Don't Burn*. His broad artistic concern is for literature and music to meet somewhere down the middle in opera apertura or lyric-epics. He works in Montclair and collects harmonicas. (247)

1.1 D. DOUGLAS GOODMAN was born in 1980 and grew up in Connecticut, Long Island, and Florida. He has held many jobs in his short life, most notably as a pizza maker, waiter, film festival manager and print runner, bartender, coffee barista, and editorial assistant. His lifelong obsessions include superheroes, Ernest Hemingway short stories, Star Wars, and the New York Mets. His stories have appeared in *Spire*, *The Square Table*, and *Dirt*. He lives in Brooklyn. (67)

1.0 Currently a photo/visual arts student in Austin, Texas, **DAVID GULLEY'S** passion for photography began nine years ago in high school, where he was awarded the role of head photographer of the photojournalism department. In addition to taking pictures, he also enjoys painting, sculpting, and cooking. (33)

1.2 JOSHUA HAGLER divides his art time between painting, illustration, design, writing, sequential art, and teaching, which he has recently come to believe are all relevant to each other. He has had work selected in *American Illustration*, shown throughout the west coast including the Museum of Contemporary Art, and appear in children's books, novel covers, editorial illustration, concept art and storyboards for film, the web, and comic books. (135)

1.3 JAN HALLE, born 1967, Denmark, based in Tokyo, Japan. BA (Hons) Photography, University of Derby, 2000. Thematically, Halle's work is concerned with exploring the multiple layers of the modern urban landscape. Specifically focusing on the ambigious and fictional quality of seemingly mundane and intermediate public spaces. Inspired by the notion of the urban flaneur. His work has been published and exhibited in solo and group exhibitions in Japan, Europe, and the USA. (154)

1.3 JESSE HASSENGER was born and raised in Saratoga Springs, NY, which is several hours away from Utica. In 2002, he graduated from Wesleyan University with a major in English and a minor in poverty. By day, he works in publishing; by later in the day, he writes. His work has appeared in *PulpLit*, *PopMatters*, and *Block*, and on www.filmcritic.com. He lives in Brooklyn, and swears he doesn't usually write about himself in the third person. (143)

1.3 MIZUE HIRANO lives and works in Tokyo, Japan. She graduated from Tama Art University. Hirano draws pictures in oil and water-colors for books, magazines, and publicity. She likes to play with images of various colors and shapes that are difficult to express by means of words or concrete figures. Those images are her special pleasure. She loves her cat "Milk"—her nature is like a cat. (156)

1.1 SIMON HÖEGSBERG, who recently left/fled School of Media in London with a Bachelor's degree in photography, is currently seated between two chairs, one of which represents his engagement in photography, the other representing his innate love for literature and the possibility of writing a novel in which he tells no lies. He hopes life will be long enough to grant him both wishes. (76)

1.2 ELLEN HONICH holds a BFA in Painting and Printmaking from Virginia Commonwealth University in Richmond, VA. She currently lives in Seattle, WA, where most of her time is spent working on graphic design and photography. Her favorite color is blue and she has a web site. (114, 131)

1.0 GABBY HYMAN has published fiction, belles lettres, and poetry in national and international literary journals. He has sold shoes, farmed bananas in the Middle East, taught fiction in a Big Ten university, and edited web copy for many existing and failed dot-coms. He has lived in Alaska and Alabama, but currently favors states that begin with the letter C. These days he is working on a chapbook of poetry and his first screenplay. When he gets to heaven, he'll look up Malcolm Lowry, Ray Carver, and Lou Gehrig. (34)

1.1 SHIN IWASAKI currently finds himself in Oakland, California trying desperately to do something useful with himself. His photographs have been widely distributed between the numerous boxes in his closet. (97)

1.0, 1.1 ROSS JOHNSON, a repeat contributor to *Dirt* and a new resident of California, has been working as a photographer for 5 years. He began using a camera to record the unique beauty he encountered in his travels to India, Brazil, Mexico, and throughout the US. Johnson's work blends reality with the abstract and intimate introductions offered in his lifescapes and portraiture. (46, 47, 62)

1.3 NICK JONES lives in Washington, DC where he is a graphic designer and frequent macro photographer of random things. An expatriate of North Carolina, he was born fourth of five to a journalist father and non-profit founding mother. He is 26 years old. (158)

1.1 Born and raised in Brooklyn, NY, Amber Stewart (**PRECIOUS JONES**) is currently pursuing her BA in Creative Writing at the New School University in Manhattan. Her poetry has been published in *Spire Press Magazine*, *Rolling Out*, an urbanstyle weekly, and featured at www.strawberrypress.net. She is the co-founder of a Wednesday night poetry group and will be participating in a poetry workshop sponsored by the LouderARTS Project. Amber also loves her three Bs: Baked chicken, Books, and Butches. (75)

1.3 JANE KIM is a designer living in New York City. (158)

1.3 SIMON LADEFOGED lives and works in Copenhagen, Denmark. He finds inspiration in urban landscapes, his beautiful wife and son, and his 1973 Ford. (162)

1.4 ALLISON LANDA is an Oakland, California-based fiction writer who likes to cheat with poetry and essay. Don't tell. She's earning her MFA at Saint Mary's College of California, has lived in the rural Midwest and Eastern Europe, and is gleefully bereft of a day job. Her work has been featured in *Clean Sheets*, *Starving Arts*, *Cherry Bleeds*, *The Ledge*, and *Poetica Magazine*. (187)

1.4 JACOB LANGVAD was born in Copenhagen, Denmark in 1977. As a graduated photojournalist he started to explore the world of art and commercial photography. Often his work is a mix from both worlds. After working as artist in residence at Fabrica, Bennetton's communication research center, he moved to London in 2005 to focus on commercial work as well as personal photographic essays. (184)

1.5 JASON LARKIN is a multi-media visual artist working from London. He's recently contributed to *Black President* and *Kin* (BITE Festival) at Barbican, *French Institute* at the Royal Academy, and *Chinese Whispers* at Battersea Arts Centre. (269)

1.0 Originally from Lafayette, Louisiana, **MIGUEL LASALA** is a high school dropout who earned a degree in architecture 7 years later from the University of Louisiana. Upon graduation Miguel moved to New York and worked for architecture firms for two years until he decided to head to Costa Rica to photo-intern for the *Tico Times*. Miguel currently lives in Carencro, Louisiana, and is considering getting into the Boudin and Cracklin business. (13, 51)

1.1, 1.2, 1.3, 1.5 BRIAN LEMOND enjoys working as an editor of Dirt Press, viewing the opportunity as a means of using his compulsive tendencies for the greater good. Brian has found the reserves of courage to begin publishing his own written work in the same arena he has offered so many critiques. It should prove interesting.... He's also a sculptor, photographer, design partner at the Brooklyn Digital Foundry, and the President of the Experimental Modern Arts Collective (XMAC). (78, 115, 147, 268)

1.3 WILLIAM AND MARY LEMOND have recently pulled up their stakes in their longtime home of Houston, Texas, and are on the way to replanting them in Fort Worth. William is a veteran of the metroplex, and Mary sees the whole thing (quite correctly) as a big adventure. (167)

1.4 NANETTE LERNER'S fiction has appeared in *North Dakota Quarterly*, *Berkeley Fiction Review*, *Pangolin Papers*, *Fiction*, and *The Minnesota Review*. One of her stories was nominated for the Pushcart Prize. Currently, she is hard at work on her first novel, *The Man Upstairs*, taking occasional breaks for sunlight and fresh air. She resides in Brooklyn. (188)

1.1, 1.2, 1.3 JOSEPH MADDALONI, a native of Brooklyn, is the New York Plan Desk Manager for an international architectural firm which, previous to the appearance of his writings in *Dirt*, had been his captive audience. In addition to his poetry, Mr. Maddaloni is also an accomplished harmonica player and amateur historian, famed for "having more stories about Ebbets Field, Luna Park, egg creams, and all things Brooklyn than the Collyer Brothers had trash." (79, 116, 159)

Ted Buenz, an architect and writer living in Williamsburg, NY, compiled and edited the work of Mr. Maddaloni.

1.0, 1.2 JOSH MAGNUSON is the best new Austin writer of the first half of the last quarter of 2004. His talents include drinking large quantities of vodka and referring to himself in the third person. He divides his time between self-loathing paralysis, counting his stock options, and completing an MFA at Texas State University. He is survived by his lovely wife and two wonderful boys. (47, 118)

1.2 JIMMY MAIDENS, a former resident of Boring, MD, now lives in the Bay Area. (126)

1.4 DAVID MAISEL is a native New Yorker, presently living in the San Francisco area. His monograph of *The Lake Project* was recently released by Nazraeli Press. He is currently at work on *Terminal Mirage*, a series of aerial images of the surreal, apocalyptic landscapes surrounding Utah's Great Salt Lake. (200)

1.4 KIRSTEN MATTHEW was born and raised in New Zealand. She lives and works as a writer in New York. (202)

1.5 GORDON McGREGOR grew up on the west coast of Scotland and now lives and works in Austin, Texas. While relatively new to photography and without any formal training, he is trying to make up for a lack of experience with a lot of enthusiasm for the subject, in particular seeking out the small details that we normally miss during the hectic day-to-day rush through life. (243, 252, 260)

1.4 JON McMILLAN is a writer. He lives and works in New York City. (209)

1.4 MAT MEJIA is the Senior Art Director at DNA Studio where he resides in Los Angeles. His work has been featured in publications such as *Computer Arts*, *Flaunt*, and *Impress Webdesign Magazine of Korea*. An avid globetrotter, much of Mat's visual style reflects his frequent travels and love for surfing & snowboarding. His most recent commercial work can be seen in campaigns for Bacardi, Cingular, and *IdN Magazine*. (205)

1.3 Born in Seoul, Korea in 1980, **YE RIN MOK** moved to Los Angeles, CA in 1992, where she lives currently. She graduated from the University of California, Irvine in 2003 with a BA in studio art. Ye Rin contributes photography to a slew of publications including *Anthem*, *Mass Appeal*, and *Metro Pop*. Recently, her work has been shown in a solo exhibition at GR2 gallery in Los Angeles. (142, 172)

1.2 CAROLINE MOORE is a new media student at the University of Maine, but her passion is photography. Moore's work consists primarily of the transformation of personal space into surreal landscapes of life. She enjoys finding beauty in the surreal, the unusual, and the awkward—to find out what happens to the visual and emotional aesthetic when things are taken out of their natural spaces and put where they traditionally don't belong. (116)

1.2 VLAD NANCA works primarily with photography and installation. His works have been shown throughout Europe including Huesca cultural center and the Contemporary Art Museum in Bucharest. Nanca is the initiator of 2020, a master plan project which is preparing the cultural revolution in Romania in the year 2020. In January 2004, Vlad Nanca started the 'incepem' e-group of Romania young (sub) culture heroes. (108, 134)

1.0, 1.3 CAMILLE NAPIER is a teacher in Massachusetts. She abuses reading like others abuse drink. She is not in denial about it. (48, 164)

1.4 MARIA NAZOS has lived in places such as: Iowa City, Iowa; Athens, Greece; Chicago, Illinois; and as of now—the Bronx. Her work has appeared in *Word is Bond*, *Earthwords*, and *Nthposition*. (218)

1.4 A regular on the pages of *PDN*, *Communication Arts*, and other commercial trade magazines, **DANA NEIBERT** is currently pursuing interested inquiries from the art world including fine art galleries and *Aperture* magazine. Much of his work is inspired by his beautiful wife and daughter who frequently appear in his images. Dana was trained as a graphic designer at CCAC in San Francisco which still plays a role in his simple, graphic, and subtle compositions. His work is regularly exhibited—front and center—on his mother's refrigerator. (214)

1.2 KIZER OHNO is an artist poet with one eye to the future and one eye to the past. In all mediums, his career is committed to expressing and exploring the vast colors of human experience. Kizer Ohno currently resides in Houston, Texas. He can be reached via his website. (115)

1.5 ERIC OLDRIN was born in Oklahoma, during the Nixon administration. Right now, he lives in South Africa. For money, he produces animation. In his spare time, he writes short stories and runs in the woods with his dog named Sit. (240)

1.1 HARLAN OVERLIKE is a Chicago-based photographer who is driven by capturing those off moments we all fear may be witnessed by others—that point in time just before sneezing, falling off the chair, or getting distracted by the telephone. Overlike's sense of observation, balance, and multiple realities meld into images that are memorable, sometimes disturbing, and always moving. Exposing randomness and freedom is one of his ongoing projects. (82)

1.0 CATHERINE EVE PATTERSON is a writer. She has lived and worked in Vienna, Paris, London, New York, and San Francisco, and is the recipient of numerous arts fellowships. She's currently at work on the second title in her crime series, *The Eight-sided Ghost*, as well as a book of essays titled *True Confessions of a Capable Girl*, postcards from the counter-cultural front, and is often found in airports, a place she affectionately refers to as zero world. (49)

.1 SARAH H. PAULSON resides in Brooklyn where she is a practicing performance artist, writer, and cofounder of P.I.T. (Projects In Transit). Paulson directs and executes movement-based, endurance-oriented pieces in constructed and restrictive spaces. Most recently, *Sunset Beach*, a collaborative performance with performance artist Holly Faurot and sound artist Joel Mellin, premiered at P.I.T. in September 2004. Paulson writes: THE DAILY RITUAL IS ACCEPTED FULLY. THE DAILY RITUAL IS FULLY BODILY. (84)

.4 Based in Brooklyn, New York, artist and musician **IDA PEARLE** exhibits and performs internationally. Using her training in painting and drawing received while at The Cooper Union for the Advancement of Science and Art, Ida has expanded her gestural and figurative work to include cut paper collage. Inspired by real and imagined events, individual collages serve as poetic vignettes that often develop into a narrative series. (216)

.0 Born and rasied in Southern California, **AARON POU** currently resides in New York pursuing photography, among other creative pursuits. (60)

.0 DAVE PRAGER lives in Brooklyn, and constantly prays for reader feedback. (54)

.2 ariane resnick holds a b.a. in creative writing/poetry from the university of californa, santa cruz. having found that to be pretty much useless, she makes a living as a model, firedancer, and nanny. she occasionally performs at spoken word events in the san francisco area, and is always on the lookout (albeit lazily) for a publisher for her book: *spikette, the missing smurf*. (125)

.2 ZEV ROBINSON—Artist, born in Israel, grew up in Canada, then lived in NY, Spain, and elsewhere. Presently in London but won't be the last stop. Painted for over 5 years, then began working on photography, video, and new media projects. (124)

.3 MATTHUE ROTH lives in California. As a performance poet, he has been featured by Rock the Vote, on Def Poetry Jam, and has toured nationally. His first novel, *Never Mind the Goldbergs*, will be released by Scholastic in January 2005, and his second by Cleis Press in September. He keeps a secret diary on his website. (166)

.1 GRAHAM ROUMIEU is a writer and illustrator whose work has appeared in *Harper's*, *The New York Times*, and many other publications. He is also the author of *In Me Own Words: The Autobiography of Bigfoot* which he recently helped adapt into a series of animated shorts for television. Graham is currently working on another major book project scheduled for publishing and release in late 2005. He lives in Toronto, Canada and hates seafood. (85)

1.1 PHILIP RYAN lives and works in New York City. Trained as an architect, he splits his time between a Manhattan architecture firm and a Brooklyn web design firm he co-founded in 1999. Photography is a method he uses for documenting the successes (and failures) of the created environment in an effort to improve his own chances of producing something worthwhile. (65, 75)

1.4 Originally from Montreal, **MELANIE SHATZKY** is a photo and video based artist currently living in New York. Her work calls attention to a pervasive sense of disconnect and an ensuing disquiet. (181)

1.1 IRA SHULL is a writer and editor living in Shirley, MA. He has been on numerous job interviews since this story was published in *Dirt*, and regards them with the same degree of enlightenment he usually reserves for the dentist, the accountant, and the sweaty guy in the cage he has to give $50 after his car has been towed. (88)

1.1 AMY SHUTT has been studying photography at university for 4 years now. She is 28 and lives in the South. Her photographs are more biographical than anything else. She shoots what she knows: the people she loves, the places she's been...the things, people, or moments she doesn't want to disappear. (91, 94)

1.4, 1.5 MARSHALL SOKOLOFF can find real beauty when there is none, and grief when there is only happiness. He's funny that way. — Marshall Sokoloff goes on about big industrial mechanization juxtaposed on the backdrop of real despair, but everyone knows he's full of shit. — Marshall Sokoloff takes brilliant photographs of industrial decay, but he wouldn't mind doing glossy editorials and hauling in the cash and the chicks. (174, 270)

1.1 SAMUEL A. SOUTHWORTH is a poet, author, and musician formerly of NYC, now living in New Hampshire. After dropping out of high school he went on to earn a BA and MA at UNH, where he later taught writing, and then moved to Manhattan, where he worked as a writer and editor. He has published four books of military history, and his hobbies are diplomacy, fencing, archery, and canoeing. (93)

1.0 REGIS ST. LOUIS is an author for Lonely Planet guidebooks and a freelance writer based in New York City. In addition to his contributions to bedside literature, he has written articles about communism, ex-girlfriends, and imported cheese. (56)

1.2 ALNIS STAKLE (b. 1975) is a lecturer of photography at Daugavpils University in Latvia. His work has been published in numerous magazines as well as exhibited in solo exhibitions across Eastern Europe and in-group exhibitions across Europe and South America. Stakle's work hangs in both public galleries and private collections. (128)

1.3 JIN SUGAHARA was born in Kurashiki, Japan in 1968 and received his Bachelor of Architecture from Yokohama National University in 1995. In Okayama, he's exhibited at *The Exhibition for 4* in 1999, *Green Away* and *AAO* exhibitions in 2001, and in the *Jiyu Bijutsu* exhibition from 1996 to 2001. He has also been featured in the *Tokyo Exhibition* in 1998. (168)

1.1 KIMBERLY A. SUTA is a writer and a filmmaker from San Antonio, Texas. She recently completed writing and shooting a short, independent film called *T.O.E.*, and is also seeking an agent for her recently completed novel, *The Rain Queen*. She is currently working on several new writing projects. (96)

1.1 ROBERT SZOT is an award-winning painter living and working in Brooklyn. His large scale abstract work has been and continues to be exhibited nationally. (98)

1.5 ANTHONY TONGAZZINI work has appeared in *Swink*, *Quarterly West*, *Hayden's Ferry Review*, *Salt Hill*, *Quick Fiction*, *Pindeldyboz*, *Mississippi Review*, *spork*, and the *Alaska Quarterly Review*, among other journals. He has received awards from the Academy of American Poets and AWP, a Pushcart nomination, and fellowships to the Prague Writer's Workshop and Ledig House Writer's Colony. He lives in Brooklyn. (253)

1.2 ERIC VAN HOVE is a Tokyo-based Belgian artist who was born in Algeria and raised in Cameroon. Upon graduating from E.R.G. Brussels contemporary art college, Van Hove continued his studies in Namur, focusing on the craftsmanship of medieval stone carving. He is currently working under the guidance of the Japanese calligraphy master Hideaki Nagano to complete his M.A. in traditional calligraphy. His works are not limited to a single medium, and include: video, drawings, calligraphy, performances, and installations. (130)

1.0 AMY E. VAN ORDEN is a managing editor in academic publishing and a New Jersey native. She holds an MA in writing and has published her fiction and poetry in numerous reviews. When in New York, she can be found at the Rose Center for Earth and Space or at the Met in front of Bastien-Lepage's *Joan of Arc*. (61)

1.5 ADAM WALKO lives and works as a freelance artist in New York City. In addition to pursuing his personal work, Adam is always searching to be involved in new and intriguing projects. (272)

1.3 CHRIS WARNER has been a teacher, journalist, and freelance editor and writer. Having grown up in Massachusetts as a Boston sports fan, Chris has had a difficult time finding the wound since the Red Sox won the World Series. He received his MFA in fiction writing from Columbia in 2004. In their four years living in New York City, he and his wife Kristen have been to the Bronx Zoo twice. (170)

1.1, 1.2, 1.3, 1.4, 1.5 DEWAYNE WASHINGTON resides in Chicago, Illinois. Although he believes in social service and works toward improving his community, Mr. Washington writes for himself. (100, 134, 173, 219, 269)

1.1 LIZ WOLFE is a Toronto-based photographer. See more of her work at her website. (70)

1.5 "To me, photography is a personal pursuit of beauty and curiosity." Born and raised in Singapore, **YANGTAN** moved to New York City in 1998 to pursue an education and career in photography. In 2003, he was part of *PDN's 30*—an annual selection of photographers to watch. A person of few words, YangTan prefers to let his audience develop their own take on the imagery, without the interference of a rationale or unnecessary art-speak. YangTan lives and works in New York City with his wife. (224)

1.2 ROSE YNDIGOYEN is a fund-raising assistant by day, drunken queer pirate/ superhero by night. She's working on a collection of stories chronicling her adventures. Not the fund raising ones. (135)

1.4 CHRIS YORMICK lives in New York City and loves art in all its forms. He enjoys watching old samurai movies and living the code of the samurai, using one swift slice to slay an opponent. He doesn't say much and prefers to stay in the shadows of the hipness. If you see him, buy him a drink and he'll get the next round. (220)

1.1 DEANNA ZANDT is a poet happily nestled in the Lower East Side of Manhattan. Her history includes a degree in linguistics, an unhealthy relationship with her computer, endless amounts of NYC trivia, and jokes about cannibals on beaches eating clowns. (101)

1.5 ANDREW ZBIHLYJ'S award-winning illustrations have been gaining international attention since they first appeared in the July 2003 issue of *Harper's*. Since then, he has contributed consistently to that publication as well as numerous others, including *Legal Affairs*, *RES*, *Punk Planet*, *The Pennsylvania Gazette*, and *American Illustration*. Most recently, his work was exhibited at Museum of the Future (Toronto), Foundation Gallery (Chicago), and Parsons School Of Design (New York City). Andrew lives and works in Toronto. (222)

Put it out there; we'll sift.
www.dirtpress.com